THE CONTRIBUTORS

JOHN AND EILEEN BARKER are long-time residents of Bournemouth, taking a great interest in the history of the town through the Bournemouth Local Studies Group. Eileen taught children with severe learning difficulties and John worked as a scientist and engineer testing and developing equipment for the Ministry of Defence at Christchurch. One of their activities is talking to local societies about the town, its history and its personalities. The talks have formed the basis of some of the booklets produced by the Local Studies Publications.

JOHN CRESSWELL was born in Bournemouth but only developed a taste for local history when an eye injury prevented his continuing practical archaeology. Then living in London, he joined a group of enthusiasts and helped their society produce a series of local histories, contributing some titles of his own. Returning to Bournemouth in 2000, he is using his experience to research his own fields of interest locally.

PETER KAZMIERCZAK is Senior Librarian: Local Studies at Bournemouth Library, dealing with family and local history. Born in Derbyshire, he has always been interested in transport, particularly railways. After working for the Civil Service, writing for various magazines and a career as a primary school teacher, he decided to change track and become a librarian.

JAN MARSH, joint editor, is an Open University graduate and until October 2009 was the Local Heritage Librarian for Bournemouth Libraries. She worked for Bournemouth Libraries for 32 years and developed an interest in both local and family history during that time, gradually building up her expertise on the history of Bournemouth. During that time Jan has also researched her own family history in Poole and Dorset going back to the early 1700s. She is currently involved with the Streets of Bournemouth project to create a virtual museum of the history of Bournemouth.

VINCENT MAY, joint editor, is Professor Emeritus of Coastal Geomorphology and Conservation at Bournemouth University. During the past 45 years, he has been involved in many aspects of the transformation of the Bournemouth Municipal College of Technology and Commerce into Bournemouth University. In 1994 he was awarded the British Petroleum Prize for Environmental Science and Management for developing teaching which exhibits the qualities attributed to the best academic research – critical thinking and creativity.

LOUISE PERRIN initially worked in the health service. After graduating from Bournemouth University in 1994, she began a new career as a museum curator, most recently at the Russell-Cotes Art Gallery & Museum. While researching her MA thesis about seaside history in Devon's museums she learned of the link between health and the origins of seaside visiting. Her first book, A Century of Bournemouth, was published in 2002. She now works freelance.

MIKE PHIPP was born in Poole, and has always lived locally. From schoolboy days he has always been interested in aviation and railways. On early retirement he was able to spend more time on his 'hobbies', becoming the Historian for Bournemouth Airport in the 1990s. In recent years he has written a number of books on local aviation subjects, including Bournemouth Airport.

JOHN SOANE previously taught at several German universities, and is now in the Faculty of the Built Environment at London South Bank University. He took his doctorate at the University of Surrey based on the historical development of Bournemouth. Dr. Soane's present interests are in the rehabilitation of historic European cities - especially Dresden.

MICHAEL STEAD works at Bournemouth Library in the Heritage Zone. His family has deep local roots and his great great great grandfather was thrown out of Holdenhurst in 1816 for being too poor.

JOHN WALKER is a local historian and author of four Bournemouth booklets. A retired Army Major and a lifelong lover of the town, John qualified as an official Bournemouth Guide in 1992. He was very honoured to receive the "Outstanding Contribution to Bournemouth Tourism" Award in 2006.

KEITH WILKES is Acting Dean of the School of Services Management at Bournemouth University. His main research is on tourism development, visitor attraction and heritage management, and tourism education. He is supervising currently PhDs in nature-based tourism, visitor motivation and behaviour at garden attractions and World Heritage Sites (Thailand and The Jurassic Coast), alongside research into urban regeneration and the 2012 Olympics and the values of UK heritage providers and consumers.

MIKE FRANCIS is Principal and SIMON FREEMAN is the Vice Principal of Westbourne Academy and Secretary of the International Education Forum. DAN FERRIS is the retired Principal of Eurocentres, Bournemouth.

Bournemouth from the pier, 1868.

BOURNEMOUTH

1810 – 2010

From Smugglers to Surfers

EDITORS

VINCENT MAY & JAN MARSH

THE DOVECOTE PRESS

Bournemouth Library

First published in 2010 by The Dovecote Press Ltd
Stanbridge, Wimborne Minster, Dorset BH21 4JD
on behalf of
Bournemouth Libraries (Bournemouth Borough Council)

ISBN 978-1-904-34976-1

Designed by The Dovecote Press
Printed and bound by KHL in Singapore

All papers used by The Dovecote Press are natural,
recyclable products made from wood grown in sustainable,
well-managed forests

A CIP catalogue record for this book is available
from the British Library

CONTENTS

FOREWORD

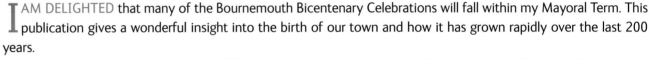

The Worshipful The Mayor of Bournemouth 2009-2010
Councillor Mrs Beryl Baxter, CMgr, MCMI

I AM DELIGHTED that many of the Bournemouth Bicentenary Celebrations will fall within my Mayoral Term. This publication gives a wonderful insight into the birth of our town and how it has grown rapidly over the last 200 years.

In reading this remarkable book, you will be able to envisage Bournemouth through the eyes of people who have lived here through the years. In particular, you will find photographic images from Bournemouth Libraries' Day Collection of 1500 glass negatives which have not been seen for many years. This collection of fragile material, mirroring the development of our town, can now be enjoyed by everyone having been conserved for posterity through the "Streets of Bournemouth" project, funded by a Heritage Lottery Fund grant.

Another heritage asset is the Russell-Cotes Art Gallery & Museum which has contributed a selection of images to this book. Sir Merton & Lady Russell-Cotes played a key role in the development of the town, as well as leaving an important cultural treasure to the Borough when they donated their home (now the Art Gallery and Museum) and their collections.

I am looking forward to the launch of the "Streets of Bournemouth" project and, when it goes live, it will provide an interactive online virtual museum devoted to the town's history, featuring many of the images found in this book. As a very exciting initiative, local people can also add their own Bournemouth stories.

I am especially honoured to have been asked to contribute to this particular book which recognises the enthusiasm and expertise of the authors of individual chapters in Bournemouth's history. I would also like to thank all the staff within the partner organisations – Bournemouth Libraries, Bournemouth Arts, the Russell-Cotes Art Gallery & Museum and Bournemouth University – and the many volunteers for their hard work and commitment, especially Professor Vincent May and Jan Marsh, the Senior Librarian for Local Studies.

KEY DATES

1802   Inclosure Act

1805   Christchurch Inclosure map identifies areas for enclosure

1810   Lewis Tregonwell rents land from Sir George Ivison Tapps

1838   Westover Villas and Bath Hotel built

1856   Bournemouth Improvement Act

1876   Boscombe and Springbourne added to The Improvement Commissioners' area

1884   Westbourne added as well as the rest of Boscombe and part of Malmesbury Park

1890   Bournemouth becomes a Municipal Borough

1900   The town becomes a County Borough

1901   Winton, Moordown, Pokesdown and Southbourne added

1914   Queen's Park, Lower Charminster and Strouden added

1931   Holdenhurst and Kinson added

1932   Hengistbury Head added

1974   Bournemouth becomes part of the County of Dorset

1997   Bournemouth becomes a Unitary Authority

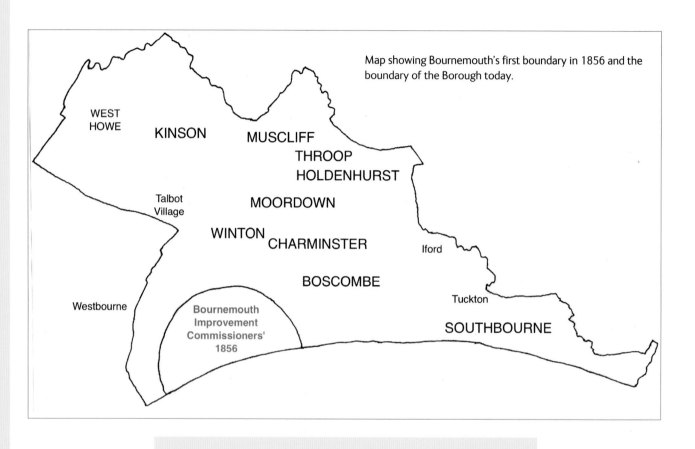

Map showing Bournemouth's first boundary in 1856 and the boundary of the Borough today.

WEST HOWE

KINSON

MUSCLIFF

THROOP

HOLDENHURST

Talbot Village

MOORDOWN

WINTON
CHARMINSTER

Iford

BOSCOMBE

Westbourne

Bournemouth Improvement Commissioners' 1856

Tuckton

SOUTHBOURNE

EDITORS' NOTE

Throughout the book, we have used the units of measurement used at the time, particularly acres, roods and square perches, pounds, shillings and pence, and miles, feet and inches. One square perch = 30.25 square yards, one rood =40 sq. poles and four roods = one acre.

However, if you want to convert to metric measure, one acre equals 0.405 hectares and one mile equals 1.61 kilometres.

PREFACE

Vincent May and Jan Marsh

THIS HISTORY OF BOURNEMOUTH has been compiled by a group of local historians and geographers who came together in 2007 as the Publications Group for the town's bicentenary. Very early in discussions, it was agreed that the book should concentrate on a number of themes which were important to the town's establishment and its transformation to its present vibrant self. Not surprisingly, within these themes there are aspects of the history which overlap with others. The history of the town is a story of interwoven ideas, actions and disputes which always had the objective that the town should stand apart from others. Indeed, that it should be Britain's premier resort, but also more than that, for its history is also marked by many events, activities and products which were the first of their kind. From its earliest days when smuggling was a vital part of the local economy to the present when surfing (electronically or offshore) offers new possibilities, the town has benefitted from nurturing its natural assets, the beaches, cliffs, chines, gardens and parks, and the creativity of its people.

The authors have written independently about themes which interest them and, not surprisingly looking at the town over its past 200 years, they have described some of its characteristics from their individual viewpoints. Some topics will be familiar to local readers but surprise visitors. One very important aspect of the book is that many of the authors write about the sense of the place and discuss how its internal patterns of roads, communities, facilities and architecture came about. So we read about how very early protests from poor people in the villages along the Stour valley led to the town's parks and how the enclosure of land at the beginning of the 19th century set the pattern of roads and estates. The early chapters describe the beginnings of the town and the people who were involved. The activities of the early entrepreneurs and the social patterns which developed as people moved into the growing town gave rise to its distinctive landscape. Each describes part of the picture, but every aspect of these patterns bears the traces of people, sometimes very far-seeing and sometimes less successful, who both as individuals and working together made Bournemouth.

The economic success and growth of Bournemouth depended in its early decades entirely upon outsiders, some living in the nearby villages and others from almost all parts of the country, who brought to the town their skills, money, influence and ability to get people working together. It was also shaped by the effects of new means of transport, the demands of war and the establishment of important industrial activities outside the town. Employment within the town has always concentrated on servicing the community and its tourism, but employment of many who live in the town has often been outside. This is not least because of a deliberate view that Bournemouth should not be industrialised. Many families in the 1950s and 1960s depended upon the combinations of working in the aircraft industry and providing holiday accommodation, and later student accommodation. Today, the income from tourism is supplemented by the very large student community of the University and language schools. Similarly, the conference business supplements the summer tourism income by providing winter visitors. A growing number of businesses now focus on ways in which the healthy and beautiful character of the town can be maintained, as its people adapt yet again to changes in its economy and wider environment.

The town continues to pride itself on its ability to adapt to change and being ahead of the market whilst retaining its healthy beautiful image.

BOURNEMOUTH 2010

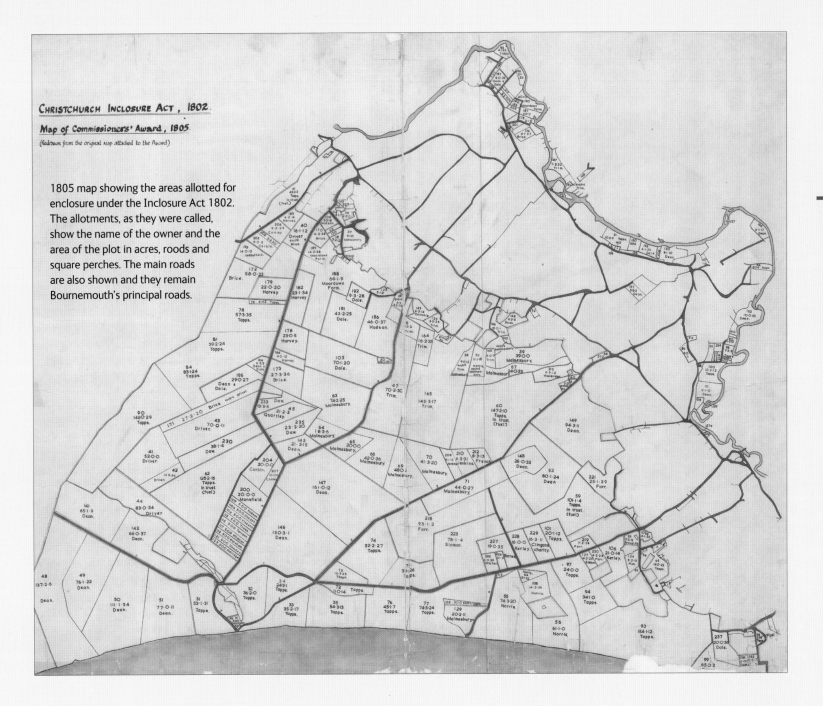

Christchurch Inclosure Act, 1802.

Map of Commissioners' Award, 1805.

(Redrawn from the original map attached to the Award)

1805 map showing the areas allotted for enclosure under the Inclosure Act 1802. The allotments, as they were called, show the name of the owner and the area of the plot in acres, roods and square perches. The main roads are also shown and they remain Bournemouth's principal roads.

ONE

TAMING THE HEATH

Michael Stead and Vincent May

Chapter One

BOURNEMOUTH today stretches from the coast to the River Stour and includes not only the former Hampshire villages along the Stour valley but also the Dorset hamlets in the parish of Canford Magna. Many of the histories of Bournemouth suggest that the landscape upon which the town was established and grew was simply empty heathland, but in fact it had been occupied by many different communities. Bronze Age barrows, Neolithic farmers' camps, Iron Age earthworks at Double Dykes and one of the earliest ports in the lee of Hengistbury Head bear witness to those early people. Hamlets and farms used the valley for farming, as the Domesday records show. Both Holdenhurst and Kinson are recorded in the Domesday Book. Between them they had 55 villagers and 21 serfs. Holdenhurst had 181 acres of meadow and Kinson 100 acres, and both villages had mills. Their inhabitants largely depended upon pigs, which were often pastured in the woodlands. Holdenhurst, which was valued at £24, also had three fisheries.

La Bournemowthe, as it was known as early as 1406, was a convenient place to reach the sea, as the valley provided easy access inland. It was also a place where, from time to time, the sea supplemented meagre food supplies. The Christchurch Priory Cartulary records that, when a fish about 18 feet long was washed up there, it was taken to the manor at Wick and 'there cut into forty pieces.'[1]

Bournemouth 1800

If we accompanied Dr Who back to 1800 and landed the Tardis on the cliff-top land above La Bournemowthe, the landscape would have been like much of the New Forest today: a vast expanse of heathland, covered, depending on the season, in purple heather and bright yellow gorse. The area would have been buzzing loudly as bees gathered pollen for their hives, which were scattered across the heath, and provided the staple sweetener – honey – for the locals who were too poor to afford the sugar then being imported from the plantations of the West Indies.

The valley of the River Stour was the site of the earliest villages. The flood plain seen here was rarely built upon except where there were crossings, such as ferries or bridges. The villages were built on low terraces above the flood plain.

There were few trees on the heath. In the past, there was woodland, but the last trees had been felled more than two centuries earlier. There were sheep, and some cattle, as the locals were allowed to graze their animals here. Ducks, amidst a wide variety of wildlife, visited a small area of enclosed wetland around the Bourne stream.

Several small chines and valleys cut into the higher

ABOVE In Kinson, which was part of the much larger Canford Magna parish in Dorset, Turbary Common is one of the areas which are still heathland, seen here with heather in the foreground. Today it is surrounded by industrial estates and by houses along Daws Avenue in the background.

LEFT As the smugglers, the Yeomanry and other travellers crossed the heathland they might have noticed the villagers' beehives sheltered by the gorse (or furze as it was called). After enclosure some of the heaths were planted, especially near the coast, with pines.

land, giving way in Kinson to the higher spurs of land, or 'howes'. The principal valleys across the land are Bourne Valley, emptying into the sea, and Longman's Bottom flowing into the Stour. As these were particularly swampy, the main tracks, which were defined as main roads in 1802 by the Enclosure Award, generally avoided them where possible. For example, Wimborne Road skirts to the east and north of Marsbarrow Valley (modern Meyrick Park) before crossing the shallower reaches of Longman's Bottom in Winton – notably at Peter's Hill. Holdenhurst

Sea Road, Boscombe. Apart from the cottage, this is the landscape that any smuggler or visitor would have walked through from the beach.

Throop Road typifies the lanes and roads which crossed the enclosed lands, although the road itself would not have been in such good condition.

Road passes to the north-west of Boscombe Chine and the valleys of Springbourne, and then to the south-east of Great Dean Bottom, now Queen's Park.

The Bourne stream rises at Knighton Gravel Hill and flows east through Bourne Bottom and Walling Ford, past Bourne Fryars, to meet with other streams that have flowed down Three Peal Bottom and Withy Bed Bottom, past Hunt Witch Hill, to carve out Bourne Chine before entering the sea at Bourne Mouth. The old names for the valleys and ridges have long passed from memory and that area is generally known today as the 'Alder Hills'.

This was all that remained of the vast Stourfield Chase,

mostly heathland that once covered this western corner of Hampshire. There were few visitors, though from time to time, Sir George Ivison Tapps went to Decoy Pond Cottage, where his hunting gear was stored, to shoot at the ducks braving Decoy Pond. Built in the 13th century, the cottage was also known in the past as Decoy Pond House and Bourne House and was located close to the present-day War Memorial in the Central Gardens. As late as 1826, Tapps' fellow local landowner, James Harris (Lord Malmesbury), wrote of shooting a blackcock on the site of what became St. Peter's Church.[2]

Along the shoreline there were few, if any, bathers. The accounts that survive suggest that there might have been the occasional gaggle of boys who stripped off for a swim, with hardly a soul to see them. Locals fishing with nets in the shallow waters had to be careful, as just getting

their feet wet could count as 'going to sea', and would be enough to give the Press Gangs an excuse to drag them off for service in the Royal Navy.

As dusk fell, some furtive figures might come ashore in tiny boats and rush into one of the dozens of small holes or fissures in the soft sandy cliffs. These were the local smugglers, bringing in contraband such as tea, tobacco, brandy and anything else with an excise duty imposed on it. Many of these men lived in the villages along the Stour valley, and they had to move their smuggled goods from shore to village hiding-place, without being discovered. The tracks that they wore across the heath would one day

become the routes of Bournemouth's main roads .

The job of stopping the smugglers rested with the Dorset Volunteer Rangers, whose role was to 'serve in case of riots and tumults . . . and in case of invasion in any part of Great Britain.'[3] They included the important families of the county, such as the Bankes, Portman, Grosvenor and Weld families: amongst them was Captain Lewis Tregonwell of Cranborne. He patrolled the area on horseback, able to call

LEFT *The Sands, Bournemouth*, an engraving by Philip Brannon in 1850, showing the first jetty. Although smugglers were no longer active when he drew this scene, it does show how they would have beached their boats at the foot of the cliffs.

BELOW A print published by R. Sydenham of Poole in 1870 showing an extended jetty inserted between the boats seaward of Brannon's original. Note how Sydenham has copied much of the detail in the earlier engraving.

ABOVE The cliffs and beaches at Bourne looking eastwards, as engraved by Philip Brannon in 1878, illustrating the opportunities for smugglers to use the gullies as temporary hiding places.

on a troop of forty men.

1800 was a significant year for the smugglers, as old Isaac Gulliver, the 'gentleman smuggler' who had decided to retire, did it in style. According to an 1867 report in *The Poole Pilot* magazine, he brought his last cargo of contraband ashore from three luggers laden with silks and tobacco close to the present site of Bournemouth Pier. The cortège which then conveyed the smuggled goods inland was two miles in length, with Gulliver riding at

BELOW Iford Bridge and the riverside hamlet of Iford, occupying land just above the flood level.

the head. The local gentry would often turn a blind eye to smuggling, in return for a small cut of the goods. Lord Malmesbury recalled one local squire who dined with his back to the windows, so that he could truthfully report that he had never seen the smugglers go past.

Others, however, remained in the business. In 1804 excise men stopped two smugglers' wagons and a cart at Boscombe and found 250 casks of spirits and a case of playing cards. Smugglers were not the only people disturbing the tranquil heath: about 1800 a group of fishermen and farm labourers were on the beach struggling to pull in nets loaded with mackerel, when they were abducted by a press gang comprising an armed party of sailors, who marched their prisoners off to Poole.

Smuggling had waned somewhat since 1783, when Prime Minister Pitt, influenced by Adam Smith's free-trade ideas, reduced the excise on various items (the duty on tea was reduced from 120% to 12.5%) and thereby made smuggling significantly less profitable. Before then, the money to be made from smuggling, by an otherwise impoverished population, sometimes justified extreme acts. About 1780 a gang of ruffians, on the orders of the principal smugglers of the region, broke into the Iford home of William Manuel, who was believed to have informed the Revenue Officers of smuggling activities. They took his son Joseph by force across the heath to the Decoy Pond House at Bourne Mouth where he was made to board a smuggling cutter, and carried away to Alderney.

There was another final procession in 1800, this time at Pokesdown. In April, Mary Eleanor Bowes-Lyon died at Stourfield House and was buried a few days later in Westminster Abbey. In her time, thanks to her father's ownership of a mining cartel in Durham, she had been the wealthiest heiress in the kingdom. Because of problems with a violent husband and many unsuitable suitors, she sought retirement in the most inaccessible place she could

Douglas House Hospital, formerly Stourfield House, home at the beginning of the nineteenth century to Mary Eleanor Bowes-Lyon.

Wick Farmhouse and Queen Anne cottage in Wick show that not all the valley villages were impoverished.

The Sanctuary, Wick Farm, Wick.

Muscliff House. In the villages along the Stour valley, many of the houses and farms date back well before the founding of Bournemouth and were often rebuilt or expanded on the sites of the older buildings.

find. That place was Bournemouth – or Christchurch as it was then called. She is of continuing interest, not only for her colourful personal life,[4] but because she is, through the late Queen Mother Elizabeth Bowes-Lyon, an ancestor of the present monarch.

Mary Eleanor's home was Stourfield House, a smart Georgian mansion on the high land at Pokesdown, at the edge of the heath, with views over the New Forest. It was owned by Sir George Tapps, the Lord of the Manor. Nearby was Littledown House, an even more modern Georgian property on the high ground overlooking Holdenhurst Village, home to the Dean family, who had been local farmers for many years. To the north across the River Stour, Lord Malmesbury lived in the more ancient Hurn Court, built on the site of the Priory House for Christchurch. To the south close to the cliffs, another smart new residence, Boscombe Cottage, was home to Philip Norris from Formby, Lancashire. It stood in several acres of land which were probably the location of 'Boscombe Copperas House', almost certainly the earliest industry in Bournemouth, since it is shown together with 'Allom house' (near Alum Chine) on Saxton's 1547 map (copperas is an old word used to describe ferrous sulphate, an iron salt which was dug out here and in Poole).

More remotely, there was a Summer House on Warren Hill (Hengistbury Head). Nearer the mouth of the Bourne, the smugglers would have seen the 18th century Bourne House, a Preventative Station. To the north-west, there was another mansion, Pelhams, at Kinson which had been built in about 1795 on land forming part of Manor Farm, owned by Isaac Gulliver. It was bought later in 1816 by William Fryer whose wife, Elizabeth Fryer, was Isaac Gulliver's daughter.

The more modest dwellings of the local farming community were in villages and hamlets dotted along the lanes beside the River Stour. Wick, Tuckton, Iford, Holdenhurst, Throop, Muccleshell, Muscliff, Redhill, Ensbury, Kinson and Cudnell were the focal points of a pastoral community, living close to poverty, who had clung on to the edge of the heath eking out a precarious living for over a thousand years. These were the people who grazed their animals on the heathland, and cut the roots of the heather to dry them into 'turves', which were used for winter fuel. They kept beehives and dovecotes,

Shelley House, Shelley Lane.

and they wore paths across the heath as they helped carry smuggled goods back from the shore. They were the folk who worked on the farms owned by the Malmesbury and Tapps families or who went looking for Mary Eleanor's pet dog when it ran off!

The heathland itself seemed uninhabited. Officially it was 'waste' – every manor had wasteland which was part

The Wilderness, Shelley Lane, Muscliff.

The caption on this photograph of an old cottage in Redhill says that this was the bakehouse which supplied the whole of Bournemouth with bread in 1800. At that time, Bournemouth did not exist but bread would have been supplied to the Stour valley villages, Redhill and Moordown.

of the economic life of the community. No one owned it outright, so everyone had some access to the land. The few people who chose to live there did so at their own risk. Early reports of the area mention mud huts as the home to various people across the heath, and some of the fanciful writings of the Tregonwell family concern 'Old Meg', who lived in her gypsy cottage on the heath. None of these mud (or cob) huts enjoyed any legal status, and they do not appear on any maps, with the possible exception of Blaeu's 1645 Map of Hampshire, which shows some sort of settlement close to the county boundary called 'Heath'. In addition to the mud huts, there were the brightly coloured caravans of the travelling diddicoys, who regularly stopped in the area on their way between the Purbecks and the New Forest. These tinkers, as well as gypsies, show up in the census returns during the 19th century, as do a small handful of tent dwellers, scattered across what remained of the heathland.

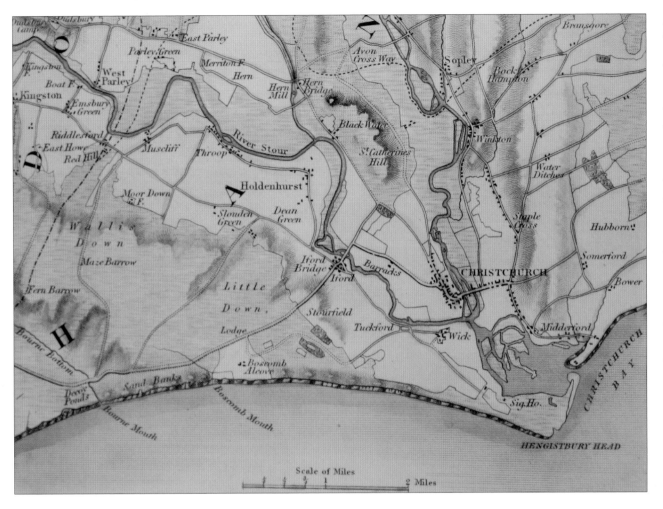

John Dower's map of the Environs of Christchurch which was engraved in 1839 for Robert Mudie's *History of Hampshire* shows nothing of the new settlement at Bourne. The Decoy Ponds and what he calls Boscombe Alcove are separated by Sand Banks.

that the Liberty of Westover (the area of Christchurch which became Bournemouth) should be enclosed.

The large scale aim was clear: to turn the commonly-held waste into privately owned farmland, at a time when there was real fear of the Napoleonic Wars causing starvation by blocking English ports. Existing rights would be compensated, roads and fields would be created, and some land sold to finance the process. The result was that some existing major landowners suddenly gained many hundreds of acres of new freehold land at virtually no cost to themselves. Some of the less appealing land (in the wet valleys that cut into the heath) was set aside for the local villagers to continue to use as before for fuel and grazing. As for the diddicoys, and occupants of the tents and mud huts, they were turned off the land, as new boundary banks, ditches and fences were put in place. The old smugglers' tracks were not used exactly, but served as guidelines for the new roads across the heath. Whereas the old track from the Bourne took a gently rising path up through what is now Horseshoe Common on to the heath, the replacement road ran steeply up Richmond Hill, making it much more difficult to get contraband to the surrounding villages.

The lines of roads and field boundaries that were drawn up under the 1802 Act, and formalised by the 1805 Award of lands, later provided the framework on which Bournemouth grew. Wimborne, Charminster and Holdenhurst Roads all date from this period. Apart from the occasional steep valley, there was no existing feature for them to divert around, and so they were all built straight and long. The Kinson enclosure in 1822 followed a similar

1802: the Beginning of Change

'Enclosure' was the means by which open areas of land were divided into smaller units to allow for a change in economic practices. The large open field systems of medieval villages had been subdivided into fields to allow for the growth of private farms. It was also possible to enclose heath or wasteland, if an Act of Parliament was obtained. One local

enclosure had allowed Stourfield House to be built, and this was sufficiently recent that the new area of parkland created out of the heath later gave its name to New Park Road in Pokesdown. By the end of the 18th century, the pace of enclosure had quickened and Acts of Parliament were passed to allow for the wholesale enclosure of land. In 1801, several local landowners including the Lord of the Manor of Christchurch, Sir George Ivison Tapps, proposed

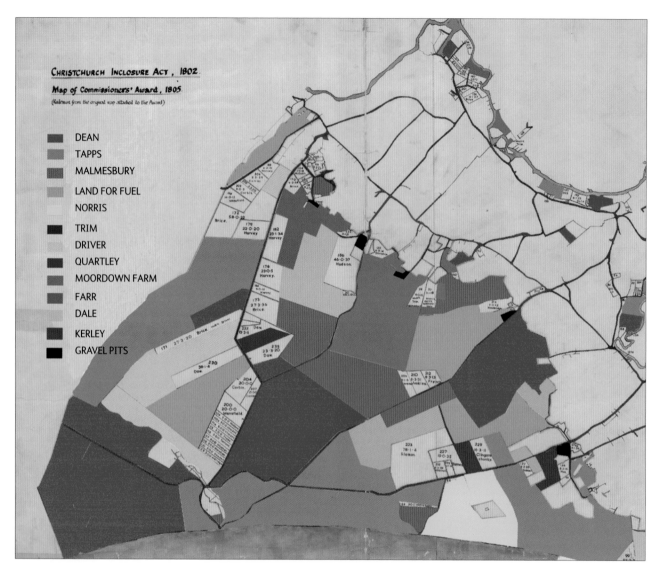

DEAN
TAPPS
MALMESBURY
LAND FOR FUEL
NORRIS
TRIM
DRIVER
QUARTLEY
MOORDOWN FARM
FARR
DALE
KERLEY
GRAVEL PITS

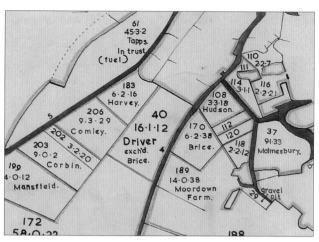

Moordown and Redhill as they were in 1805.

Throop had just a few cottages along the lane in 1805. Tapps, Dale and Dean acquired plots on the floodplain.

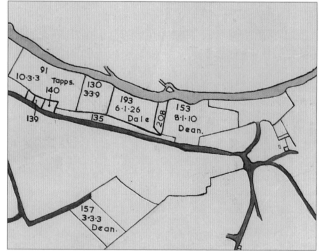

This map shows the ownership of the enclosed areas within the Liberty of West Stour in 1805. Several landowners, especially William Dean and Sir George Tapps, owned large areas of the cliff top land around the Bourne valley.

pattern, providing the lines for Wallisdown, Columbia and Kinson Roads.

The major parks of Bournemouth were also delineated at this time. The cottagers in the villages had used the heath for cutting turf as a source of fuel. They feared

that their ancient rights of cutting turves would be lost when the heath was enclosed and so persuaded William West, a Muscliff farmer, to help them prove their claims and put their concerns to the Inclosure Commissioners. As administrators of the 1802 Enclosure Act, the

Commissioners allocated five enclosed areas, 424 acres in all, as 'turbary' or 'poor' commons to 86 qualifying cottagers in the villages and hamlets between Muscliff and Wick, including Pokesdown, for fuel. These are now Bournemouth's parks: Redhill, Meyrick, King's and Queen's Parks, and Seafield Gardens (in Southbourne). A similar area of 'turbary' land survived the later enclosures in Kinson as the present-day Turbary Common. An area at the top of Richmond Hill was considered not worth enclosing and divided into nine strips of five acres each, allocated to cottagers at Muscliff.

Over two centuries, most direct evidence of the enclosures has vanished as the land has been developed. There is the occasional low ridge, running through Meyrick Park or Strouden Park, to show where an enclosure bank once ran. Elsewhere the old boundaries are 'ghosts' that lie behind the paths of other roads. Woodland Walk in Boscombe follows the edge of enclosure 56. Portman Road divides enclosures 228 and 229. Queensland Road comes to an abrupt end where it meets the long-gone boundary of allotment 127, awarded to Rachel Sabben, widow. Allotment is not the modern meaning, but the land which was allocated to the new owner. Richmond Park Road once separated the allotments of Lord Malmesbury to the south from those of Cornelius Trim to the north. Meanwhile, in Moordown, Rose Gardens exists as an isolated pocket of housing, as it was built to give access to two small enclosures (112 and 120).

The way in which the various parcels of land allotted in 1802 later changed hands had a significant effect on the shape of the development of Bournemouth.

The Award of 1805 records, in passing, various names that have since been lost. Ensbury Park was once Quomp Corner, and Redhill Avenue was Redhill Lane. Bournemouth School for Boys stands on a site once known as Gallopers Breath, whilst the lower end of East Way was Dominie's

Southbourne in 1900.

Lane, named after William Dominie, who owned land nearby at Pick Purse and Honey Hill, also called Hungry Hill. Castle Lane was Wimborne Road in 1805, and Woodbury Avenue was Sheep House Lane. Dean Drove Gate and Castle Gate Close were names that preserved the location of two of the gates into the long-vanished Stourfield Chase. The two main valleys running through Queen's Park were Longman's Bottom and Great Dean Bottom. At Throop, a small branch of the river was known as Harbridge Stream, or the Lidden Stour. Scattered around Holdenhurst, we find Bickerill Folly, Cutter Slade and Pistle Barrow (now Thistlebarrow Road) which originally indicated stopping points where an epistle would be read from the Bible whilst beating the village bounds. These were the familiar

The Gables, Sea Road, Southbourne-on-Sea, c.1900, looking towards Hengistbury Head. There are few early photographs which show the enclosed landscape away from the growing Bourne and Southbourne-on-Sea.

old names of the landscape known to the local inhabitants as they became used to the new division of enclosures.

In the short term, the enclosures did little more than turn the tent dwellers and gypsies off the land. The major landowners had little money to spare to improve the land, and less inclination to invest in it. Once the Napoleonic threat abated, there was little incentive to convert the heathland into farms, and so Sir George Tapps gladly sold several acres to Captain Tregonwell, so that he could build

Portman Lodge in 1863, originally built in 1810 by Tregonwell for his butler Thomas Symes.

his house, initially called The Mansion, in Exeter Road. The only enterprise of note, seemingly instigated by Tapps, was the planting of pine trees, reportedly to harvest their resin and timber. A contemporary account reports that local labourers planted them in their thousands, for a pittance of a wage, little caring if the branches or roots went into the soil. It was only some very wet summers around 1816 that prevented the entire crop from dying.

For much of this period, the agricultural land and the various farms remained central to the economy of the area. The farms gained a good reputation if they were successful and productive, and a new owner often retained an existing name. When Charles Hicks moved from Holdenhurst to Muccleshell, his old farm kept the name Hicks' Farm, and he lived at King's Farm, which only became Hicks' Farm when he finally died in 1857.

Even after Tregonwell arrived, there was little change to most of the heathland. Even thirty years later, when the next great survey for the Tithe Awards took place, it was only at Bourne that there had been any noticeable change to the landscape.

Tregonwell began by buying several parcels of land in what we now think of as the town centre, and which was then a marshy ford far from anywhere. He built a handful of buildings north and south of the river, which could be rented to prosperous friends to provide a small income. Pretty gardens, an orchard and woodland walks were added. There was also West Cliff Farm built where St. Michael's Road now runs.

A map of Bourne Tregonwell in 1835. Although land near the cliff top had belonged at the time of enclosure to Sir George Tapps, he had sold land to T.S. Erle Drax by 1835. None of Tregonwell's land had direct access to the cliff top.

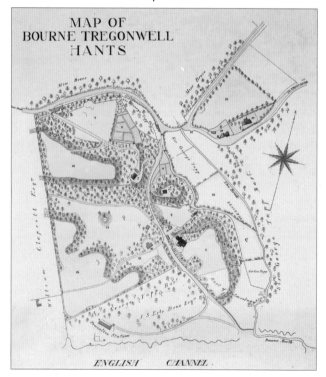

The Tapps Inn had been built as a public house, supplanting the 18th century Bourne House, a Preventative Station from which coastguards could prevent landing by smugglers. However, it has often been suggested (but without any specific evidence) that Tregonwell actually controlled the smuggling with the help of these coastguards, and the Tregonwell Arms, as it was renamed, provided their retail outlet.

The Tregonwells' enjoyment of Bourne lasted for a quarter of a century. Although Edmondsham remained their principal home, Tregonwell's widow Henrietta was living at Bourne with her Portman relatives in 1841 and died there in 1846. Tregonwell's estate remained an unremarkable location within the ancient tything of Holdenhurst. The roads leading towards Bourne also took the names of ancient hamlets such as Muscliff.

The Marine Village

The principal impetus to change at Bournemouth came in 1835, with the death of Sir George Tapps, who had sold land to Lewis Tregonwell. His 40-year-old son, another George, took possession of the estate, and engaged locally born architect Benjamin Ferrey to design a 'Marine Village' to be built beside Tregonwell's Bourne.

Ferrey produced various plans and paintings showing how the development of Tapps' land, the present-day East Cliff, could look. Thanks to his father and the Enclosure Commissioners, Tapps owned all the cliff top land as far back as Christchurch Road, from Bournemouth to Boscombe Chine. Ferrey planned to cover the whole of this with elegant Georgian crescents, but little was actually built. Westover Road was constructed to open up the land east of the Bourne, and a row of Italianate villas was built, with the Bath Hotel built at the seaward end.

Littledown House, home of the Dean family.

The hotel opened in the summer of 1838, on the same day that Queen Victoria was crowned. Fireworks echoed across Poole Bay in celebration. Any seagulls startled into the sky by the coronation fireworks would have flown over a settlement on the threshold of a new age. Westover Villas would have shone brightly in the sun and on the hill behind them surveyors were measuring out land for a second phase of villas, named Poole Crescent.

To the west, other surveyors were measuring out the land for villas up Nurses (now Richmond) Hill and along Gordon Grove (St. Stephen's Road). This work was undertaken for Mr William Gordon, who had become the owner of Bruce's Wood, a sizeable estate assembled by Patrick Crawford Bruce when he bought land north of Poole Road. The estate eventually reached from Nurses Hill to Alder Road, but only six villas were built in Nurses Hill.

By 1840, Ferrey had moved away from the area, and George Tapps, by then called George Gervis, brought in

A drawing of the proposed Gervis estate at Bourne 1837 which looks across the Bath Hotel and up Bath Hill. Everywhere are curves – the streets, the paths and the layout of the gardens.

'Plan of building land at Bournemouth near Christchurch, Hants, showing the New Marine Village of Bourne and the Baths now erecting March 1838.'

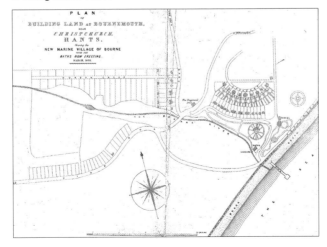

Decimus Burton, who had laid out Hyde Park, to design gardens and wooded walks between Westover Road and the Bourne. Gervis died in 1842, leaving his estates in the possession of his 15-year-old son, who became George Meyrick, in order to inherit a large estate from his Meyrick maternal great grandfather. William Gordon ran out of money trying to build villas on Nurses Hill and ended up increasingly in debt to George Durrant. Thanks to the financial ineptitude of William Clapcott, the only other major landowner in the vicinity, his son, William, was left with hundreds of acres of land that he could not afford to develop.

At the start of the 1840s, as the first guide books to Bournemouth were being published by John Sydenham of Poole, the development of the settlement was grinding to a halt. The quietude suited Sydenham. He invented Bournemouth's earliest mythology, erasing the history of smuggling and cattle-grazing by the poor and hunting by the rich, providing a blank past for Bournemouth, where Squire Tregonwell's footfalls of thirty years earlier broke a centuries-old silence in an uninhabited wilderness.

Sydenham's map of Bournemouth, showing it at the convergence of several roads and tracks, surrounded by

Lower Charminster Road in about 1900 looked very like most of the rural lanes would have a century earlier.

The first church in Bourne near the Square in 1838.

Holdenhurst church and surrounding fields today: a landscape which would have been familiar to the early 19th century villagers.

hundreds of acres of heath, intimated at the grander plans of Gordon and Gervis, rather than the modest success they had achieved. The growth of Bournemouth slowed to a trickle, with no new roads, and buildings appearing slowly in areas already opened for development.

There was only one builder in Bournemouth at the time, David Tuck, who built the first Westover villa, and laid several of the earliest roads. In the 1840s, the most significant developments were the construction of St. Peter's Church (replacing the chapel that had been established in Bourne House) and the development of Commercial Road with houses, a school, an inn and a laundry. The only noteworthy development in the wider area was Boscombe (or Heath) Farm in Richmond Park Road, occupied by David Tuck's nephew William.

The rest of Westover remained just as the Enclosure Commissioners left it 35 years earlier. The Stour valley was still a working farming area, with at least six farms clustered around Holdenhurst Village Green. Whilst the landowners at Bourne were concerned with roads and villas and visitors, along the Stour the landowners such as the Dean family of Holdenhurst, Lord Malmesbury, Sir George Gervis, the Harvey family of Muccleshell, and the Aldridge family of Muscliff were concerned with fields and crops and cattle. Most farms consisted of long strips of fields and larger areas still called 'acres' from the time they were enclosed. Many of the names of the older fields may reveal a little of their history. For example, what lies behind the names of some of Clapcott Dean's older fields,

'Hard Acre Camp', 'Pistle Burrow', 'Harpway', 'Spite Fields', 'Folly', 'Bee Garden' and 'East Kite Land'?

In Kinson, across the county boundary in Dorset, there were different landowners, George Bankes, of Kingston Lacy and William Fryer, grandson of Isaac Gulliver the smuggler. Kinson was divided into several farms, at East Howe, Howe and West Howe, Ensbury and Kinson Manor.

By the end of its first thirty years, Bournemouth had come into existence, but it was still small. The 1841 Census records 165 inhabitants living in 34 households. Already known for its sea-bathing, it was attracting small numbers of visitors and had two hotels, the Bath and the Belle Vue, a library

Pier Approach from the west in about 1855, probably the earliest photograph of Bournemouth, with the Belle Vue Hotel on the left.

and reading room, and two cottages in Orchard Lane which provided a school for 18 children and a temporary church. A Dr Granville described 'its yet unformed colony' in 1841 as

By the time, this sketch was drawn the houses on Westover Road had been built and some of the pines of the cliff top had been cleared to make way for them.

The Jetty and the Belle Vue Hotel in 1855. The jetty had been built to provide access for larger boats and to avoid having to beach them. One of the priorities for the Improvement Commissioners was to replace this simple wooden structure with a more substantial pier, thus bringing the town in line with other seaside resorts both in England and on the Mediterranean coast.

capable of becoming England's foremost sea-watering place and winter resort.[5] This put the possibility of long-lasting change and development of the place into the minds of some local people. Two other developments occurred at the same time. The first was the consolidation of the existing estates, for example Stourfield, into small growing settlements such as Pokesdown and Winton. The second was the continuing but slow growth of the valley hamlets and villages. The villages were already beginning to establish schools which, together with the churches and chapels, became focal points in the development of the outer town. By 1841, there were four schools, at Kinson, Pokesdown, Bourne and Winton.

These two developments provided some of the pioneering inhabitants, whose arrival in turn influenced the design and growth of the new town. They also fixed the pattern of main streets linking the growing town with the outskirts. From the very first days, the new settlement needed craftsmen and servants. They could only come from the surrounding areas and some of the impoverished farm workers found work as carpenters, gardeners and bricklayers. However, unlike many other growing resorts, at Bournemouth they had an almost blank canvas on which to build the new place, but it took almost two more decades for the town to gain formal recognition as a separate place with its own legal identity. The next 15 years shaped and consolidated the community and urban landscape of Bournemouth.

TWO

PEOPLE WHO MADE THE TOWN

Eileen and John Barker

Bright's 1903 map shows the Improvement Commissioners' unusual circular boundary of 1856 (in blue) and the County Borough boundary of 1901 (in red). Bournemouth now includes Winton, Springbourne, Boscombe and Southbourne. Westbourne, the area around Horseshoe Common and Dean Park and the West and East Cliffs have large detached houses in large gardens. The areas outside the 1856 boundary have much denser housing. Below the inset map, Talbot Village and Highmoor are isolated from other settlements. Reproduced with the kind permission of the Ordnance Survey.

Chapter Two

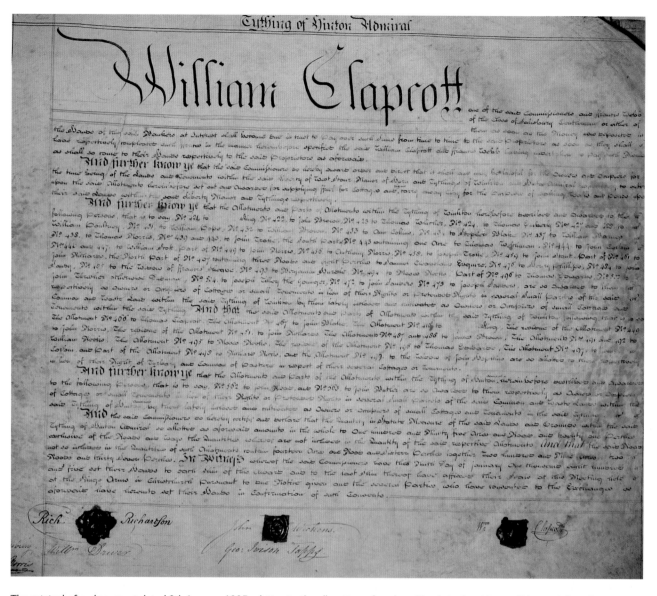

The original of a document dated 9th January 1805 relating to the allocation of enclosed lands in the tithing of Hinton Admiral. At the bottom are the signatures of Inclosure Commissioner Richard Richardson together with those of William Clapcott, William Driver, Philip Norris and Lord of the Manor George Ivison Tapps, all of whom acquired land in Holdenhurst parish.

AT THE BEGINNING of the 19th century, the stretch of heathland between Poole and Christchurch was uninhabited apart from a few wattle and daub cottages, the settlements of Moordown and Pokesdown on the escarpment above the River Stour and two large houses: Littledown, occupied by William Dean and Stourfield tenanted by the Countess of Strathmore. Within the fertile valley of the river, there were a number of hamlets including Kinson, Holdenhurst (the largest), Throop, Iford and Wick.

An extract from the Tithe map of Ensbury. Plots 458 to 461 were owned by the Rev. Charles Bowle, who had been given them by the smuggler Isaac Gulliver. The adjoining plot 461 was owned by William John Bankes (owner of Kingston Lacy), who patrolled the coast immediately to the west of Tregonwell's patrol area.

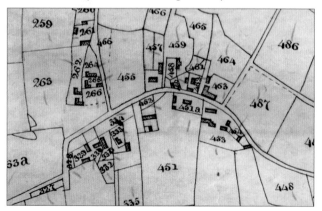

Enclosure and the Rich and Poor

In 1801, local landowners led by Sir George Ivison Tapps, the Lord of the Manor of Christchurch, lobbied Parliament to enclose large areas of the heathland, some of which was the source of turf for the cottagers, their main fuel for heating and cooking. One of the most important events in the history of the town now took place. A crowd of graziers and turf cutters and their supporters from the Stour valley villages went to the Muscliff farmhouse of William West, described as an educated farmer. Such an assembly of workers about their working conditions could lead to imprisonment under the Combination Law of 1800. So they were taking a considerable risk by gathering together and walking as a crowd to his farm. However, they persuaded him to put their concerns to the Commissioners appointed to administer the 1802 Act of Inclosure.

The three Commissioners were William Clapcott, son-in-law of William Dean, who lived at Littledown, Richard Richardson, a London barrister, and John Wickens of Mapperton in west Dorset. They ruled that 425 acres in five locations could be allotted to occupiers of cottages and tenements which were less than one acre in area. They had to be on 'ancient sites' or have been occupied for more than 14 years. These 'turbary' commons subsequently became Bournemouth's parks.

Without the villagers risking imprisonment, and William West agreeing to help them, five of the most important parts of the landscape and recreational facilities of Bournemouth would probably not exist and would almost certainly have been built upon. Land at the top of Richmond Hill was allocated to nine cottagers from Muscliff, including three widows, Mary Vincent, Mrs. Tarrant and Martha Watton and three labourers, William

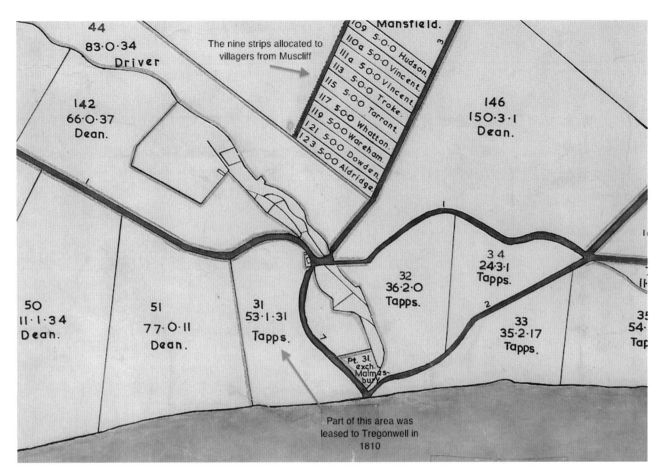

Extract from the 1805 Enclosure map showing ownership around the town centre. Part of Plot 31 was where Tregonwell first rented land from George Tapps in 1810. The narrow plots, 109 to 123, had been allocated to a group of Muscliff cottagers.

Troke, Peter Wareham and William Dowden.

The area subject to the Inclosure Act, 5084 acres 1 rood and 9 square perches, was divided into 241 plots. Of these, 29 plots were allocated for roads, mainly along the existing tracks, and gravel pits to supply road-building materials, plus one for clay. Just over 1258 acres were sold to meet the expenses of administering the Act and purchased by seven individuals for a total of £4100 14 shillings and 11 pence. The largest areas, totalling a little over 764 acres went to Sir George Ivison Tapps, Lord

of the Manor and living at Hinton Admiral, the Earl of Malmesbury who lived at Hurn (or Heron) Court on the far side of the River Stour and William Dean who acquired just over 500 acres on the West Cliff and around King's Park. Probably the most significant for the early development of

A portrait of Lewis Dymoke Grosvenor Tregonwell who was described as the Founder of Bournemouth. An oil painting after Thomas Beach. Photograph reproduced with the kind permission of the Russell-Cotes Art Gallery & Museum.

Bournemouth was the 205 acres bought by Tapps on the cliffs around the Bourne valley. A further 240 acres went to Tapps as compensation for loss of rights and interest in soil and the loss of common rights, and 316 acres to Lord Malmesbury in lieu of tithes. Tapps thus gained more land between Boscombe and the Lansdowne.

The four others included William Driver who bought about 246 acres at Redhill and Moordown and Philip Norris who acquired 141 acres at Boscombe and 11 acres at Strouden. Cornelius Trim bought a little over 82 acres and Arthur Quartly, a physician in Christchurch, bought about 21 acres near Stokewood Road. Tapps paid £5 2 shillings per acre, but William Dean paid much less: £1 8 shillings per acre. Although some forty people in all gained from the sale, the main beneficiaries were Sir George Ivison Tapps and William Dean, with 1149 acres 2 roods and 34 square perches and 1137 acres and 14 square perches respectively. These similar holdings were subsequently managed quite differently, but had a very substantial effect on future development of the town.

In 1810, Lewis Tregonwell, a Dorset landowner and officer in the Dorset Yeomanry, while staying at Mudeford with his wife Henrietta, explored the coast towards Poole and, delighted by the scene where the Bourne stream enters the sea, bought a plot of eight and a half acres from Sir George Tapps on which to build a house. When completed in 1812, and named Exeter House, it was said to be the first house in Bournemouth although not far north was the Tapps Arms (see page 31), a public house built in 1809 near where the track from Christchurch to Poole crossed the Bourne. Tregonwell extended his estate to 36 acres over the next twelve years, building a number of cottages to let to visitors, together with one for his butler, Thomas Symes (see page 22), and another for his gardener.

William Dean died in 1812, leaving a will which expressly prevented land from being developed for residential buildings, and also made his son-in-law, William Clapcott, his successor in the Christchurch, Wimborne and Ringwood Bank. His daughter, Mary Clapcott, and her husband William now owned a large estate, but could not benefit from rising land values. George Bruce's book *A Fortune and a Family: Bournemouth and the Cooper-Deans*[1] describes in detail the financial difficulties that followed. By 1820, the Clapcotts had accrued substantial debts, largely as a result of William's banking losses. Then in 1825, the London bank, Pole & Company, failed owing £300,000, mostly due to bad overseas government debts

Exeter House, the house completed by Lewis Tregonwell in 1812, and generally regarded as the first house to be built in Bournemouth. Parts still survive, incorporated into the Royal Exeter Hotel.

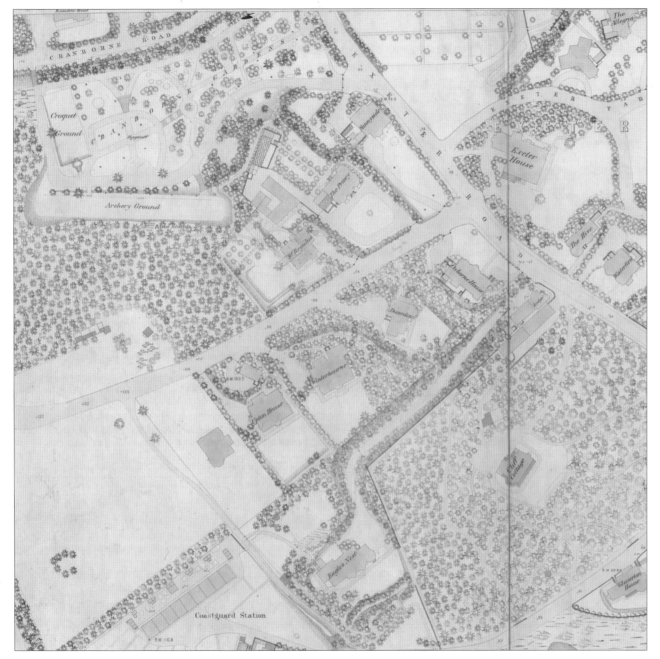

and speculation in South American mines. The impact on many smaller banks across the country was disastrous. The Bank of England had to draw upon its gold reserves to meet the debts and prevent panic in the financial markets. William Clapcott's debts continued to rise, so that he and his wife had almost no ready money: hardly enough to pay their estate workers. After he died in July 1833, Mary set about freeing her and her son, William, from the mortgages which so restricted their ability to capitalise on the now rising land values. She arranged in 1839 for 714 acres, which included now valuable land fronting several hundred yards of the coast, to be released from a mortgage. She had also invested in life insurance so that when she died in 1854 it became possible for William to be freed from the burden of mortgages which had bedevilled

LEFT A detail from a map showing Exeter House, Cliff Cottage and the Coastguard Station in 1870. Reproduced from the (1870) Ordnance Survey map with the kind permission of the Ordnance Survey.

BELOW The boards outside the Tregonwell Arms in 1883 include notices about Bournemouth's Government School of Art and the South American Missionary Society: all beneath the inn's own signs for a choice of Ale and Stout from the wood or bottled.

James McWilliam, one of the founders of Bournemouth. He appears here in his uniform as colour-sergeant in the 19th Hants Rifles Volunteer Corps. He was a long-serving member of the Board of Commissioners and its Chairman in 1874/5. He was the provisional Mayor of Bournemouth when the town was first incorporated and Captain of the newly-formed Fire Brigade.

the family for almost four decades. William nevertheless also had to change his name to Clapcott Dean in order to secure his inheritance. The scene was set for development of his land near the growing resort.

Forming the Town

In the meantime, other changes were taking place and other players were becoming involved in the new town. In the mid-1830s, Tregonwell brought William Rebbeck from Cranborne to manage his estate in Bournemouth. Rebbeck founded an estate agency in 1845 to manage other estates. In 1851 Sir George Gervis granted him a 99 year lease of the westernmost portion of the triangular piece of land opposite the Tregonwell Arms, where he built his first office. This became known as Rebbeck's Corner. Rebbeck also took on other tasks: he raised money for a jetty at the mouth of the Bourne, he was a rate collector for five years, and the first Parish Clerk to St. Peter's Church.

Sir George Gervis, the son of Sir George Tapps, succeeded to his father's estate in 1835. He was keen to develop the land on the eastern bank of the Bourne into a fashionable watering place and resort. His Christchurch-born architect, Benjamin Ferrey, produced plans for the estate which included a row of villas and a hotel overlooking the sea (see page 21). These were to become Westover Road and the Bath Hotel respectively. David Tuck, a local bricklayer, his son Peter and foreman James McWilliam built the hotel, the first of the villas and the Belle Vue boarding house by the mouth of the Bourne. Another builder, Robert Kerley from Sturminster Newton, was developing the Tregonwell land on the western side of the Bourne. Kerley Road on the West Cliff is named after him. The prospect of work attracted builders and labourers from Hampshire and the neighbouring county of Dorset to the growing village.

Encouragement came from an outside source when Dr Granville, author of *The Spas of England*, visited the area in 1841 and wrote that its climate and position made it an 'ideal place for invalids and those of delicate constitutions requiring a warm and sheltered locality in the winter season.'

In 1851, the marine village had a population of 598 of which only 15 had been born there and they were all less than 15 years of age. Approximately a quarter of the inhabitants came from Dorset and one seventh from Hampshire, the rest from much further afield. The migrants were mainly tradesmen, skilled artisans (builders), shopkeepers and labourers.

Sir George Gervis built the first church of St. Peter in 1843. It had no permanent clergy until 1845 when the Reverend Alexander Morden Bennett was appointed as perpetual curate. The church had not yet been consecrated. On his arrival he said, 'The benefice was so uninviting in every respect that no clergyman could be found to take charge of it. There was no parsonage house, no school and a very small endowment. However I resolved to take charge.' Later that year the church was consecrated and the endowment increased. Bennett then built a school and a vicarage for the church. Soon afterwards he met George Edmund Street, an ecclesiastical architect who was to enlarge the church, add a tower and finally the spire. Bennett was concerned not only with the parish of St Peter but also with the spiritual and moral life of the outlying districts. With Street he built a small chapel at Moordown, St. John in the Wilderness, as well as another at East Parley. He founded a Mission Church of St. Michael on the West Cliff and St. James at Pokesdown and established a number of church schools. He died in 1880, much respected and revered despite his austere character. Sir Henry Taylor, a retired diplomat and poet, said of him, 'He was like the commination service incarnate – so little addicted to flattery of his human fellows, it was difficult to believe he could find it in his heart to praise God.'

In 1852, Christopher Crabbe Creeke, an architect and surveyor, who was to have a great influence on the future shape of the town, arrived to work on Sir Percy Florence Shelley's house in Boscombe. One of his first jobs was supervising the building and layout of the grounds of Branksome Towers for Charles Packe, MP for South Leicestershire. He designed the original Richmond Hill Congregational Church on a site overlooking the central gardens and Bourne Avenue. In 1854 he was a member of a committee, chaired by Morden Bennett, set up to obtain an Act of Parliament to secure the improvement and better regulation of Bournemouth. The other members were builders David and Peter Tuck, estate agent William Rebbeck, Samuel Bayly, a retired Christchurch draper, James McWilliam, banker George Ledgard, resident physician Dr Mainwaring and Henry Blacklock. Creeke was tasked with producing a map of the district and procuring boundary stones.

The Improvement Commissioners set to Work

The Improvement Act of 1856 (Section Two) defined Bournemouth as the area within 'a circle of the radius of one mile, whereof the centre is the front door of the Belle Vue Hotel'. Thirteen Commissioners were appointed who were authorised to improve the roads and drainage, to build a pier or jetty, to provide street lighting, a market place and to levy a rate to meet expenses. The Commissioners included the Lord of the Manor and his nominee. Of the original committee, only George Ledgard, Samuel Bayly and David Tuck became Commissioners. The others were William Clapcott Dean, John Tregonwell, Charles William Packe, Robert Kerley, William Robson, Thomas Shettle, Samuel Thompson and William Esdaile Winter.

At their first meeting at the Belle Vue Hotel, the Commissioners appointed Creeke as Surveyor and Inspector of Nuisances. He also had to assess the rateable

RIGHT Christopher Crabbe Creeke, an architect and surveyor, was appointed by the Improvement Commissioners as the first Surveyor and Inspector of Nuisances in 1856.

BELOW Southbourne Terrace, the first parade of shops, with St. Peter's Church on the far right seen from Exeter Lane in 1865.

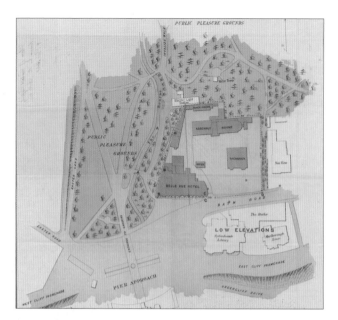

A plan of the Belle Vue Hotel advertising its sale freehold in 1906. Compare this with the photograph on the right showing the same buildings 40 years earlier.

East Beach, with the remains of the 1861 jetty on the left, the Belle Vue Hotel in the centre, and the Baths and Sydenham's Library on the right.

value of the properties in the district. Mate and Riddle in their history of the town[2] say of his task, 'There was no proper system of drainage; the roads were in a chaotic condition. It took the Surveyor some years to put them in order. His early years were devoted to levelling the surface of the roads – gravelling and kerbing them and throwing the spare soil over the cliffs. With an eye to the artistic he designed winding and tortuous back roads'. They go on to say, 'Creeke's idea was to avoid a straight road.'

In 1857, William Clapcott Dean engaged him to manage his estate. Here he produced the circular cricket ground, Dean Park Crescent and Horseshoe Common. His architectural practice designed the Almshouses for Talbot Village, the Lansdowne Baptist Church, a homeopathic nursing home, Hahnemann House, and several villas on

the West Cliff as well as extensions to the Bath Hotel. In 1877, he laid out the grounds of the Wimborne Road Cemetery and designed the chapel and mortuary. He was buried there in 1886.

The duties of the Inspector of Nuisances were to inspect and report on defective drains, foul closets, uncovered night soil and overflowing cesspits. In 1857 Creeke reported a defective privy belonging to Henry Joy. There were complaints about the smell arising from pigs kept in the town centre. Another Inspector, Mr. O'Connell, reported that a shed had been converted to a slaughterhouse with putrid offal and a dead horse left in the open. Dairyman William Batten of Springbourne was charged in 1885 with unlawfully keeping 47 pigs, 6 horses and 5 cows in his garden. A later visit found several dead

pigs and an offensive smell from unsanitary pig sties. He was fined £2 with £1 16 shillings costs.

In 1855, the 100-bed National Sanatorium for sufferers of tuberculosis was built overlooking the Central Gardens on land donated by George Durrant, owner of the Branksome Estate. It was the first purpose built sanatorium in the country on a site chosen because of 'its healthy situation – dryness, equability and mildness of temperature.'

In 1870, Dr John Roberts Thomson, a Scot and physician at the cottage hospital in Madeira Road, was appointed as a resident surgeon to the National Sanatorium. His concern about the inadequacies of the cottage hospital for the growing population of the town led to the building of the Royal Victoria Hospital on Poole Road between Westbourne and the Square. Later a branch of the hospital was built to the east in Lowther Road. Further lobbying resulted in both hospitals being amalgamated with the Boscombe and West Hants Hospital in Shelley Road.

Thomson also advocated secondary education for boys which resulted in the founding of Bournemouth School in 1901. For these services to the town and his role as Commanding Officer of the Volunteers (the fore-runners of the Territorial Army), he was made an Honorary Freeman of the town.

One of those attracted to Bournemouth was the carpenter Henry Joy, who moved his family from Chalbury just north of Wimborne into the town in 1847. His obituary said of him, 'He first came to the town carrying all his fortune with him – not a big bank account, but health, indefatigable energy, indomitable will and the valuable gift of foresight which enables a man to see the possibilities of business or to spend money and time developing projects, that, to the less prescient, appear hopeless.' The next few years saw him raising capital by speculative building until he could start on his first major project still standing, Southbourne Terrace overlooking the Square (see page 31).

He went on to build the Arcade, which bridged a

The National Sanatorium, which opened in 1855 overlooking the Central Gardens

ABOVE & RIGHT The Arcade in 1878, and today. It runs between Gervis Road (shown in the 1878 photograph) and Old Christchurch Road.

stream joining the Bourne, an act that was seen initially as vandalism of a favourite beauty spot but later as an asset to the town. He repeated its success by building another arcade in Westbourne. Henry Joy was typical of many working class craftsmen who moved to the town and used their entrepreneurial skills to make their fortune and create a new town. At first, he lived in Terrace Road where his neighbours were building workers, domestic servants, stone masons, a blacksmith and a dressmaker.

The better roads and drainage brought about by the Improvement Act attracted people of all classes to settle in and around the Marine Village. Invalids and the upper classes were drawn by the mild climate and, for the latter, the respite it provided from the London Season. Villas, hotels and boarding houses were erected to house these visitors and invalids. Terraces of smaller houses were built close to Commercial Road and at West Hill Place, at the top of the hill, for the living-out domestic servants, artisans and labourers required to meet the needs of the

new arrivals. Among the inhabitants of West Hill Place was Mr. Whitty, a collector of road tolls. By 1851 a number of shops had opened on the western side of the Square at the lower end of Commercial Road. There were butchers, grocers, bakers, dressmakers and a chemist.

The second half of the 1850s saw the first landing stage for pleasure boats built, and the preparation of a path through Westover Gardens to be known as 'Invalids Walk'

The Almshouses, Talbot Village, part of the model village created by Georgina and Marianne Talbot, which when finished in the 1860s included six farms, a church, school and 19 cottages as well as the almshouses.

(later renamed Pine Walk). The area around the crossing of the Bourne at the foot of Richmond Hill became known as The Square and the first newspaper, *The Visitors Directory*, was published. It listed the arrivals and departures for the week and where they were staying, enabling cards to

be sent to those one wished to contact. Sir Henry Taylor grumbled that 'Two doctors, three widows and six old maids made up the sum total of possible acquaintances.' Among the arrivals it reported in 1846 were the Duke and Duchess of Montrose, Lord and Lady Lytton and the Marquis of Westminster. But amongst the apparent affluence were some glaring instances of dreadful poverty.

The Misses Georgina and Marianne Talbot were the daughters of Sir George Talbot, who owned property in London and Surrey. On his death, the women inherited a

considerable fortune and moved to a large house called Hinton Wood on the East Cliff. Here they were disturbed by crowds of families shouting for food and begging for work. In 1850, Georgina Talbot bought some 350 acres of land to the north of the town to build a small village with cottages and farms to provide work and homes for some of the poor. All but one of the cottages in Talbot Village were set in an acre of land with a pig sty and a water supply. The occupants were expected to be self supporting, to abstain from alcohol and to move on when they had sufficient means. The building of the cottages, which were completed by 1862, was undertaken by James McWilliam. Almshouses, St. Mark's Church and School were added in succeeding years. The Talbots also owned land on the eastern side of Wimborne Road and in 1865 built artisans' cottages between what is now Brassey Road and Calvin Road. This formed the core of the present suburb of Winton.

As the town expanded from 1860 onwards, many of the builders from the early years continued to work in the trade. James McWilliam who helped to build Westover Villas went on to supervise the building of Talbot Village and Winton. The development of Winton as a working class suburb was paralleled by similar developments in Springbourne, Pokesdown and parts of Boscombe. Springbourne started on the south side of Holdenhurst Road on land allotted to Dr William Farr, the Earl of Malmesbury and John Sloman of Tuckton and Wick, as compensation for loss of rights of common. Dr Farr lived at Iford House. When he died in 1863, his son, William Deale Farr, inherited the estate and leased the first plot in 1864 to Nicholas James, a bricklayer who used it as a brickyard for some ten years. Other plots were leased to William Lane and to a partnership of Peter Tuck and James Druitt, a Christchurch solicitor.

Peter Tuck, the son of David Tuck, succeeded his

In his day Joseph Cutler was a local (Bournemouth) celebrity. He was a member of the governing party, an alderman, a volunteer fireman, a sergeant in the Bournemouth Artillery Volunteers, and promoter of the first Regatta in 1871.

father as a contractor to the Gervis Estate. At this time he was an Improvement Commissioner (1861 to 1877) and Chairman of the Board in 1869. He died in Bournemouth in 1896 aged 74.

Bournemouth at this time had a number of brickyards near the town centre, at Boscombe, Springbourne and Charminster which exploited the local clay deposits. William Mabey, a carpenter from Beaminster in Dorset, in his reminiscences of Bournemouth in 1868, writes of a brickyard in Madeira Vale, the area around the Lansdowne, and of another near the entrance of Boscombe Chine. He describes Madeira Vale as the 'home of lodging men, flocking in from all parts to work in the clay and gravel

pits,' and saying to their mates, 'does 'e think' e can go to Madra Vale? He can get good diggins go woam drunk any hour and none word zed.'

This is the time when many builders were making their way to the expanding town. One of these, described as 'one of the liveliest and provocative personalities in the public life of the town', was Joseph Cutler. Born in Christchurch in 1830, the son of a fisherman, he left school, 'not having mastered the alphabet nor reaching the three times three in the multiplication table.' He was apprenticed as a glazier and plumber in Lymington. After working in Australia and London, he moved to Bournemouth in 1865 as a builder.

Among the buildings he erected was Cumnor, a house in Old Christchurch Road overlooking Horseshoe Common. Later he replaced it with the five storey terrace of seven shops with living accommodation which still stands. Farther up the road he bought and completed an unfinished terrace of six shops which became known as 'Joseph's Terrace'. Separating the six properties were tiled panels, each of which included a portrait of Cutler. His contemporary, Henry Joy, noted that the tiles included 'the crack in the head'. Cutler was elected an Improvement Commissioner in 1881 and celebrated by presenting the town with sixty horse chestnut trees which were planted on the north side of the Bourne from Invalids' Walk to the present tennis courts. Earlier, after a dispute with the Burial Board, he supplied the Monkey Puzzle trees that lined the main drive of the Wimborne Road Cemetery. The Municipal Corporation Act of 1882 led him to campaign for municipal status for the town, which was refused at first but granted at the third time of asking. He also advocated votes for women, cheap return tickets on the railways for

Sir Henry Drummond Wolff, K.C.M.G., M.P., in a cartoon from *Vanity Fair* in 1874. He played a significant part in the development of Boscombe and in particular of Boscombe Chine gardens.

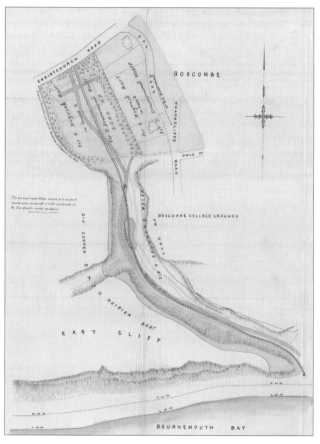

Winter Gardens. He and his wife sponsored a number of agricultural shows in the area and, when he became MP for Christchurch in 1874, donated to many local charities. He later returned to the diplomatic service, but retained his interest in the estate until his death in 1908.

Among the many upper class people who made their homes in the town was Lady Georgiana Fullerton, granddaughter of the 5th Duchess of Devonshire. She had from an early age been concerned with alleviating the sufferings

Plans for the development of the pleasure gardens in Boscombe Chine in 1884.

The thatched Spa at Boscombe in 1876, with the Chine Hotel in the background.

working men and an independent police force, and was a member of the fire brigade and the artillery volunteers. His many letters to the press included one complaining about pig keeping in the town centre. Cutler served the newly created Municipal Borough as a councillor and later as an alderman. He died in 1910 and is buried in Wimborne Road Cemetery.

Although much of the development of the town was undertaken by builders, Boscombe Spa was the project of a retired diplomat and protégé of the Earl of Malmesbury, Sir Henry Drummond Wolff. A grandson of Horace Walpole, he joined the Foreign Office at the age

of sixteen after his handwriting was approved by Lord Palmerston. After service in the eastern Mediterranean, he retired and bought an acre of land from Malmesbury in the area bordered by Boscombe Chine and Sea Road, Boscombe and built a house there. It was close to a spring which, reputedly, provided mineral water similar to that of Harrogate. William Mabey claimed it improved his eyesight. Wolff decided to exploit it as a spa and bought the rest of the land between Owls Road and the sea, and later leased the remaining land between Christchurch Road and Owls Road from Sir George Meyrick. He proceeded to build large villas and hotels in the estate and to develop Boscombe Chine as a pleasure ground. Unlike some other landowners of the time, Wolff did involve himself in public projects to enhance the district, investing in Boscombe Pier and the

Lady Georgiana Fullerton was a very important Roman Catholic benefactor for the poorer communities in the town, providing support for schools as well as other needs.

of the sick and poor in Europe, in this country and in London. She gave them practical help by herself helping scrub or sweep floors, light fires and make beds. To finance this work she wrote novels, biographies and poetry. In Bournemouth, she founded St. Joseph's Home in Madeira Road for poor Catholics from London with tuberculosis. A group of ladies including the Duchess of Norfolk and Lady Kirwan supported her. The home closed after her death in 1885, but her husband funded the opening, in 1888, of another home in Branksome Wood Road and invited the Sisters of Mercy to run it. Among her many friends were the Countess Pauline Von Hugel who established the Church of Corpus Christi in Boscombe and Sir Henry Taylor with whom she enjoyed literary discussions.

ABOVE Looking inland along Boscombe Chine in 1875, we can just make out St. Clement's Church on the horizon. To the right are some of the earliest villas along Spa Road.

BELOW Further east by 1900, at Southbourne, Dr. Crompton's dream of a separate resort was crumbling into the sea as the promenade was undermined by storms. His original plan was for houses such as these along the whole length of the promenade. Only 6 were built. The foundations of the sea wall were for many years still visible at the end of the modern groynes.

RIGHT Details from the portraits of Annie and Merton Russell-Cotes in 1895, painted by John Henry Lorimer. Both photographs reproduced with the kind permission of the Russell-Cotes Art Gallery & Museum.

ABOVE Father Christmas has just flown in on his way to Beale's in 1912.

LEFT Beale's first store 'Fancy Fair' in 1881.

BELOW LEFT The Beale family in 1905.

BELOW One of Beale's delivery vans in 1924.

The suburb of Southbourne was the creation of Dr T. A. Compton who bought 230 acres of land in 1870 with a mile of seafront between Boscombe and Hengistbury Head. There he built a pier, a sea wall and an esplanade with a terrace of villas. All were destroyed by south-westerly gales within the next twenty years. He built Tuckton Bridge and a winter garden for his wife to exercise in by horse riding but he also opened it to the public.

The last decades of the 19th century saw more shops being opened on the eastern side of the Square. Frederick Bright, a former missionary, opened a haberdashery in the corner of the Arcade in 1871 and John Elmes Beale, a draper from Weymouth, leased a shop just to the east to sell a variety of goods under the name 'Fancy Fair'. He took advantage of the increasing number of visitors coming by train to Bournemouth and offered wooden spades, buckets and toy boats for children going to the beach. Both shops expanded into large department stores. Percy Bright, who succeeded his father in the business, always left his office door open for any member of staff who wanted a chat.

Merton Russell-Cotes came to Bournemouth in the

ABOVE The Russell-Cotes Museum & Art Gallery today and (LEFT) as it was in 1907 when it was still called East Cliff Hall.

RIGHT An early view of the Royal Bath Hotel.

1870s to improve his health and in 1876 bought the Bath Hotel. He added two wings designed by Crabbe Creeke, redecorated and re-opened it in 1880 as the Royal Bath Hotel. He and his wife Annie were great travellers and filled the hotel with artefacts collected on their travels to the Far East. Behind the hotel they built East Cliff Hall which was to be left to the town with their collections as a museum and art gallery. Russell-Cotes was a leading advocate of an undercliff drive, a promenade, a pavilion and a direct railway to London. He and his wife founded a nautical

Police Sergeant Coles, head of Bournemouth Police 1863. At the period there were three policemen stationed at Bournemouth, Sergeant Coles and two constables. These men were the sole police for the care of Bournemouth. Note the sergeant's beard, also the long tightly buttoned frock coat form of uniform. In those days any person who was under arrest was remanded in custody in Christchurch and then brought before the Hampshire magistrates sitting at the Town Hall.

school for boys at Parkstone which eventually passed to Dr Barnado. He and his wife were made Honorary Freemen of the town in 1908. Merton served one year as Mayor and was knighted in 1909.

Horace Dobell was one of the many doctors who sang the praises of Bournemouth as an ideal place for the sick.

Bournemouth Police Station (seen here in 1875) was, like many other buildings, built away from the centre of the new town.

In his book, *The Medical Aspects of Bournemouth and its Surroundings*, he examined its climate and geology and concluded it to be suitable for treating many ailments. He was not in favour of young children paddling in the sea because it resulted in congestion, headaches and bilious vomiting. An enthusiast for the 'Mont Dore' treatment, he welcomed the opening of an hotel to provide this cure.

At first the Commissioner's district had one policeman, P.C. Smith, who was attached to the Ringwood Division and responsible to the Chief Constable at Winchester. Requests for better cover brought, in 1862, two more

constables and a sergeant and eventually a permanent station in Madeira Road. Joseph Cutler pressed for a Bournemouth force independent of the county but this did not occur until 1948. Much of the crime was petty but the last offence of poaching, unusual in this town, was heard by Bournemouth Magistrates in 1932. Mr. Keats, a local carpenter, recalled serving as a special constable for the Guy Fawkes celebrations in the 1880s when extra police were drafted into the town. Lighted tar barrels were rolled from the top of Commercial Road to the Square and shopkeepers had to board up their shops. The crowds were large and lively and occasionally out of hand, with some of those taking part assaulting the Police. After one court case, the Chairman commented that 'Bournemouth

Fire Brigades were almost always dependent on volunteers. In 1894, Capt. W. J. Worth was responsible for the Bournemouth Volunteer Fire Brigade.

ABOVE The Bournemouth Volunteer Fire Brigade turn-out parade at the new fire station in Holdenhurst Road in 1902.

ABOVE RIGHT Bournemouth's first steam-powered Fire Engine.

RIGHT The Ambulance Section making a Chair Knot and the Chair Knot in use for moving injured or ill people from buildings.

has for some years had an unenviable notoriety in regard to firework disturbances on Guy Fawkes day.' Keats said that not all the rioters were Bournemouth people but some came from as far as Newton and Moordown.

As more large houses, hotels and shops were built in the town centre, the potential danger that fire presented was recognised because the nearest fire engines were at Poole and Christchurch. Joseph Cutler agitated for a fire fighting service for the town. His pleas fell on unheeding ears until a serious fire occurred on Richmond Hill. A Bournemouth-based fire service was seen as a necessity and a volunteer force was formed under the leadership of James McWilliam. It expanded over the years ahead but remained largely a volunteer force until the 1930s. The first paid fireman was James Paradine who had experience with the London Fire Brigade. Henry Robson, a Yorkshireman, joined the Volunteer Fire Brigade soon after his arrival in the town

in 1891. He became its Captain in 1912 and oversaw a number of improvements to the service. Robson, who founded a grocery business in the Triangle, was Mayor from 1915 to 1917, an officer in the Boys' Brigade (he attended the first Scout camp on Brownsea Island) and was made an Honorary Freeman of the town in 1930.

Developing the Borough

In 1890, the town was incorporated as a Municipal Borough with a Mayor elected from eighteen councillors. The first Mayor was Thomas Hankinson, the last chairman of the Improvement Commissioners. Born in Norfolk, he came to Bournemouth in 1858 to improve his health.

He set up as an estate agent, printer and auctioneer and managed the Durrant estates in the locality. Of the next 87 mayors who served until the year 2000, twenty one were shopkeepers, seven hoteliers, seven builders, six estate agents and six doctors.

Of the hoteliers, the most influential were probably Sir

ABOVE The staff of local builders and contractors, George and Harding, outside their premises in Lansdowne Road.

BELOW The Duke of Gloucester with Mayor Alderman Cartwright on the way to a ceremony at the War Memorial on 19th March 1929.

The Provisional Mayor, James McWilliam, and the Bournemouth Commissioners 27th August 1890. Alongside McWilliam are Mr. T.J. Hankinson, Chairman, 1876 and 1890, and Chairman of the Society for Promoting the Incorporation of Bournemouth, Mr. H.T. Trevinian, the Society's solicitor and Mr. J. Druitt, Clerk to the Board and Provisional Town Clerk.

Heavyweight Champion in 1948.

Deric Scott, the 50th Mayor, funeral director and descendant of an old Tuckton family, became the Chairman of the new Dorset County Council after Bournemouth was absorbed into the county. He was appointed High Sheriff of Dorset, a post later filled by his son, Adrian.

Of the many clergymen who served the churches of Bournemouth in the first years of the 20th century, one of the best known was Rev J.D. Jones C.H., M.A. D.D. The Minister of the Richmond Hill Congregation Church for 39 years, he was a world-renowned preacher and administrator. He was an influential member of the Bournemouth Education Committee. In 1927 he became a Companion of Honour, and in 1930 the first minister of religion to be made an Honorary Freeman of Bournemouth.

There were no major manufacturing industries in the town. The main employers were builders, department stores, bakeries, laundries and dairies. For working men there were jobs in the building trades and for women the choice was domestic service or work in a shop or laundry.

Charles Cartwright and Frank McInnes. The former, unfairly described as an uneducated pot boy when he arrived, was shrewd enough to become the owner of a number of hotels. One was the Mont Dore, which in 1922 became the Town Hall. He championed the building of the Pavilion and was Mayor in 1929 when it was opened by the Duke of Gloucester. He was Chairman of the Finance Committee for many years and at the start of the Second World War was Group Controller of the Air Raid Precautions service. McInnes, a former soldier and gymnast, at one time owned the Norfolk Hotel on Richmond Hill. He was a friend and supporter of boxer Freddie Mills from Terrace Road who became World Light

Nellie Hoare, born in 1898 in Winton and the youngest but one of nine children, recalled that her father was a labourer working outside on roads, putting in kerbstones and laying drains. In 1912, he earned, in a good week, about 30/-, half of which he gave to his wife and the other half he kept for his beer and tobacco. Her eldest sister went into service when she was eleven years old, getting up at 6.30 am and preparing and lighting the fires before breakfast. She was paid 1/6d a week but got her meals free. When she was fifteen, she left to become an ironer in a nearby laundry for 5/- a week. Nellie left school when she was fourteen to work in Castle Laundry as a calendar maid. She left after

Alderman Percy M. Bright, Mayor of Bournemouth in 1934. Photograph reproduced with the kind permissionof the Russell-Cotes Art Gallery & Museum.

collapsing in the heat and then worked as a daily maid doing housework in the morning and taking children out in the afternoon for 2/6d and lunch. When the First World War started, she was sixteen and, with the shortage of young men, she was able to take on a milk round complete with horse and float. For that she earned 18/- a week plus a pint of milk a day. After eighteen months, she moved to a bottle washing plant in the brewery in Holdenhurst Road. Eventually, as the youngest daughter, she had to give up work to look after her mother.

The Prince's Tower built in The Square for the visit of the Prince of Wales in 1890.

In 1923, at age fifteen, Kenneth Blakey joined an estate agent as an office boy. The wages of 5/- a week were not enough to help his widowed mother so he joined the provisions merchant, Sainsbury's, as a grocer's assistant for 25/- a week. After two weeks training in London, he was employed in one of the Bournemouth branches. The working hours were from 8am to 6pm on Monday, Tuesday

ABOVE The opening of Kinson Community Centre by Mayor Harry Mears and Councillor Bessie Bicknell in 1964.

LEFT The Bournemouth Unemployed Ex-Servicemen's Organisation was one of many organisations which provided support for the unemployed during the 1920s and 1930s.

and Thursday: until 7pm on Friday and until 9pm on Saturdays. Wednesday was a half day, closing at 1.30pm. One year's service entitled him to one week's holiday with pay. At the age of twenty one, wages increased to £3 per week, but it was usual to dispense with staff of that age to reduce costs: a common practice in many large shops.

Apprentices before the Second World War were often used for mundane tasks such as sweeping floors, making tea and cleaning machines before any craft training was given. John Miles, a Boscombe boy, was apprenticed to a joinery shop where his main tasks were to make sure the glue pot was hot, sweep the floors and to paint with pink primer any wooden structure required for house building. Dissatisfied with this, he moved to become a 'bound' apprentice stone mason. His wages were 3d an hour for

Flower sellers in the Square in 1950 carrying on a long tradition of produce being brought into the town from the Stour valley farms and the surrounding countryside.

the first year rising to 7d an hour for the fifth and final year for a forty hour week. In 1938 the hourly rate for a fully qualified mason was 1/6d. Common practice in all building firms was not to pay 'wet time' – time taken for preparing materials. Also the hourly rate meant acceptance of an hour's notice of dismissal. In the last hour before leaving, a tradesman was allowed to sharpen and clean his tools.

All the above were in work, but in the 1920s and 1930s, there were many unemployed. Among them was George Veal who described the queue at the Labour Exchange in Yelverton Road as four deep and stretching from there down to Old Christchurch Road and up as far as Dalkeith Steps. A gap was left outside the Cadena Café for the morning coffee trade. 'Signing on' was a twice weekly ritual. Walking back to Pokesdown, Mr. Veal and others would scour the roads for enough 'fag ends' to make a cigarette. At the Pokesdown Technical Schools, they could buy a cup of tea and a bun for a penny and if they were lucky get one free. This was a time when street singers, buskers and pedlars were a common sight.

There were several schemes to provide work. One was the creation by ex-servicemen of the Fampoux Gardens in Lower Charminster to commemorate the Hampshire Regiment's stand against the last German push in 1918. Another was the preparation of the racecourse at Ensbury Park. This was the work of Frederick Etches, a professional photographer with a keen interest in flying. In 1915, he became manager of the Bournemouth Aviation Company which ran a flying school on the Talbot Village estate to train pilots for the allied air forces. When the site proved too small, he and Bernard Mortimer bought the Ensbury Farm Estate and moved the school there. From 1917, it was known as RAF Winton. It was relinquished in 1919 and became a civil airfield. Etches and Mortimer were keen to establish a racecourse on the land. Kinson Parish Council agreed, as it would provide work for many of the unemployed.

After a number of delays, the racecourse opened in April 1925. Mr. Mortimer, expounding on the difficulties they faced, said of Bournemouth, 'The fairest town in the South is where until a few years ago the Council would not light the streets on a Sunday and on that day kept the trams in the sheds just to annoy visitors and residents.' During the next three years, there were National Hunt races, two air shows, grass track and greyhound racing. The racecourse described potentially as the 'Ascot of the South' attracted large crowds but too few for the venture to make money. Eventually it became a housing estate. Mr Etches went on to build many bungalows in north Bournemouth. He died in 1959.

The Second World War brought many more people flooding into the town. Airmen and soldiers were billeted on local families whilst training. The threat of air raids led to Civil Servants from London and schoolchildren from Southampton, Portsmouth and elsewhere being evacuated to Bournemouth for their safety. Many hotels were requisitioned as accommodation. Small workshops took on war work such as mending seamen's boots. There was a test tank for small boats at 'Harvey Nichols' in Commercial Road and a torpedo factory in Westover Road. Schools were closed after Dunkirk to accommodate returning troops.

One of the early casualties of bombs dropped in the

The brick-built Bournemouth International Centre (BIC) and West Beach from the Pier.

town was Cumberland Clark whose artless verse celebrated the town. His memorial has the largest angel in Boscombe Cemetery and was erected before his death as he 'didn't want his relatives to spend their inheritance on a brand new motor car.'

Sir Alexander MacLean, who founded the manufacturing chemists of that name, retired to Bournemouth and funded many charities for the elderly and infirm. During the Second World War, he gave money to launch the National Services Club at the Lansdowne and provided mobile canteens for use by Civil Defence in Bournemouth and Poole. These charitable activities were recognised when he was made an Honorary Freeman of the town.

Four other prominent citizens were similarly honoured in the post-war years. Harry Mears, cinema owner, farmer and horseman, was a member of the Council for over forty years and Mayor three times. He was awarded the OBE for his work as Civil Defence Controller during the war. An enthusiastic supporter of foreign language schools, he was opposed to a subsidised conference centre.

Affectionately known as the 'Mayor of Kinson', Harold Benwell, was a Londoner who convalesced in the Mont Dore Hotel after being wounded in the First World War. After discharge, he joined a local insurance firm and moved to Redhill, then in Kinson. As a Parish Councillor, he proposed many improvements to the village but opposed its move into Bournemouth. When Kinson joined Bournemouth in 1931, he became a Councillor and served as Mayor twice. In the Second World War he was in the Auxiliary Fire Service and was awarded the British Empire Medal.

The stonework for the Echo Offices, the Westover Ice Rink, the Council Chamber and many other buildings in Bournemouth was supplied by Templeman and Sons in Windham Road. Philip, the third generation of the family, became a Councillor and Chairman of the Welfare Services Committee. With the advent of the National Health Service, which wanted to use the Fairmile Workhouse in Christchurch as a properly equipped hospital and the abolition of the Poor Law, the occupants of the building had to be re-housed. Overnight more than one hundred

Miss Margaret Rainey was 100 years old when this photograph was taken in 1862. She was the daughter of a farmer and was born in Ireland. She lived to be 103 and was buried in St. Peter's Churchyard.

were moved into newly built old people's homes. In the ensuing years, Templeman established many more homes for the elderly and disabled. In 1970 he became the first Bournemouth-born person to become an Honorary Freeman of the town.

The building of the Bournemouth International Conference Centre (BIC) was a culmination of the desire to provide a venue for large conferences which could not be accommodated in the Pavilion or the Winter Gardens.

A strong advocate for such a centre was Councillor Bill Forman who was Chairman of the Hurn Airport Management Committee for ten years. He was also associated with the rebuilding of the Pier and its Show Bar.

The people mentioned here are just a few of the many who came to Bournemouth during the last two hundred years to build a town and a community where they could find work, prospects and enjoy a mild climate and healthy sea air.

Most of the early arrivals came from Dorset and Hampshire. Many of these were trades people, domestic servants and builders. Few were classed as 'gentry'. Thirty years later, every part of the British Isles was represented by 'incomers'.

Between the two World Wars, Spaniards escaping from the civil war in their country and many refugees from Eastern Europe arrived in the town, amongst them Ludwig Loewy who founded a successful engineering firm and Dr Alfred Steiner who went on to teach French, German and mathematics at Bournemouth School. In the 1950s, many Europeans who served in the allied forces saw business opportunities in an attractive town and stayed rather than return to their war-torn countries. They contributed to the present cosmopolitan aura of the town, augmented now by students from all over the world attending Bournemouth University and the many language schools. These, together with the development of the conference business and the re-location of major financial institutions, provide a constantly changing population which enriches the town and its culture.

THREE
AN UNEQUALLED CLIMATE

Vincent May

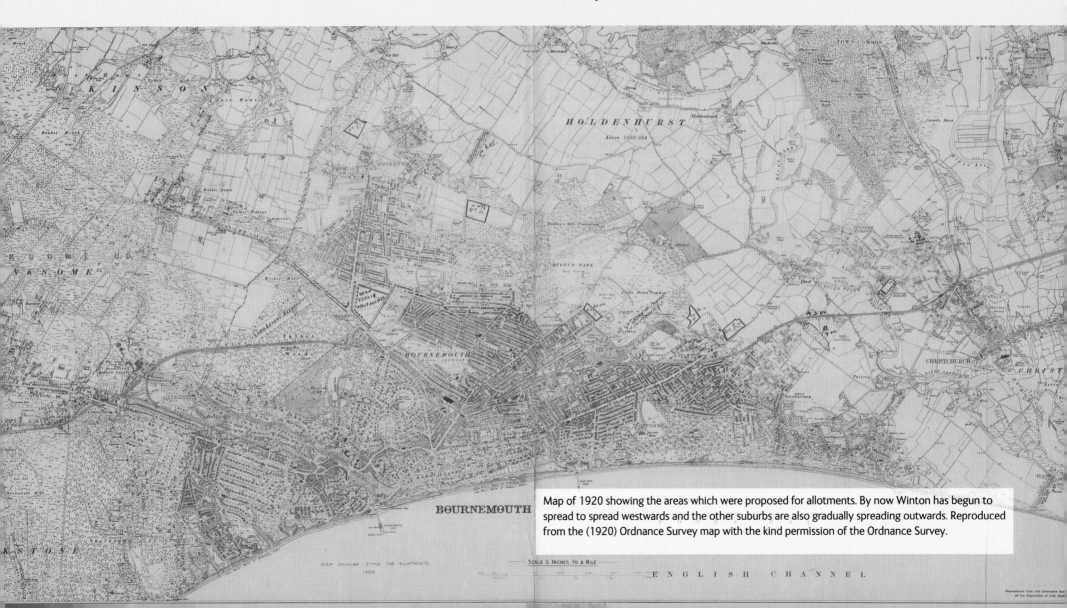

Map of 1920 showing the areas which were proposed for allotments. By now Winton has begun to spread to spread westwards and the other suburbs are also gradually spreading outwards. Reproduced from the (1920) Ordnance Survey map with the kind permission of the Ordnance Survey.

Chapter Three

FROM THE EARLIEST DAYS of Bournemouth's development as a resort, its climate was amongst its greatest assets. It was regarded as a unique feature that made Bournemouth especially important for its pre-eminent role as a health resort. By 1841, in his very influential *The Spas of England*, Dr A.B. Granville emphasised that Bournemouth had the greatest potential to be England's most important 'winter residence for the delicate constitutions requiring a warm and sheltered locality'.

Such a positive view of the town was often repeated, for example by Dobell in 1886: 'its softness, its freshness, its purity, and its antiseptic properties – a combination peculiarly difficult to obtain.'[1] Harries urged in 1914 that the town '. . . should be content with its unique position in the climatic scale, which is not equalled by any other town'[2] and the Medical Officer of Health noted in 1934 that 'gentle breezes from the sea temper the air.'[3] However, not all agreed that the climate suited everyone. Hawkins, for example, emphasized in 1923 that the climate was 'unsuited for growing and healthy children; for those with rheumatism, neuralgia, or an irritable cough; and for all who cannot go out of doors'[4] and, according to Burney in 1885, 'It would be an error to regard Bournemouth as a

Invalids' Walk in 1875. Dr Horace Dobell thought the aroma of Bournemouth's pines made it perfect for those with chest complaints and 'delicate constitutions requiring a warm and sheltered locality.'

The classic view of Bournemouth. Blue skies and a sandy beach.
The pier and beach from East Cliff.

Snowy winters were more common in the late 19th century. Belle Vue Road in 1895.

<table>
TABLE 1: Bournemouth's climate since the mid-nineteenth century
</table>

Years	Mean annual temperature (˚C)	Annual rainfall (mm)	Annual sunshine (hours)
Published records			
1862 to 1879		721.2	
1867 to 1884	9.97	759.0	
1879 to 1884			1532
Official records			
1900 to 1909	10.36	807.4	1855
1910 to 1919	10.08	889.8	1766
1920 to 1929	10.24	729.4	1730
1930 to 1939	10.46	801.8	1671
1940 to 1949	10.58	741.3	1734
1950 to 1959	10.37	817.0	1783
1960 to 1969	9.98	845.2	1721
1970 to 1979	10.19	778.1	1785
1980 to 1989	10.45	789.2	1724
1990 to 1999	10.99	764.7	1858
2000 to 2009	11.47	779.0	1882

perfect winter climate, which, indeed, it is far from being.'[5]

Granville, however, had stressed in a speech at a public dinner in 1841 how the differences of climate between the higher ground and the valleys gave the 'as yet unformed colony'[6] an unrivalled opportunity to attract the wealthy consumptives instead of them spending their money on the Continent. One of his audience, a Dr Aitkin, was sceptical about Granville's assertion. Aitkin had already read a paper to the Provisional Medical Association in 1840 in which he referred to the remarkably low rainfall and dry atmosphere at Bourne.[7] However, he wrote in May 1841 that he had decided to see if there were measurable differences in the temperature. On his first observation (at 1 p.m. on 8th March) on the West Cliff with a fresh breeze from the southwest, his thermometer 'sheltered from the wind and in the shade, stood at 49 degrees (Fahrenheit)' and another reading nearby was 50 degrees. 'In the different glens it ranged from 58 to 60 degrees. By repeated subsequent observations I note similar differences.', [8] i.e. about 5 degrees Celsius. Almost two decades later, regular readings supported Aitkin's description of the microclimatic variation which became so important for the future of Bournemouth.

As early as the 1850s, the town's new residents had begun to record the weather systematically. In 1868, the newly formed Bournemouth Meteorological Society reported that records were being kept at ten locations and each of these records was then used to provide an overall value for Bournemouth. Mr. Charles Dales began regular records in 1877 and was appointed Borough Meteorologist when Bournemouth joined the UK

Climatological Network in 1901. He continued to make observations at the instrument enclosure in his garden at 5 Nelson Road until his retirement in 1938 at the age of 87, when he was believed by the Meteorological Office to be its longest serving observer.

The early records reveal considerable variation in the local climate, an important consideration when showing how different places in the town provided better conditions for some medical conditions than others. Changes in recorded climate can be the result of the change in location rather than changes in climate, and the location of the meteorological instruments has changed during Bournemouth's history in an attempt to maximise a favourable climate.

Rainfall records in the official register in the 1920s show that rainfall at the official station in the Pleasure Gardens near the Pier was lower than at Firvale on the cliffs. For example, January rainfall in 1928 was 4.42 inches (112.3 mm) at the Pleasure Gardens, but 5.58 inches (141.7mm) at Firvale. Both were recorded in the newspaper report for the month. The siting of the official sunshine records was of particular importance to the town as part of its image. During the 1960s, the official site was placed in Meyrick Park, but a continuing debate about the location of the sunshine recorder led to the installation of a trial recorder on Bournemouth Pier by the Public Health Department to test the suggestion that the pier was a sunnier location than the park. However after recording from 22nd June 1964 until 21st June 1965, Meyrick Park had received 103.2 hours more sunshine than the pier and it remained the official station. The summary of the comparison stated that the differences were due to 'sea mist, or chance obstruction by cloud formations. It is worthy of note that the most marked differences occur at the change of the seasons. The largest difference, in April this year [1965], was due to sea fog, which was unusually persistent.'[9]

The winter of 1962-3 was especially memorable because it was both very cold and the freezing conditions lasted from Boxing Day until March. The photograph above is of St Mary's Road, whilst the Upper Gardens are shown on the right.

The difference was in fact 21.3 hours, almost 43 minutes daily. However, July, August and September lost a daily average of 26.8 minutes, far too great a difference in the annual competition between resorts for the title of sunniest seaside resort. Meyrick Park ceased to be the official site for sunshine records in the late 1970s, when the site was moved temporarily to the Dorset Institute of Higher Education (now the University) site (in Poole!) and then to King's Park where all the official climatological information for the town is recorded.

The early reports of the Bournemouth Meteorological Society note the great variability of the weather from year to year. 1868 was 'a very extraordinary year, and it will long be remembered for its eight months of unusual heat, its great drought, the dashing rain of August and

The local weather patterns were seen by the Victorians as a very important asset for the town and it is still common to find one part of the town in sunshine while another is under cloud. Here we can see cloud and showers over the sea and the Isle of Purbeck, whilst it is clear and sunny at Bournemouth.

September, the enormous rainfall of December, the peculiar character of its gales, the winter thunderstorms and the earthquakes.'[10] Yes, even earthquakes! On the 29th October, there were two shocks, followed by others on the 30th and 31st. 1868 was the wettest year since 1862 with 876.3 mm (34.5 inches), but between 25th May and 5th August only 40.1 mm rain was recorded, with over 13 mm on June 21st. Between 21st November and 31st December, 268 mm (10.55 inches) of rain fell. 1869 had a particularly cold June

and 'in consequence of this unseasonable weather large numbers of swallows died in many places from cold and want of their usual supply of insect food. The temperature of the longest day in 1869 was "almost identical with that of the shortest day in 1868.'[11]

National surveys of the climate in spas and coastal resorts emphasised Bournemouth's special climatic qualities. Writing in 1914, Harries described the town as 'blessed .... with a rare combination of sea air and pine-wood air, a combination which is of inestimable value'[12] so that the visitor or resident would always be able to find protection against the wind wherever it blew from. The British Medical Association meeting in Bournemouth in 1934 made much of the health-giving attributes of the resort. In 1886, Dobell had explained Bournemouth's

value as a health resort as the result of the combination of:

(a) moisture-laden sea-breezes coming in from the south;

(b) diluted and partially dried as they are in the manner described, by condensation of moisture on the face of the cliffs, and by admixture with the upper, drier, and less saline atmospheric strata, as they rise to the tops of the cliffs;

(c) the important chemical changes which take place when the watery vapour mixes with the terebinthenate (Turpentine) emanations from pines;

(d) the incident absorption of all redundant moisture by the soil;

(e) the dryness of the soil with the rapid percolation of the absorbed moisture to a great depth from the surface, and the numerous subterranean conduits by which it finds its way to the sea;

(f) abundance of sunshine from the wide expanse of sky, and the catching of clouds by the Rain-Traps; free circulation of fresh air in consequence of the houses being built upon an elevated plateau, instead of under the cliffs or upon sea-level flats, and the heathland character of the surrounding country and

(g) the protection afforded by the pine-woods which give the climate of Bournemouth at once its softness, its freshness, its purity, and its antiseptic properties - a combination peculiarly difficult to obtain.'[13]

When the separate resort at Southbourne-On-Sea was being developed, it was more concise, advertising a 'Salubrious Climate', 'Gravel Soil' and 'Full south exposure'. Gravel meant well-drained soils and so little dampness in the air. 'Full south exposure' assured plenty of sunshine and healthy sea air. To provide both shelter and more exotic sub-tropical conditions, a Winter Garden was built, but is now gone.

The Sea's Influence

Measurements of air temperatures taken along Boscombe Pier and up the Chine to the north side of Christchurch Road during calm high pressure conditions in winter have shown that there is often a fall of temperature along this transect of as much as 4 degrees Celsius. With the sea relatively warm compared to the cold frosty land under these conditions, such differences are not surprising. Go further inland and the records at Hurn often report the lowest minimum temperatures in lowland England. Winds blowing on-shore from warmer seas during the early part of winter have a similar warming effect. In contrast, in summer, sea mists can leave the coast several degrees cooler than the clear sunny skies just inland from Christchurch Road – they were a common feature of the summer. Rainfall is generally slightly lower at the coast than further inland, but the higher inland rainfall is more likely to be a result of the greater altitude.

These effects depend to some extent on the differences between the temperature of the sea and the land at different times of the year and the day. Official records of sea temperature begin in 1970, but there are many earlier reports. For example, in 1934, it was reported that sea temperatures varied from 10°C in May to 16°C in July and 18°C in August. The mean sea temperature between April and September, the main period for sea bathing, was 17.6°C in 1868, but only 14.3°C in 1870. The comparable value for the period 1971 to 2004 was 13.7°C, with the warmest April to September sea occurring in 1976 when the mean was 14.9°C. The mean sea temperature is recorded during the daytime and is similar to the mean maximum land temperature. In 1976, they were 14.9°C and 14.3°C respectively. In contrast, in 2003 (the warmest year) they were 13.3°C and 15.5°C respectively.

TABLE 2: Bournemouth's Climate: extreme years

WETTEST YEARS	Total rainfall (mm)	DRIEST YEARS	Total rainfall (mm)	WARMEST YEARS	Mean annual temp (°C)	COLDEST YEARS	Mean annual temp (°C)	SUNNIEST YEARS	Total hours
1960	1226	1921	448.1	2007	11.9	1963	8.89	1911	2137
1912	1099	1973	539.0	2002	11.9	1919	9.06	1959	2083
1951	1080	1995	544.0	2006	11.8	1916	9.11	1990	2076
1937	1041	1953	586.7	1949	11.7	1962	9.17	1949	2057
1904	1039	1933	591.1	1989	11.7	1979	9.30	2003	2039
1915	1007	2003	603.6	1995	11.6	1917	9.33	1989	2029
1993	994	1945	620.5	1993	11.6	1956	9.50	1995	1999
1914	991	1971	622.0	2004	11.5	1931	9.67	1976	1987
1939	977	1938	623.8	1921	11.4	1965	9.67	1933	1984
1966	976	1964	629.0	2005	11.4	1986	9.60	1921	1971

The general increase in air temperature in the 1990s and 2000s is larger than in sea temperature, with the effect that there is a greater difference between them.

Has Bournemouth's Climate Changed?

Climate is always changing: we remember extremes, for example, the 'Great Snowstorm' of 25th April 1908, with the snow captured in a photograph of the Central Gardens (see page 53), the long cold winter of 1962-3 when streams froze and temperatures remained below freezing for several weeks, the hot summer of 1976 or the so-called 'hurricane' of 1987. Very dry, wet, hot or cold days or months are recorded in the meteorological records, but they do not necessarily reflect long-term trends in climate.

For those, we can look at over a century and a half of records collected daily (Table 1). The most striking feature is that of the 10 warmest years, seven occurred since 1993, but only one year in the same period (2003) is among the sunniest (Table 2). The mean annual temperature for 2008 was 10.9°C, 1 whole degree lower than the mean for the previous decade. Wettest, driest, coldest and sunniest years do not reveal any particular trend, but are noteworthy for clusters of extreme years. For example, three of the coldest years were 1916, 1917 and 1919 and 1962, 1963 and 1965. 1912, 1914 and 1915 cluster as wettest years. The means for each decade do show some trends. The most obvious is the progressive increase in mean annual temperature from the 1980s to the present: but it was not until the 1980s that the temperatures of the 1930s and 1940s were exceeded. Sunshine amounts have

In contrast to the photograph on page 54, low cloud over Bournemouth, but sunshine breaking through on to Purbeck.

only returned to the level of the 1900s since the 1990s. The mean annual rainfall for 1990 to 1999 and 2000 to 2008 is almost exactly the same (764.7 and 764.6 mm respectively). Recent rainfall amounts are comparable to those of the later decades of the 19th century. The total rainfall for 1864 was the fourth lowest recorded (551.2 mm), but has not been included as it is not in the period of the official standardised records. Although the 1930s were amongst the warmest years, they were also the least sunny.

Bournemouth's climate is still an important part of its image and its attraction, but we know less about it in detail than our Victorian counterparts. Their network of recording stations would have allowed us to detect subtle changes within the town as it became more and more built-up. The construction of taller buildings has changed the way the wind blows through the town and some areas lie in shade. The Victorians would have been much better able to comment on the present-day changes. At the same time, although they would have been concerned about the medical implications of changing temperatures, they might have also seen the recently steadily increased warmth as an opportunity to draw people to Bournemouth all year round. However, the importance of the weather to the town's reputation remains important. In 2009, Bournemouth's Director of Tourism claimed that 25,000 visitors shunned the town on the May Bank Holiday Monday because the Meteorological Office and the BBC forecast constant thundery showers, when it was the hottest day of the year until then. Since day visitors spend on average £41 per head, that represented a loss of just over £1 million.

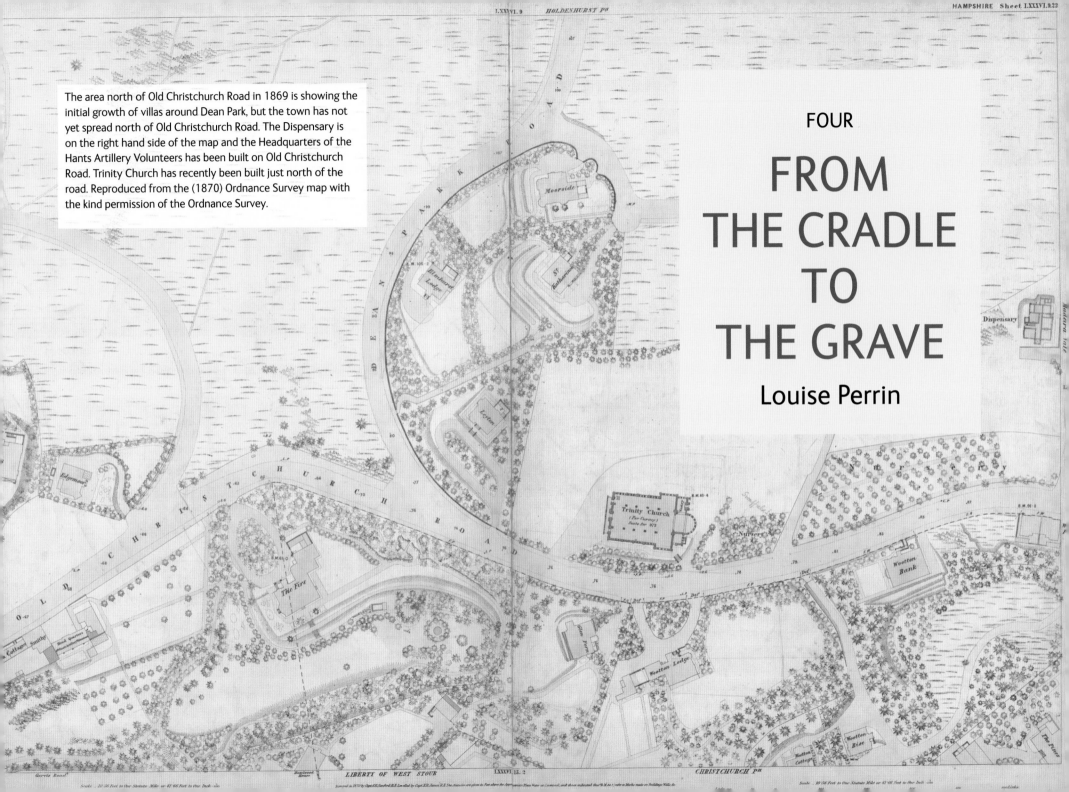

The area north of Old Christchurch Road in 1869 is showing the initial growth of villas around Dean Park, but the town has not yet spread north of Old Christchurch Road. The Dispensary is on the right hand side of the map and the Headquarters of the Hants Artillery Volunteers has been built on Old Christchurch Road. Trinity Church has recently been built just north of the road. Reproduced from the (1870) Ordnance Survey map with the kind permission of the Ordnance Survey.

FOUR

FROM THE CRADLE TO THE GRAVE

Louise Perrin

Chapter Four

IN 1810, MEDICAL TREATMENT was little different from earlier centuries. Caring for the sick was usually the responsibility of women in the family, few people had access to doctors and those doctors were not qualified in the way we understand today: a patient's recovery was often due to luck rather than the skill. Surgery was brutish and only undertaken as a last resort.

When Lewis Tregonwell bought the land on which to build his seaside home the understanding of disease processes and the ability to either prevent or cure disease was only just beginning. The English physician William Harvey had identified how blood was pumped round the body by the heart and published his theories in 1628. Over 150 years later in 1798, Edward Jenner published his research into smallpox and its prevention by vaccination. Germs had not been discovered and there were few effective medicines. Childbirth continued to be the most hazardous life event, both for mother and baby.

Prayer, Purging and Powders

In 1810, people lived mainly in rural communities but within 100 years half of the population had moved to the towns to work in factories. The growth in urban populations led to overcrowding and, combined with poverty, the lack of clean water and poor sanitation resulted in endemic diseases such as smallpox, typhus, tuberculosis and cholera, a 'new' disease which had spread from Asia earlier in the century.

So what could doctors do for their patients? The options available were limited, to use laxatives or emetics in a treatment known as 'purging', bloodletting into a cup or by using leeches, or simply praying until the 'crisis' had passed. There was not a lot in the doctor's bag of much use, he might offer a 'powder' made up to his own prescription. There were no adequate painkillers until opium and its derivatives, such as morphine, became available in the nineteenth century. Laudanum, a mixture of alcohol and opium, was available without prescription over-the-counter. Physicians used the drug as a panacea for a wide range of illness in adults and children, with the consequence that patients frequently became addicted to it.

Bournemouth's future prosperity would be founded on the needs of invalids, especially those suffering from lung diseases. The town acquired a reputation for treatment and convalescence, recommended by medical practitioners such as Dr Dobell. Later, trains would bring many holidaymakers seeking fresh air and relaxation by the sea, whether for a day, week or longer.

'The very first sea-watering place in England'

The curative use of water or hydrotherapy had been known since Roman times when citizens visited thermal and mineral springs across the empire. In England during the Middle Ages people visited holy wells or springs dedicated to particular saints to obtain relief from illness. During the reign of Queen Elizabeth I, it became popular for the aristocracy to visit the thermal springs at Bath, Bristol and Buxton. Visiting spas for health continued up until the beginning of the nineteenth century, and has recently seen a revival.

A tentative fashion for sea bathing in Scarborough, Brighton and Margate became the vogue following the publication by Dr Richard Russell in 1750 of a book entitled *A Dissertation on the Use of Sea Water in the Diseases of the Glands*. People began to seek both health and pleasure in the fishing villages

Pulchritudo et Salubritas and the 'health-giving' pines. An early 20th century souvenir from Bournemouth in the shape of a pine cone decorated with the Bournemouth crest.

around the coast that were to become new spas-by-the-sea. Visitors would undertake their health regimes in the morning leaving the afternoon and evenings for more pleasurable entertainments.

Health was at the forefront of Bournemouth's ascendance and, in particular, the new fashion for sea-bathing. The first house in modern Bournemouth was in fact a second home built for Lewis Tregonwell as a holiday retreat for his wife Henrietta. Bournemouth could have continued in this very small way except that Sir George William Tapps-Gervis saw a commercial opportunity to build an exclusive watering place, similar to the fashionable resorts of Weymouth and Brighton. He inherited the Meyrick Estate in 1835 and within four years, two hotels had opened and apartments for visitors were established along what is now Westover Road. The Marine Village of Bourne soon had the requisite features of a spa-by-the-sea, bathing machines, hot and cold water baths, a circulating library and a room at the Belle Vue Hotel which acted as an assembly room where people could gather.

Shortly after this, in 1841, the new resort of Bournemouth was mentioned in a survey of English spas, *Spas of England and Principal Sea-Bathing Places,* written by Dr A. B. Granville as a travel guide for those seeking a health-cure. In the first paragraph he writes 'I look upon Bournemouth, and its yet unformed colony, as a perfect discovery among the sea-nooks one longs to have for a real invalid . . .' He identifies the incipient town as having the 'capabilities of being made the very first invalid sea-watering place in England; . . . but what is more important, a winter residence for the most delicate constitutions requiring a warm and sheltered locality at this season of the year.[2]

The infrastructure of the town developed to accommodate invalid visitors, their carers and companions, and the associated service industries. For the new town, health meant wealth.

The First Hospitals

The 18th century saw the beginning of hospitals for the deserving poor, firstly in London and then in the provinces. These were privately funded charitable asylums for the sick or those people who, in the language of the time, were either mad, idiots, or cripples. The services provided were less about cure and more about relief of symptoms and were frequently places of last resort. Operations were performed at the patient's home or in the premises of barber-surgeons.

Thirty years after Tregonwell built his house, the census of 1841 counted 905 inhabitants living within the parish of Holdenhurst, an area much larger than the little cluster of new villas centred around the Bourne stream. At this time, residents and visitors had to seek medical assistance from either Poole or Christchurch. The following year, an advert appeared in the *Salisbury and Winchester Journal* on 16th May 1842; 'a resident surgeon now affords the patients at Bourne what was before much needed, the opportunity of a skilful hand.'[3]

Bournemouth's First Dispensary

The earliest dispensaries were not chemists' shops but a place where poor people could attend as out-patients or be treated at home if they were seriously ill. The Bournemouth Public Dispensary opened at 2 Granville Cottages, Yelverton Road on the 17th October 1859, offering advice and free medicine to the poor of Bournemouth and its neighbourhood. Between 1851 and 1861, the population of Bournemouth trebled and the successful Dispensary quickly outgrew the site and moved in 1868 to larger premises in Madeira Vale near the

junction of modern-day Stafford and Lorne Park Roads. It provided in-patient wards for male and female patients and accident cases. Boscombe opened its first dispensary in 1876 at 4 Gervis Place opposite the Palmerston Hotel. It later became the Boscombe Hospital and Provident Dispensary in Shelley Road and the forerunner of hospital facilities on that site.

The National Sanatorium for Consumption and Diseases of the Chest

A contributing factor to the growth of Bournemouth was the opening of the National Sanatorium in 1855 (see pages 35 & 60). As it was the first Sanatorium for the treatment of tuberculosis in the country, it drew attention to Bournemouth's climate and setting. Tuberculosis, TB or consumption was one of the most feared diseases of the 19th century. TB is a wasting disease of the lung caused by bacteria passed on through spitting, sneezing and coughing. It was a major cause of death in Victorian England amongst people aged 24-45. The disease could lie dormant for several years and when it appeared was almost certainly fatal: there was no treatment or cure. While it affected all classes, poverty and poor nutrition exacerbated its spread and because it occurred in overcrowded conditions people thought it was hereditary. It was not recognised as an infectious disease until 1880.

Sufferers would try any remedies. One quack doctor made a 'cure' mainly consisting of brown sugar and eating live snails. The first vaccine was discovered in 1921. The real breakthrough came in 1943 with the discovery of the antibiotic streptomycin.

The Brompton Hospital in London chose Bournemouth as the location to build the National Sanatorium as the climate was considered ideal for people recovering from

One of the earliest photographs of the National Sanatorium from a stereoview by the photographer Frank Mason Good about 1865.

tuberculosis.[4] The Annual Report of 1864 records the counties from which patients were admitted: two people came from as far away as Aberdeen. Interestingly, the occupations of patients were listed. The highest figures recorded included 11 dressmakers, 11 labourers, 14 menservants and 29 maidservants.

Dr Willoughby M. Burslem was the first doctor of the National Sanatorium for Consumption and Diseases of the Chest. Born in Portsmouth in 1819, he was educated at the Edinburgh Medical School and was particularly interested in the cause and treatment of TB and published a book *Pulmonary Consumption and its Treatment* in 1852 based on his experience working in other hospitals.

Over 150 years later, it is easy to forget that the

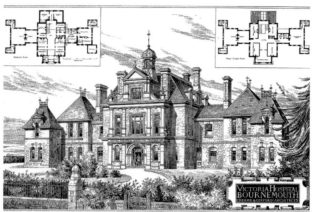

In 1890 the *Building News* published this print showing the front view and internal layout of the Victoria Hospital, Poole Road.

Sanatorium existed entirely on charitable donations and a weekly fee of 3s 6d paid by the patients towards their keep.[5]

Developing the Infrastructure

Although Bournemouth's position as a place to recuperate from TB and other lung diseases brought people to the new town, other factors contributed to further rapid growth in the population, especially between 1871 and 1881, not least the introduction of public holidays and the development of a rail network bringing a day at the sea within the reach of many working people. The town has always had to cater for visitors who become ill while on holiday.

From being a part of the larger parish of Holdenhurst, residents began to consider self-government and acquiring the formal infrastructure of a town. The Bournemouth Improvement Act 1856 allowed for the building of a pier to enable the landing or departing of visitors by sea. The

pier quickly became a focus for taking gentle exercise and breathing in sea air, something we still enjoy today. Improvements also included responsibility for sewerage and cleansing. A Board of Commissioners was appointed to oversee the work. .

The first Public Health Act in 1848 empowered local authorities to appoint a Medical Officer of Health and Inspector of Nuisances. The Inspector of Nuisances was an early form of Environmental Health Officer and nuisances were any kind of insanitary condition which could endanger health. The Inspector would check living conditions in houses, the state of outside toilets and drains, refuse piles and dung heaps, and sheds and yards where animals, such as pigs, were kept and steps would be taken to resolve the nuisance. Christopher Crabbe Creeke became the first Inspector of Nuisances in 1856.

The annual reports of the Medical Officer of Health (MOH) provide a fascinating glimpse into the town's health over the years. The reports identify particular areas of concern and record the number of births, marriages and deaths. Dr Kinsey-Morgan, the MOH in 1890, records 582 deaths during the year and a death rate of 15.5 per 1,000 of the population.[6] He notes that one-third of these are 'strangers', presumably visitors to the town. Sadly, there were 122 deaths of children aged one year and under in 1890.[7] A report from the Inspector of Nuisances is included: in 1890 this was William Geoffrey Cooper. In 1891, someone is reported as adding 2% sand to powdered cinnamon and milk containing 20% added water. The reports also recorded annual temperatures and rainfall.

The legal framework in which Dr Kinsey-Morgan worked was reinforced by the Infectious Disease (Notification) Act of 1889 which obliged doctors to report certain diseases to the authorities, these being smallpox, cholera, diphtheria, membranous croup, erysipelas (St. Anthony's

Fire), scarlatina or scarlet fever, typhus, typhoid, enteric fever, relapsing fever (from bacteria associated with rodents and lice) and puerperal or childbed fever. The Act was adopted by the Bournemouth Commissioners in 1890 and is first referred to in the report for the year ending 1891 in which 86 cases were notified and referred to the Bournemouth Sanitary Hospital for Infectious Diseases on Gloucester Road.

Pulchritudo et Salubritas

When Bournemouth became a Municipal Borough in 1890, it adopted the motto *Pulchritudo et Salubritas* (Beauty and Health) 'indicating two of its chief characteristics and principal claims to renown'.[8]

At the end of its first century, the town had many medical institutions. These were funded by the generosity of the townspeople, former patients, or sometimes in memory of someone who had died. Some were set up by external charities that chose to provide facilities for their own clients in Bournemouth. Their names may seem stark to us now. Care and kindness are not obviously suggested by such names as The Victoria Home for Cripples in Alum Chine (a branch of Ragged School Union in London), or the Convalescent Home for the Sick and Afflicted.

The First Home For Cases of Advanced Consumption, founded in 1868, is what we would now call a hospice for people in the terminal stage of the illness. The rules stated it was for advanced cases of chest disease 'which required removal from any of the institutions in Bournemouth intended solely for convalescents, preference being in all instances given to patients from the Royal National Sanatorium.'[9] and 'Advanced cases of chest disease, if resident in Bournemouth at least one month.'[10] Of the 32 cases admitted in 1917, 23 people died. The Annual

The Earl of Pembroke laying the foundation stone of the Herbert Memorial Hospital in 1865.

The Herbert Memorial Hospital on Alumhurst Road in 1895.

Report lists the names and amounts of the subscriptions and donations including anonymous poignant donations 'In Memoriam F.V.I.' or 'In Memory of H.F.'.

Bournemouth had a Homeopathic hospital. The Hahnemann Convalescent Home and Homeopathic Dispensary opened on 3rd June 1879. It was established for the recuperative care of TB patients. The doctors were medically qualified and the clientele were mainly aristocratic, wealthy or professional people.[11] The Thirty-

ninth Annual Report issued in April 1918 is similar to that of the First Home, listing subscribers by name and the amount paid, and detailing the number of patients treated in both the outpatients department and people visited at home.[12] The names of the president, the committee, the chaplain and the medical staff are listed, as are the bankers. Most of these people and their families lived within the town, and would need schools and all the requirements of everyday life. It is not surprising the town continued to grow.

And as for those Pine Trees . . .

One aspect of life in Bournemouth that featured in many descriptions of the town was the plantations of pine trees growing around the district. It has been estimated that 3 million were planted during the Victorian period, and their beneficial nature was frequently quoted as central to the health-giving character of the resort. First mentioned in 1886, Bright's 1898 *Guide to Bournemouth* devotes a whole page to the subject and mentions the 'antiseptic properties of the volatile substances which the pines exhale . . .'.

Doctors of the day stressed the benefits from the pine trees, some referring to the quality it gave the air, others that the trees simply protected against strong winds in the winter and the hot sun in summer. Pine oil had been used in the home to alleviate the symptoms of respiratory infections and lung congestion. As its mild antiseptic properties became known, it was used as a disinfectant and included in household cleaning agents and soaps. Visitors could even buy decorative bottles of pine crystals to take home as a souvenir.

The pine trees continued to be used in advertising well into the 20th century, if indirectly. An advert for a guest-house, the Westgate, in the 1932-33 *Bournemouth Guide*, describes itself as situated 'in the heart of Pineland'.

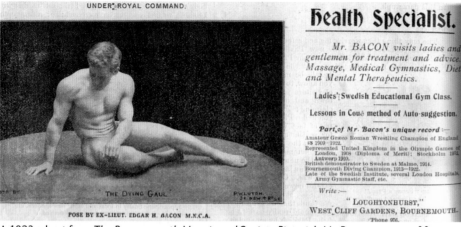

A 1923 advert from *The Bournemouth Magpie and Society Pictorial*. Mr. Bacon was one of five brothers who were all wrestlers. The pose replicates a famous ancient Roman sculpture known as the 'Dying Gaul'. The Coué Method was an early form of psychotherapy. In the years between the two World Wars, fresh air and exercise were seen as key to a healthy lifestyle.

The New Era of Medical Science

When Mate & Riddle published their history of Bournemouth in 1910, medical science was entering a new era: the social standing of the medical profession was higher than it had ever been. A fall in the mortality rate of the United Kingdom from 23 per 1,000 in 1855 to 18 per 1,000 in 1895 was ascribed by contemporaries to the improvement in sanitary and hospital conditions, nursing skills, and the general course of medical progress. The long view now suggests that simple improvements in nutrition were far more significant, as more people had access to decent food, drink and housing.

The Mont Dore Hotel

The rise and fall of the Mont Dore Hotel straddles the end of the 19th and beginning of the 20th centuries. It opened in 1885 as a first class bathing establishment and hotel and offered all manner of hydropathic treatments for guests and residents. Seawater and fresh water from the Bourne stream were pumped into the basement of the hotel. Curiously the hotel was offered for sale in 1890, suffering perhaps from changing tastes and people no longer seeking water-cures.[13] Furthermore, in a prime location overlooking the Upper Gardens the hotel also happened to be immediately next door to the National Sanatorium. The Sanatorium had adopted the open-air method of treatment consisting of quiet, rest, wholesome food, and plenty of fresh air. Day huts were built in the grounds of the Sanatorium and eventually sleeping shelters were introduced so patients could sleep outside. Extensions to the hotel brought TB sufferers into view of hotel guests who could also hear them coughing. As the infectious nature of TB came to be understood, there were concerns that the Sanatorium was not only catering for convalescents but some people in the acute stages of TB. After several years, it came to a head in 1906 when both parties consulted their solicitors. The Mont Dore was not the successful party.[14]

At the outbreak of the First World War, the British Red Cross and the Order of St John formed the Joint War Committee (JWC). Volunteers, who received training in first aid and general nursing, were organised into Voluntary Aid Detachments and worked alongside the professional nurses. Very quickly Bournemouth was able to provide beds for the influx of wounded soldiers even if these were in tents in the hospital's grounds. The JWC administered auxiliary hospitals and convalescent homes. Such was the pressure for beds that six Auxiliary Home Hospitals were set up in Bournemouth: the St John Ambulance Brigade Hospital at 2 Bodorgan Road, the Crag Head Red Cross Hospital in Manor Road, Stourwood House Hospital in Grand Avenue, Boscombe Wentworth Lodge, Grata Quies in Branksome Park and Branksome Gate (for officers). Even private homes with rooms large enough to be converted into wards were commandeered. The Mont Dore Hotel was requisitioned as a military hospital, and Boscombe Military Hospital at the Royal Victoria and West Hants Hospital in Shelley Road were both under direct control of the War Office. After the war, the Mont Dore was bought by the council and after extensive renovations it re-opened on 1st October 1921 as the Town Hall, which is what it remains today.

Soldiers from the Indian Army wounded while fighting on the Western Front were sent to the Royal Victoria Hospital in Netley, Hampshire, but when this became overcrowded, patients were sent to other hospitals on the south coast including Bournemouth. There was local concern about whether English nurses should be permitted to care for the Indian soldiers. Some of the soldiers who died in Bournemouth's auxiliary and private hospitals are buried in Bournemouth East Cemetery. One of these is Private W. F. Stevens, the first soldier to die of wounds at Boscombe Hospital.[15] Although Private Stevens was born in Gloucestershire and served in the Wiltshire Regiment, he died in October 1914 from a gunshot wound in the thigh and is buried in Bournemouth so we can rightly consider him an adopted son of the town.

During the year ending October 1st, 1904, Donations and Subscriptions have been received amounting to £57 19s. 6d. Various articles of linen have also been received to the money-worth of £17 45. 2d., making a total value of _£75 4s 2d., collected in money and kind by the Association. A very gratifying result for seven months' work.

The articles received are as follows : — 3 dressing gowns, 14 sheets, 27 pillow cases, 4 bolster cases, 6 blankets, 12 mattress covers, 30 hand towels, 20 bath towels, 12 dimity curtains, 9 round towels, 17 tea cloths, 4 medicine cloths, 23 glass cloths, 6 patients' table cloths. In addition (making a grand total of 461 articles) the following have been purchased, with part of the funds in the Treasurer's hands, at a cost of £42 5s. 4d :— 18 patients' quilts, 13 staff ditto, 56 sheets, 36 pillow cases, 83 bolster cases, 50 mattress covers, 5 coloured curtains, 1 table cloth, 12 pudding cloths.

This extract from the First Annual Report of the Ladies' Household Linen Association in 1904, shows how vital their work was in providing basic supplies for the Royal National Sanatorium.

The Royal National Sanatorium in 1908. It has recently been converted into flats.

A postcard of the open air shelters or 'chalets' at the National Sanatorium in 1911. The sender of the card was less delighted by the joys of outdoor living. 'Five weeks today,' he wrote, 'still jogging about as usual. We get a lot of cold and wet weather. Not at all nice for living and sleeping outdoors. I would give anything to sit by a fire or even see one. Very often cold for hours at a time.'

The School Health Service

Head teachers recorded day-to-day events in a school log book. The Somerset Road (Freemantle) Infants School in Pokesdown opened in April 1897. The schoolmistress was Amy Evans. By 11th May, she had 47 pupils, 32 of whom were infants: 'The attendance is very irregular, several children absent through sickness; two cases of whooping-cough.' And in May 1900, 'The attendance is not so good this week owing to several of the children being sick with whooping-cough and measles.' In 1910, there were approximately 1,000 deaths a year from measles in children under 15 in England. On 6th February 1902, the head teacher wrote in the log book 'Although the gas has been burning the whole day and the fires as large as the grates will allow the thermometer has marked 51° (Fahrenheit) at the highest.'

Absence of children due to general illness, bad coughs and colds occurs regularly, but illnesses such as whooping-cough, scarlet fever, mumps, chicken pox, and ringworm all receive specific mention. The School Medical Service was established in 1907 and the first reference to a visit by Dr Edwards, the School Medical Officer, is logged on 18th September 1908.

A postcard of staff at the National Sanatorium about 1911. Their names are listed on the reverse. Top row L-R Nurses Edwards, Vickers, Tate (?), Bright, Stephenson and Young; Front row L-R Nurse Cox, Sister Bell, Matron, Dr Halroyd, Sister Scott, Nurse Smith.

From Invalids' Walk to Pine Walk

A quick survey of Bournemouth in 19th century guidebooks reveals Invalids' Walk as one of the town's chief attractions. The earliest mention is in Heywood's 1886 *Guide to*

ABOVE A waiting room at the Royal Victoria and West Hants Hospital during the First World War. Reproduced with kind permission of The Royal Bournemouth & Christchurch Hospitals NHS Foundation Trust.

ABOVE RIGHT The headstone marking the grave of Private William Stevens in Bournemouth East Cemetery. He was wounded in France and was the first soldier to die at Boscombe Hospital when it was taken over as a military hospital in the First World War.

LEFT Convalescent soldiers at the Mont Dore Hospital in June 1916.

RIGHT Disabled soldiers and sailors from the Winton Workshops on Peters Hill.

Bournemouth but was ultimately to have its own section in Mates' *Beautiful Bournemouth* 1897 guide, declaring itself in capital letters and describing the delights of promenading in the 'balmy exhalations', 'protected from cold in winter and the sun in summers'.

For almost 20 years Invalids' Walk was accepted as a major asset of the town: there were clearly no misgivings about the name. But almost quietly, lost amidst all the news of the First World War, there was a very brief paragraph in the *Bournemouth Daily Echo* in January 1917, 'Tomorrow is the last day on which the "Invalids' Walk" at Bournemouth will be officially known under that title. After Sunday the famous pine-strewn avenue from the Arcade to the sea will be known, officially at any rate, as "The Pine-Walk"'.

In contrast, the *Manchester Guardian* of the same date has a much longer article, clearly stating that the town wanted to rid itself of its 'old character of a resort for consumptives and bronchially affected' not least because of changes in the treatment of the disease. Although published in Manchester, this was a newspaper of national standing and many of its readers would travel by train to holiday in the seaside resort.

1918-1919 Influenza Pandemic

Influenza or flu is a highly infectious illness which spreads very rapidly through coughs and sneezes of people who are already carrying the virus. Until the virus was identified, people did not know what caused influenza and often came up with very strange ideas. At one point, it was thought to be caused by the bodies of seven million Chinese people who had died when the Yellow River had burst its banks producing a 'vast burden of poisonous organisms by which to devastate the world'.

The pandemic ran from the middle of June 1918 until the following May. There were 189 recorded deaths in Bournemouth. The Medical Officer of Health reported to the Borough's Health Committee on 11th October 1918 that there had been 'a number of cases of influenza in the town'. Action taken by him, including the closure of schools, was approved. At the next meeting on 1st November 1918, the minutes record 'A letter from the Medical Officer of Health and report was read.' The contents of the letter are not included but the Town Clerk was instructed to 'communicate with all proprietors of cinemas'. Warnings about kissing in the back row perhaps?

The school logbooks of the time are tantalisingly brief as well, outlining events but not giving any insight into the human experience. The headmaster of Alma Road School writes in the logbook on 27th September 1918 'There have been several cases of influenza during the past week.' On 4th October, he records 'Owing to the outbreak of influenza the school closed today at noon by order of the Medical Officer of Health.'

The 1918-19 influenza pandemic killed 20 million people around the world: there have been further outbreaks in 1957, 1968 and 1977. Because influenza is caused by a virus, it cannot be treated by antibiotics and recovery is reliant on a person's own immune system. A flu vaccine is now available for high-risk groups, such as people over 65, care workers, or people with impaired immune systems, although during the winter of 2008/09 Tesco's supermarket was offering a 'flu jab' for £10 at its in-store pharmacy.

Sun is good for you - isn't it?

The health benefits of fresh air and sunshine had been promoted since the beginning of the 20th century

The headstone marking the grave of Edward Harold Dimmock who died at the Mont Dore Military Hospital. Lieutenant Dimmock died of pneumonia in 1919. He was a 'flying soldier' and lived to see the formation of the RAF in 1918.

especially in connection with treatment for tuberculosis. Spending time outdoors and sunbathing were actively promoted by health experts.

When Bournemouth Pier Approach Baths opened in 1937, the Borough was keen to advertise the new sun terrace and solarium with due South aspect. Other facilities included Turkish Baths and the exotically sounding Na-Ki-Dal baths – 'The Latest Form of Spa Treatment highly recommended for Rheumatism, Sciatica, and allied complaints. Invaluable in cases of general fatigue, tiredness, overwork etc'. The *Bournemouth Daily Echo* proudly announced on Wednesday 24th March 1937: 'Baths opened at the Pier Approach – Bournemouth's Contribution to The Physical Fitness Campaign'

Amongst the many column inches recorded in the *Echo* a small sentence from Councillor Wilkinson, chairman of the Baths Committee, might almost go unnoticed:

'Bournemouth is the premier health and pleasure resort.' Mental and physical health were interlinked. The Borough Engineer, Mr F.P. Dolomore, wrote 'The health resort of today is more concerned in providing recreation and amusement as a stimulus to both mind and body, to keep the machine in good condition rather than wait for the inevitable breakdown, and then attempt a cure.'

The Typhoid Epidemic of 1936

A year before the opening of Pier Approach Baths in 1936, an outbreak of typhoid occurred in Bournemouth, Poole and Christchurch.; doctors began to see people with symptoms from 4th August onwards. In total 718 cases were reported, 51 people died locally and some 20 people elsewhere, mainly visitors who returned home.

The outbreak was caused by contaminated milk being delivered to homes across the conurbation and traced to an inadequate sewage tank at Merley House, where the carrier of the disease lived, discharging into a stream above a small dairy farm. The milk was sent to Frowd's Dairy in Parkstone where it was mixed with milk from other farms. Although the dairy had strict hygiene controls it did not pasteurise the milk and the entire delivery was contaminated. Pasteurisation would have killed the bacteria but this was not a legal requirement in the 1930s and many people were not in favour of it. A full report on the outbreak was issued in 1937.[17]

A National Health Service

From the beginning of the 20th century, it was increasingly believed that a fair society was one that cared for its citizens from the cradle to the grave. Medical services gradually opened to all classes, not just the 'deserving poor', who could receive treatment in charitable hospitals, or the very poor who obtained care in workhouse infirmaries. Early legislation provided medical insurance for working men over 16 years of age although not for their dependants.

The nationwide abolition of workhouses in 1926 resulted in the closure of the Christchurch and Bournemouth Workhouse which had existed since 1835. Bournemouth Council took over the running of Fairmile House, as the workhouse had been renamed in 1914. It was renamed again as Fairmile Hospital when the National Health Service was introduced, and ultimately became Christchurch Hospital.

When the NHS was born on 5th July 1948, the townsfolk of Bournemouth, as elsewhere in the UK, were to have access to free health care. After almost 150 years of assorted charitable and municipal health provision, everyone would have their own GP, free dental and optical care, hospital and specialist services. It was also the beginning of specialist services where the GP would refer patients to out-patient specialists and no longer looked after their own patients in hospital. The Annual Report of Bournemouth's Medical Officer of Health for 1948 makes moving reading 'Mr. Mayor, Ladies and Gentleman, I have the honour to present my Annual Report for 1948, a year during which there have been momentous changes in the administration of the Public Health Services. The statistics for the complete year include the infant and maternal death rates which are remarkably low even for Bournemouth. They are the results of many years of patience and perseverance and show what can be achieved when the services for Prevention and Treatment are co-ordinated.'

The infant mortality rate was the lowest ever recorded in Bournemouth, with only one death associated with childbirth. Remarkably, no child under two died from diarrhoea, previously a major cause of death.

House Beautiful – the Sunday Schools Union Childrens' Convalescent Home at the corner of Carlton and Derby Roads 1903.

Dr H.Gordon Smith took the opportunity, while 'having regard to the new order of things', to comment that 'as a large County Borough with visitors as the greatest industry Bournemouth has its peculiar health problems.'

All Change in 1974

Twenty-five years later, the Medical Officer of Health, Robert H. Browning, delivered his annual report for 1972 ahead of another major change to health provision in Bournemouth, when local government reorganisation removed Bournemouth's status as a County Borough and placed it in the County of Dorset. Dr Browning had a wider worldview, stating that the health and sanitary provision of Bournemouth compares well with those of other European towns. 'Unfortunately that is not to say that all is well, indeed, we still face a number of serious problems.'

Poster advertising a fête to raise funds for the local hospital in 1930. The fête was opened by the renowned pilot Amy Johnson, who arrived by plane.

He echoes the comments of his 1948 predecessor as health service provision in the town is 'one and a half to two times the national average...because of the enormous elderly population and to a smaller extent because of the seasonal influx of holidaymakers. While the number of TB cases is quite small the number of people with alcohol problems could well exceed a thousand in this town,

and there is the problem of illicit drugs as well . . . I, like many others, still do not know how to prevent them.' Dr Browning remarked on the number of legal abortions being quite small, but noted that the illegitimacy rate was nearly double the national average and pointed to the need to spend money on an effective Family Planning Service.

Key priorities for Bournemouth

The Bournemouth Public Health Report 2005/6 published in March 2006 identified priorities for improving health in Bournemouth based on local needs within the framework of government policy on health.[18] The priorities were as follows: health inequalities, reducing smoking, tackling obesity, improving sexual health, improving mental health and well-being, reducing the harm caused by alcohol, children and young people, older people, health protection.

In 2009 Bournemouth residents can receive a wide range of services including family health services, community health services, local hospital services, local mental health services, and continuing healthcare as well as GP care from the Dorset Healthcare NHS Foundation Trust, The Royal Bournemouth and Christchurch Hospitals NHS Foundation Trust and the NHS Bournemouth and Poole, until recently Bournemouth and Poole Teaching Primary Care Trust. It can be very confusing.

Full Circle

Bournemouth developed from an idea for a spa-by-the-sea. An Internet search using the words 'spa' and 'Bournemouth' results in over 2,000,000 hits. There are many hotels and leisure centres with spa facilities offering a 'spa leisure day with use of indoor pool, sauna/steam

Children and staff from the Victoria Home for Crippled Children in about 1940.

room, jacuzzi/spa and gym': well-being in a package and at a price. Where the Mont Dore Hotel may have failed at the end of the 19th century, hotels in Bournemouth today are taking up where it left off, offering a variety of packages for the over-stressed, over-indulged, or simple mother and daughter 'pamper days'.

In 2001 national newspapers reported an outbreak of TB in a school in Leicester. Responding to local concern, Dorset Health Authority said there had been a lapse in its own prevention programme due to a shortage of the vaccine. A local Poole Councillor stated 'we cannot pretend this disease is a thing of the past.' A further concern today is evidence of drug resistant strains of TB. In 2006 the Health Protection Agency reported that levels of TB had been increasing year on year since the late 1980s.

On 29th September 2004 the *Daily Mail* printed an article with an astonishing headline: 'Pine cones could kill

A health
information
poster from the Second
World War about spreading disease.
Crown copyright.

Catch it, Bin it, Kill it

In the 2006 Public Health Report quoted earlier, there is one section headed 'Planning for Pandemic Influenza'. In April 2009, a strain of flu virus was identified in Mexico and became known as swine flu as it is thought to have originated in pigs. Plans for dealing with a possible pandemic, including mass vaccination of school children, were prepared in anticipation of a national outbreak in the autumn of 2009.

Time for a health-giving stroll along Pine Walk perhaps?

The former Grovely Manor, better known as Shelley Park and, as from November 2009 the Shelley Park Medical Centre.

superbug MRSA.' Scientists discovered the cones from common conifers contain antibacterial agents that help destroy the bug. The researchers from the School of Pharmacy at London University hope to isolate compounds from pine cones to create new drugs effective against the bacteria.

The great behemoth that is the Royal Bournemouth Hospital in 2009, part of the Royal Bournemouth and Christchurch Hospitals NHS Foundation Trust.

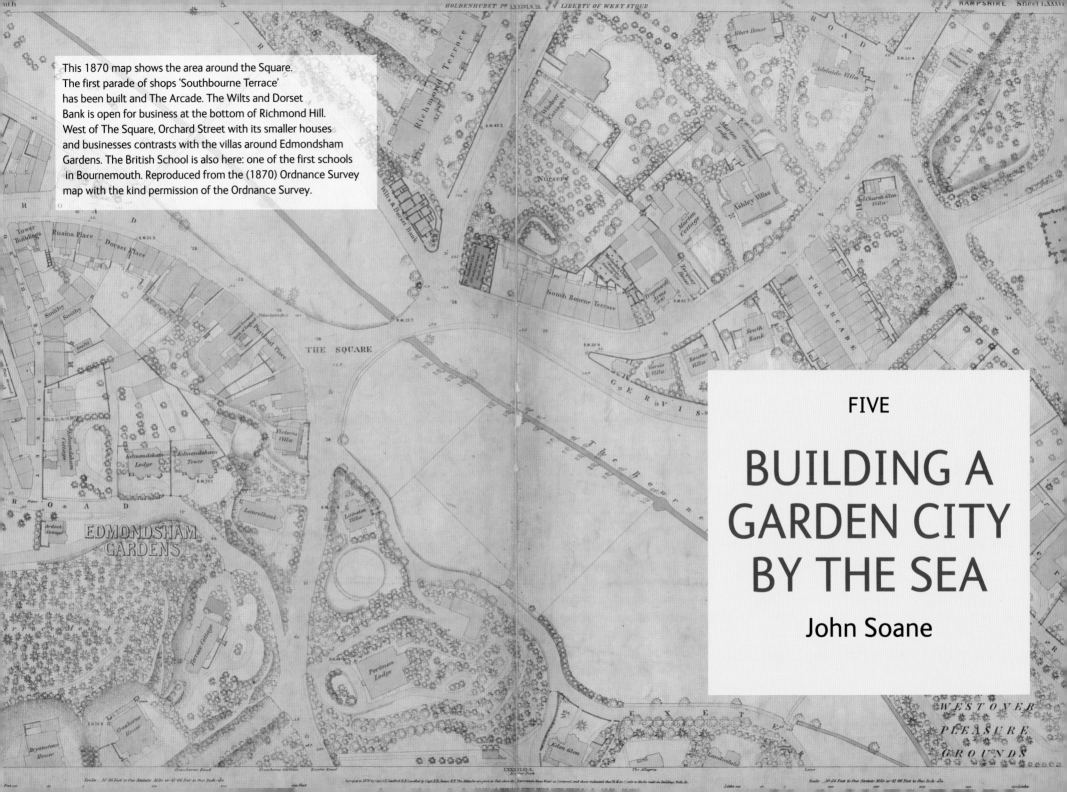

This 1870 map shows the area around the Square.
The first parade of shops 'Southbourne Terrace'
has been built and The Arcade. The Wilts and Dorset
Bank is open for business at the bottom of Richmond Hill.
West of The Square, Orchard Street with its smaller houses
and businesses contrasts with the villas around Edmondsham
Gardens. The British School is also here: one of the first schools
in Bournemouth. Reproduced from the (1870) Ordnance Survey
map with the kind permission of the Ordnance Survey.

FIVE

BUILDING A GARDEN CITY BY THE SEA

John Soane

Chapter Five

Benjamin Ferrey's proposed design for Gervis Place in 1838.

THE ARCHETYPICAL STREETSCAPE OF BOURNEMOUTH – outside the principal parks and the Central Gardens – consists of small to medium-sized detached houses and bungalows with relatively compact front areas and larger, more varied open spaces for greenery and other functions at the rear.

What is so special about this? After all, similar layouts of residential areas exist around London and many other British towns. The unique feature about the townscape of Bournemouth is not so much its distinctive physical structure, but rather the topographical situation and its effect on people's attitudes to it.[1]

From its earliest days, the town was designed and built with a considerable degree of aesthetic sensitivity. The pattern of residential streets, service and administrative areas and green spaces, plus the liberating influence of the open sea, meant people of every sort have been able to live alongside each other without the stresses of a town dominated by industry. A distinctive balance was achieved between man-made structures and the space which surrounds them. The exceptionally low density of the built-up areas of the resort has tended to encourage a more individual sense of space and a shared sense of place. That such a unique atmosphere remains present across much of the built environment of Bournemouth is in no small measure due to the founding of the resort in 1810 during

the time of the Romantic Revival. Changing attitudes, especially towards picturesque scenery, stimulated the creation of a new and highly original residential townscape of elegant and refined detachment. The growing numbers of successful individuals, in effect a new social class born out of the world industrial dominance of Britain, wanted a more secluded and less pretentious seaside resort than was offered by the more formally planned streets and crescents of Brighton and other similar watering places.[2]

The basic plan for the initial layout of Bournemouth owed a great deal to the landscape ideas of Humphrey Repton and his principal disciple, John Loudon, the leading authorities on Picturesque-Gardenesque design. This was a style of garden design which represented the natural world through artistic composition. Repton believed that an idealized, more intimate townscape could be achieved on a relatively small scale by the judicious planting of well-selected trees and shrubs near any detached residence.

This would soften the arbitrary relationship between built structure and open space. Loudon also suggested that the visual relationship of several houses or 'villas' could be enhanced by using imaginative plantings to create natural progressions of greenery, such as parks or foliated avenues to similar residential areas.[3]

These principles were followed from about 1838 when the first buildings began to appear on the slopes of the Bourne valley. Over the next three decades, a local architect from Christchurch, Benjamin Ferrey, laid out the centre of Bournemouth in the form of large villa plots on either side of the lower Bourne valley and around Crichel Mount.[4] After Sir George William Tapps-Gervis died in 1842, the estate was managed by trustees with the well-known architect and town planner Decimus Burton as their consultant.

In establishing the new townscape of the infant resort, apart from Sir George Gervis' insistence, following the fashion of contemporary building estates, that properties should be detached and in their own grounds, full use was

made of dramatic locations on high vantage points near the sea, especially along the cliff top. At the same time, no development was allowed at the very centre, for according to Burton: 'The wooded valley through which the Bourne Rivulet flows to the sea is and must always constitute the principal object in the landscape, and therefore any work undertaken there should be most jealously watched and every endeavour made to preserve the natural beauty of the valley . . . for the characteristic which distinguishes Bournemouth from most other watering places is its rusticity. This individuality should be maintained and a class of visitors attracted who cannot find the same elsewhere.'[5]

In zealously promoting a romantic face for this new watering place, Burton was following landscape practices that were increasingly being applied in the laying out of well-to-do early 19th century maritime resorts. Whereas villas near the coast were favoured by natural topographical advantages, on other villa sites further inland, the proportions of built or un-built land, the

ABOVE LEFT Brookside from Exeter Lane 1870.

ABOVE Villas in central Bournemouth in 1879. Looking seawards over Westover Road, the Bath Hotel (left background) and the Baths and original jetty (right background).

RIGHT The villa next to the Hermitage Hotel is the sole survivor of the picturesque residences that were spread informally alongside the lower Bourne valley between 1840 and 1860. Its combination of classical Georgian restraint with an Italianate tower was a common feature of the original Westover Road.

average plot size and the relationship of all the plots to the road system and the surrounding parkscape were kept as regular and simple as possible. In this way the generally accepted principles of villa estate development would not conflict with the overall picturesque grouping of the entire resort.[6]

As a result, an amazing degree of architectural variety became possible. According to a contemporary guidebook from 1856: 'Numerous detached villas have been constructed on the slopes, crests and retired dells

TOP Granville Cottages on Yelverton Road display a simple balance of features and a delicacy of design in 1862.

CENTRE 1 Adelaide Villas on Old Christchurch Road in 1862 is notable for the asymmetry between bays, windows and roofs at both ends of the building.

BOTTOM Terrace Cottage in 1870.

of the hills which form this valley. The designs are very varied, chiefly Italian, thatched, and Elizabethan cottages, or rather mock Gothic, or as an architectural friend of ours calls it, the 'The Bourne Style'.[7]

The only surviving example of the informally spread out picturesque residences that once dotted the lower Bourne valley between 1840 and 1860 is the villa adjoining the Hermitage Hotel in the Lower Pleasure Gardens (see previous page). The building combines classical Georgian restraint with an Italianate prospective tower: an architectural combination that was quite common in the original appearance of Westover Road. The evergreen landscape in combination with the surviving houses along Tregonwell Road is probably the only place in the town centre which gives some idea of the vanished romantic character of the early Bournemouth.

Twenty years after the first villas were built, Bournemouth offered its first wealthy residents a very comfortable and extremely secluded place in which to live. This fitted perfectly the more assertive character of the many self-made businessmen, members of the professions and colonial expatriates who wanted a less hectic and more leisurely environment in which to retire or to conduct their business. By 1851, Bournemouth had no fewer than eight annuitants, two bankers, three house proprietors and two retired members of the East India Company in residence.[8]

Transformation into a Resort 1860 – 1880

The rapidly expanding British economy was producing ever-more wealthy people who wished to escape the increasingly polluted centres of industry and commerce. Yet, as healthier more informal lifestyles within contrived rustic settings became more popular, the growth of new working suburbs could not be ignored. As they were built to accommodate the growing service sector, and in order to ensure that they did not become the breeding grounds of endemic disease, these neighbourhoods had to be integrated with the initial romantic vision of early Bournemouth.[9]

Between 1860 and 1880, villas owned by the wealthy spread rapidly in all directions. From the lower Bourne valley along new serpentine roads across the East and West Cliffs and around the embryo Dean Park, new detached houses covered most of the area between Horseshoe Common, St. Paul's Road and Wimborne Road as far as the new cemetery. A cramped group of artisan dwellings also appeared behind the first terraces of shops and purpose-built apartments between the Square and Poole Road. The construction of more spacious retail premises along Old Christchurch Road and an entire low-density suburb of semi-detached cottages for labourers at Springbourne near Holdenhurst Road provided improved facilities.

Not surprisingly, the aesthetic appearance of new buildings changed distinctly. As the resort expanded, the visual ambience of the Marine Village had faded away to be replaced by the architectural character of a more extensive residential seaside town. Inevitably the need to build commodious villas that might be used equally as an hotel, as apartments or as single family houses led to a greater standardisation of architectural design, but with more distinctive stylistic categories than was apparent a

Predominant social groups in real estate investors	Areas	Social structure (class) %	Price range of property £	Owner occupiers %	Rent per annum (range) £	House occupiers in 1903 in same property in 1911
Upper echelons of entire social groups	Bournemouth Southbourne Cliffs	A. 100	1167 to 5503	52	70 to 330	60.0
Middle to upper echelons of rentier social groups	Central Branksome Estate Dean Estate S W Boscombe	A. 93.7 B. 2.2 C. 2.1 D. 2.0	1163 to 3329	41.5	65 to 180	56.6
Middle to lower echelons of rentier social groups	Westbourne South Winton Charminster North Central Dean Estate N W Boscombe West Southbourne	A. 79 B. 5 C. 6 D. 10	656 to 1875	13.9	35 to 100	45.6
Miiddle to lower echelons of small-scale building entrepreneurs	Pokesdown East Boscombe	A. 12.8 B. 17.6 C. 28.8 D. 30.4 E. 4.8	283 to 849	27.0	15 to 45	48.0
Middle to lower echelons of entire rentier/entrepreneurial population sectors	Springbourne Malmesbury Park	A. 30.6 B. 20.4 C. 28.5 D. 14.2 E. 6.12	244 to 357	4.8	13 to 19	29.7
Upper to lower echelons of small-scale entrepreneurs/capitalists	Winton Moordown	A. 9.8 B. 23.5 C. 25.4 D. 27.4 E. 13.7	242 to 526	35.2	13 to 28	43.7

Key to Column 3   A Capitalists (including "gentlemen" occasional investors of more limited independent means)
B Petty capitalists of professional status
C Non-manual workers
D Independent artisans
E Unskilled
Sources: Kelly's Directory 1903-11: County Borough of Bournemouth General Rate Book 1911: Various Indentures of Lease

generation earlier. On the West Cliff, all-purpose seaside accommodation was built which combined Italianate stylistic features with a more robust approach to vernacular architectural form. However, increasingly, in the newer, well-to-do residential neighbourhoods further from the sea, as in the southern section of Dean Park, more assertive Gothic-style influences with prominent gables and distinctive roofs appeared.

As retail and commercial premises increased, their builders favoured the late Georgian idiom. Elegant examples may still be found at West Hill, at Southbourne Terrace in the Square and especially between the Gervis Arcade and the Lansdowne.

The Climax of Building Activity 1880-1910

Following the arrival of the railways, there was a very rapid increase in the population from 5,896 in 1871 to 78,766 in 1911. Within three decades, the distinctive visual characteristics of the infant resort were successfully integrated into the most dramatic transformation of its appearance. Bournemouth experienced a level of growth almost unmatched in Britain, as road after road of solidly built residential and commercial properties spread remorselessly inland. The open heathland, the agricultural hamlets along the old Muscliffe Road, the expanding centres of Westbourne, Springbourne, Winton, Boscombe and Southbourne, and the scattered brickyards and market gardens of Charminster and Stourfield were swallowed up by the spread of the town beyond the Bourne valley. The present extent and characteristics of the built-up area of modern Bournemouth were in place within little more than

ABOVE LEFT Contrasting styles of houses on the south-east side of Holdenhurst Road in 1862.

ABOVE Holdenhurst Road: houses on the north-west side, some still under construction with strong brick pillar and rails boundaries in 1865.

LEFT The central Cooper Dean Estate from the tower of St Paul's Church in 1888.

30 years, an unparalleled achievement. From then until the outbreak of the Second World War, the pattern of well-to-do tenure near the town centre with a patchwork of residential areas of varying socio-economic status inland typified Bournemouth's further expansion.

By the 1880s, the evolving urban environment of the town continued to appear as 'a pyramid based on its apex . . . a superabundance of commodious mansions with few houses for the working classes.'[10] Exceptional contrasts of townscape densities were avoided, in no small part due to the generally dispersed nature of the early settlement pattern. Increasing numbers of working residents found places to live in newly built neighbourhoods across Bourne Heath. This, together with the ever present Romantic-Gardenesque ambience in urban design, not only prevented the further spread of traditionally deprived artisan areas, but also encouraged, even during the breakneck growth of Boscombe during the 1890s, the construction of relatively spacious residential districts throughout the resort.[11]

This exceptional momentum of resort development, both on the English South Coast and in similar benign locations in Europe, which Bournemouth shared, provided for their inhabitants a sense of the victory of technology and urban innovation over the travails of domestic life before the 19th century.

As the number of dwellings increased from 519 in 1871 to 14,225 in 1911,[12] attitudes to social, economic and environmental changes merged, allowing, as in other expanding resorts, the relationship between the size and appearance of the new houses in their overall settings to be considered. In Bournemouth especially, as more of the resident population acquired the economic means to aspire to middle class status, social distinctions based solely on class were replaced by more pragmatic criteria based on occupation and place of residence. The basic difference between many of the more fashionable neighbourhoods nearer the sea and the less pretentious suburbs further inland was less their appearance than their different uses. So the owner of a villa might use his ground to create an ornamental garden to attract visitors, whereas a builder living near his men would have sufficient room on his elongated plot for a small yard with space left over for a small vegetable patch or flower garden.

In the later 19th century, in order for the unfolding townscape to enhance, rather than dominate, the advantages of natural topography precise planning concepts were needed that fixed clearly the relationship between the incoming inhabitants of Bournemouth and their surroundings. The highest priority for the town's administrators and the building entrepreneurs was to ensure that a reasonable balance was maintained between the new residential areas and their general setting. With

few exceptions, the construction of high-density all-purpose apartment blocks in the inner town was to be restricted. Further expansion took the form of individual plots set out on parallel or right-angled roads where houses could only occupy between 40% and 60% of each plot.

Notwithstanding the existence of shopping parades and the fact that permission was sometimes granted for two houses to occupy three consecutive plots, the result of these planning impositions was the evolution of a large garden city, where, apart from the most affluent districts, a relatively narrow range of plot size (between 3,600 and 5,700 square feet) typified most neighbourhoods. The design and appearance of particular residential undertakings (including road widths and building heights) were regulated by general agreements and legal documents between the municipal authorities, landowners and building entrepreneurs. In general, building leases controlled the size, area and hypothetical value of the structures to be built. Further conditions of tenure were applied according to the expected level of affluence of the particular area under development. As the spatial structure and appearance of the expanding urban environment became ever more precisely regulated, the resulting hierarchy of house types owed more to economic realities than to social considerations.

Bournemouth's phenomenal expansion between 1880 and 1910 induced several freehold land development companies to hold building plot auctions (on occasion laying on special trains from London for the benefit of potential buyers), especially in Boscombe and Southbourne and to a lesser extent Alum Chine. These companies included on their boards mainly prominent members of the local community, active in business and professional affairs, and some outside investors, mostly from London. Two of the most active development agencies were the South Coast Land Society, run by

A house in the Arts and Crafts Style on the corner of Clarendon Road.

local builders and specialising in cheaper artisan houses at Moordown and later at Stourfield, and the Boscombe Conservative Co-operative Land and Building Society, which was principally interested in land speculation. Its board included an estate agent and an hotel owner. Their principal area of operations was Boscombe Spa, Boscombe Manor and Boscombe Park, originally part of the Shelley Estate between Christchurch Road and Boscombe Overcliff. Plots generally sold for between £125 and £160 per site for villas to be built for between £500 and £800. Other development agencies offered easier terms to builders in less expensive neighbourhoods, such as Winton, Moordown and Stourfield, where houses were priced at about £400.

By the late 1880s, the most fashionable new areas of the town were on the West Cliff near Poole Road, and in the more northerly sections of Dean Park around the new cricket ground. The large villa in Clarendon Road is typical of the new Arts and Crafts influence from

TABLE listing the main land development companies, their board members and their principal estates in the late 19th century.

Norman Shaw that was now beginning to influence the appearance of well-to-do villa estates. These houses had more neo-vernacular decorative features, including more distinctive roofscapes and a greater variety of contrasting architectural features, such as subsidiary bays, towers and high chimneystacks. These are still visible north of the Lansdowne between Cavendish and Wellington Roads. However, most other residential buildings during this period appeared either as single houses, a pair or more of semi-detached houses or more rarely as terraces.

An increasing number of villas were constructed for the middle-class housing market proper in a broad arc in central Bournemouth close to the fashionable coastal districts. Mainly medium-sized, square-shaped houses, with two to three bay windows, they were usually of two or more storeys with doors, windows and half-timbered gables of considerable architectural pretentiousness all put together in a restrained Arts and Crafts style.

Such properties, built mainly for the holiday trade, quickly became popular as family and retirement homes amongst the increasingly numerous professional and commercial classes. They became so popular that they were built in considerable numbers, especially in the newly developing area of Southbourne,

Developing agency	Date established	Board members	Trade or profession (where known)	Activities	Area
Bournemouth Gas & Water Company	1863			Supply of gas and water	Central Bournemouth
Bournemouth and Christchurch Building Society	1866	Elias Lane and other members of Lane Family of Christchurch	Grocer, then speculator		
Consolidated Land Society	1880s	Jones and Murin families	Builders	High density terraced houses	Westbourne
Bournemouth Land Society	1881	C.A. George James Druitt E.W. Rebbeck	Builder Solicitor Estate agent	Artisan housing	Winton
Southbourne-on-Sea Land Company	1883	T. Compton Baring Young Hon. E. Douglas Col. Brander Capt. Wollaston James Druitt McEwan-Brown Charles Wyatt	Medical Doctor M.P. for Christchurch and banker Solicitor Estate agent Estate agent	Well-to-do villa residences	Southbourne-on-Sea
Bournemouth and Boscombe Conservative Cooperative Land and Building Society	1888	Charles Collins Charles Dacre Charles Wyatt	Hotel owner Estate agent	Lower middle-, middle- & upper-middle class villas	South Boscombe between Pokesdown and Boscombe Chine
Bournemouth & District Electricity Supply Co.	1890	London Board including A.J.Sanderson R.P. Sellar	Local businessman Local businessman	Supply of domestic and public electricity	Bournemouth
Westbourne Park Estate Company	1893	William Dixon Thomas Warren Henry Jenkins C.A.George	Businessman Estate agent Builder Builder	Middle-class villas	Westbourne
South Coast Land Society	1898	3 members of the Lane Family of Christchurch E.W.Jenkins W Hoare V.A.Slater A.H. Abbot	Builder Builder Builder Estate agent	Artisan and lower-middle-class houses	Stourfield, north Winton and Moordown
Bournemouth & District Property Company	1900	T.J. Hankinson G.J.Lawson J.J. Allen J.E. Beale E.W. Jenkins W.J. Reynolds S.J. & G.A.Mate	Businessman Businessman Store owner Store owner Builder Printers	Conversion of well-to-do villas into hotels and boarding houses	Mainly East Cliff
Stourcliff Estate Company	1911	Seat of Board Faringdon Street, City of London		Terraced houses	West Southbourne

West Cliff, Voyseyesque Style.

ABOVE Lansdowne from Richmond Gardens, 1870.

RIGHT This villa (later named 'Southlea') on Durley Road on the West Cliff was designed for a Mr. Clarke by Christopher Crabbe Creeke in 1876. Creeke was also responsible for laying out many of the curvaceous roads of the West Cliff in particular.

BELOW A view towards East Common from Holy Trinity Tower 1878.

when areas further west were being constructed in the more fashionable Voyseyesque Style. Charles Voysey favoured 16th and early 17th century vernacular styles which preferred white roughcast walls, horizontal ribbon windows and large pitched roofs. It used materials typical of English farmhouses. One exception was a well-designed cluster of seaside apartment blocks, built exclusively for the holiday trade, in West Cliff Gardens during the 1880s.

The largest concentration of artisan areas was in east Boscombe and around the ancient hamlet of Pokesdown, between Ashley Road and Leap Hill Road north of Christchurch Road and between Parkwood Road and Southbourne Roads to the south. Visual aspects of status mattered, even in Bournemouth, mattered: roads of greater

Typical of some areas are large two-bay houses. The varied chimney styles are one of the most distinctive features of much of the local urban skyline.

San Remo Towers above Boscombe Spa.

Alumhurst Road (at the Poole Road end in Westbourne) in 1870 with distinctive architectural styles which typify much of the area towards the West Cliff.

architectural pretentiousness tended to be nearer the retail facilities of Christchurch Road, with more utilitarian roads closer to Pokesdown Station. Most houses here were modelled on variations of the standard two-storey, bay-windowed, detached/semi-detached, already common in London and southeast England. Some had more elaborate lintels over windows and doors and relatively elaborate gables over the front bay window. The more utilitarian neighbourhoods built by local builders for the working classes and for small investment opportunities, as at Malmesbury Park, had very little architectural significance. However, there is clear evidence from the contemporary local press that many of the first occupants who worked in the building industry were generally quite content, especially as the majority of houses came with generous sized long plots.

By the end of the 19th century, an extensive and very personalised structure of social contacts and building entrepreneurship had grown up as Bournemouth spread rapidly outwards. This cut right across the formal structure of socio-spatial hierarchies common in most resorts of that period. Indeed it was especially at fashionable expanding resorts such as Bournemouth that the outward appearance of residential neighbourhoods of different status could mask economic realities. A wealthy villa owner with sea views might enjoy income from property in an artisan area which equalled that of a successful contractor who lived in the same district. At the same time, income could be derived from houses built in the most opulent districts of the town. There is also evidence that many individuals of independent means were active in a great variety of part-time endeavours that further reduced the formal relationships between the working populations and the visitors and wealthier residents that they served.

ABOVE Sandy Bay on the Southbourne Overcliff Drive with distinctive corner architecture gaining wider views from within.

LEFT St.Catherine's Road in 1910 has a curved frontage of shops with residences above which have ornate balconies and distinctive single bays with four narrow vertical windows. The bays on the top storey are only glazed on the street face. The carter is advertising the Ceylon and India & China Tea Association. The first building is the Post Office which advertises that horses and carriages are for hire and bicycles can be stored.

The Early 20th Century

At the beginning of the 20th century Bournemouth was characterized by residential areas occupied by different socio-economic groups. A fair number may be described as rentiers, i.e. people who lived on dividends from property and investments. Areas such as the centre of the resort and the Bournemouth and Southbourne Overcliffs were dominated by these wealthy capitalists, but also by occasional investors (often gentlemen of more limited but independent means). These were the locations of the most expensive properties and highest rents. Other neighbourhoods, such as Boscombe, Charminster, Malmesbury Park and Winton, were being created, owned and lived in by a much more socially and economically varied population, including rentiers and entrepreneurs, as well as artisans and the unskilled.

Between 1900 and 1920, a growing pattern of well-integrated life styles ensured that the most distinctive changes to the urban environment appeared in a series of exceptionally well-designed 'gentlemen's' residences in the town centre. They were influenced by the house designs of Charles Voysey. They appeared mainly around Meyrick Park (the area of Saint-named roads) and rather less elaborately on the West Overcliff and between Wellington and Stewart Roads. The best examples of this style were individually built, erected in many cases by people who had benefited from access to the gold fields of the Transvaal after the Anglo-Boer War. There was a strong emphasis on simplicity and rationality, with traditional building materials were used wherever possible.

As the town's general level of consumer demand grew, so did its retail needs. From the turn of the century, several elegant shopping parades were built, notably Poole Road, Westbourne, along Christchurch Road either side of Boscombe Arcade, Southbourne Grove and to a lesser extent through Winton and Charminster. This final spurt of Voyseyesque/Arts and Crafts elegance in Bournemouth was almost the last manifestation of the grand villa style. Bournemouth was one of the first places after 1890 where the domestic and formal living arrangements of houses of varying size gradually became similar, but without any sacrifice to modern comfort. However, these developments could not have come about without a realisation by the newly urbanising classes of their

Shelley Road, Boscombe, in 1910.

Social and Urban Change between the World Wars 1920 – 1940

By the early 1920s, all over northeastern Bournemouth, in Wallisdown, west Winton, Moordown, Redhill, north Charminster and Iford, former building trade workers with borrowed capital were constructing hundreds of small detached houses for sale freehold at between £200 and £300 on deposit of £100. In keeping with more restricted budgets, these family homes were smaller than the standard pre-1914 artisan houses, but this difference was lessened by the continued provision of generous building plots. During the 1920s, the number of small builders rose from 62 to 266 and the average number of houses completed rose to well over 1000 per year.

This new inter-war townscape, constructed mainly in a vernacular Tudor revival style, resulted in completely new neighbourhoods, especially between Withermoor Road and Harewood Avenue respectively and Castle Lane. Architecturally there is nothing to distinguish these houses from thousands of others in the south of England. What is important is that for the first time people of ordinary means were striving to be in a position to either build or purchase their own home in an hitherto quite exclusive seaside resort.

At the same time, the established social structure in Bournemouth continued to have considerable, if declining, importance. An influx of former landed gentry ensured that a series of fine well-built houses in the mature Voyseyesque/Arts and Crafts style was built at Talbot Woods, and replicated on a lesser scale on the Boscombe Manor, and the Portman and Wentworth estates.

The dramatic urban changes in the northern part of Bournemouth during the 1920s made the Borough Council feel obliged under the new Housing Acts to provide a considerable amount of social housing or housing subsidies at Carbery and north Charminster. Dr. Bodley Scott, then Mayor of Bournemouth, acknowledged that the resort could no longer be considered such a prosperous watering place but would be obliged to change both its appearance and social attitudes to accommodate poorer visitors. For him, the town had to become 'the great pleasure and resort of tired and overworked industrial England. Partly owing to the war and partly to the great democratic change of life all round, the (class of) people who (visited) Bournemouth 40 or 50 years ago when it was a health resort of the orthodox millionaire and his family is now extinct.'[13]

During the 1930s, holiday habits changed and holiday excursions became more common, with coach excursions to Bournemouth rising from 19 in 1933 to 799 in 1935. The original domestic scale of the townscape in central Bournemouth altered to meet these changes. In 1926, after the Meyrick Estate had sold 419 leaseholds in central Bournemouth, the *Bournemouth Echo* wrote: 'The town's amazing expansion has brought new conditions involving changes which do not harmonise with the old order of things. Bournemouth's growth has been mainly in areas remote from the seafront, yet it is our beach, pier and promenade attractions that have been elaborated to cater for the increased thousands.'[14]

The last remaining 'cottage orné' villas in Westover Road were replaced by a terrace of neo-Georgian shops and offices as well as a skating rink, two cinemas, the multi-storey Palace Court Hotel and opposite, in the Lower Pleasure Gardens, a very large 2000 seat Art Deco theatre/ concert hall: the Pavilion. Nearer to the West Cliff, the new Winter Gardens heralded an era of more profound cultural provision for the resort.

The great question now was how to adapt the more formal central townscape created between 1890 and 1930

enhanced material state. This feeling of self-fulfillment amongst the lower income groups, much enhanced by widespread property speculation on a small scale and by more assertive political activity, was hugely radicalised by the dramatic social consequences of the First World War. Their impact on the future urban environment of Bournemouth was very significant.

As hundreds of war-weary soldiers returned from the battlefields after 1918, there was a general demand for 'Homes fit for Heroes'. This meant that in Bournemouth the pent-up need for new houses, especially for the lower income groups, could no longer be governed by the uncertain patronage of wealthy businessmen, a chronic shortage of working capital or what were now seen as increasingly outdated working practices.

to the demands of modern less affluent visitors. During the difficult 1930s, the urban environment began to change to serve two quite distinct entities: an extensive residential town and a fully developed holiday resort. Bournemouth could no longer ignore the distinction between the need to provide more conventional amenities for the working population and to take a more professional approach towards the enhancement of the town as a tourist centre in its own right. As one writer said in 1934 'We see her as a modern child of modern times without the legacies of yesteryear. She was created as a resort; she has never known an existence other than as a holiday and residential centre. There is a choice of home in the larger house near the centre, the modern villa or bungalow on the outskirts, in modern flats of which large blocks are now in process of construction'[15.]

Changes after 1945

The Second World War changed fundamentally how prosperous modern seaside resorts would be perceived and inhabited by modern industrialized societies. The gently decaying gardenesque neighbourhoods of Bournemouth could no longer be secluded from the contemporary world. Although the resort survived the conflict with relatively little damage, the Borough Council bowed to general pressures of social reform and urban renewal in the immediate post-war years. In 1946 the distinguished planner Sir Patrick Abercrombie was invited to assess the development prospects of what was now an extended coastal conurbation that stretched across the Dorset-Hampshire border (see also Chapter 11).

Abercrombie's suggestions did not reflect the historic development of Bournemouth, where fine villas and labourer's tenements existed side-by-side, just as they did at those country estates on which Bournemouth had been modelled – so that the fine villas of the West Cliff were mere yards away from the warren of workers' terraces at West Hill. This mixture did not appeal to Sir Patrick, for Bournemouth had 'large and somewhat incoherent areas of building of mid-Victorian and later eras . . . these areas do no credit to towns like Bournemouth . . . their shops are strung out in ribbons along main traffic arteries, their architecture and layout is depressing'. Abercrombie was 'confronted at Bournemouth and its immediate neighbourhood by a pompous array of some three to four thousand large and often pretentious villas . . . the now obsolescent opulence of a departed day.'

Bournemouth, he said, 'failed through a lack of planning typical of its period and in spite of some attractive gardening to make the best use of its natural beauties of pine woods, sand and sea, of the great sweep of Poole Bay with its

This 1921 sale plan of Lots 181 to 379 of the Bournemouth Estates of Sir George Augustus Eliott Tapps Gervis Meyrick shows the range of plot sizes in streets around Bournemouth Central Station, reflecting the differences in date and building style. Reproduced with the kind permission of the Ordnance Survey.

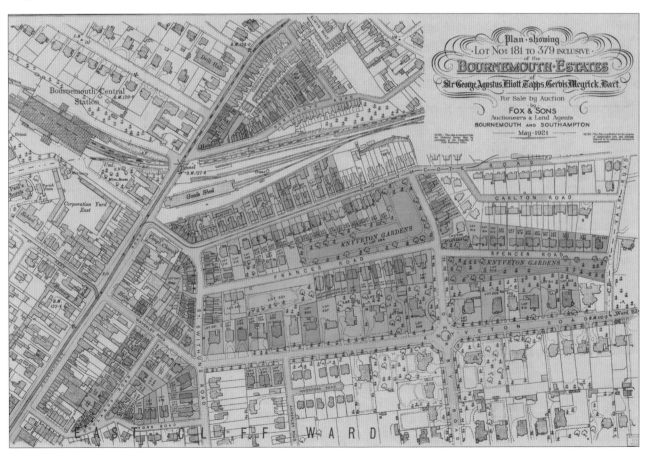

high coastline of precipitous sandy cliffs . . . no ordered planning, alas, brought any cohesion to this attempt at rapid and wholesale provision for a mild riviera life . . . an incomparable opportunity was thus wantonly thrown away.' He then contradicts himself by commenting that 'we find here no attempt adequately to take advantage of or to express the really dramatic contours of the land and coastline.'

Abercrombie's principal recommendations were aimed at turning the entire area into an efficient administrative and economic centre, while at the same time modernising the well-established leisure industries. In line with the planning orthodoxies of the time, he wished to alter completely the linear early 19th century spatial character of the town centre by the construction of a large civic centre near the Lansdowne on the East Cliff, and the replacement of many villas in central Bournemouth by a variety of different sized serpentine-shaped apartment blocks.

However, far from providing a simple solution for Bournemouth's future development, his conclusions caused much soul-searching and confusion. While there was a general feeling in the town that more integrative planning, especially to provide a more efficient transport infrastructure, was necessary, many people found it very hard to accept the complete replacement of the low density, quasi-romantic ethos that had been the principal creative force in the town's evolution.[16] Examples of the proposed massive structures constructed in the prevalent Modernist style proved to be totally at odds with the morphology of the existing built environment.

Consequently for two decades after the end of the Second World War, with the resort seemingly secure and prosperous, but without any coherent plan for future development, the extensive late Victorian and early 20th century neighbourhoods ceased to be considered amongst

ABOVE Sir Patrick Abercrombie's 1946 design for the centre of Bournemouth which suggested a network of roads around the town centre. The present town centre by-pass and some other roads in the town centre partially mimic Abercrombie's suggestion, but not completely so that some remnants of the original 'garden city' survive today.

BELOW The Albany flats built on the East Overcliff Drive in the early 1960s were potentially the start of a cliff top dominated by multistorey blocks which would have completely altered the appearance of the town not only from the sea but also inland.

the most important assets of the resort. Instead during the 1950s and early 1960s, apart from the construction of social housing estates at East and West Howe and Kinson, a fair number of medium-priced houses and chalet bungalows were built on the edge of Talbot Woods and between Queen's Park and Castle Lane. Numerous less expensive bungalows also began to spread along the northern edge of Bournemouth.

The rise of land prices after rent control was relaxed in 1956 encouraged landlords in Bournemouth to seek the vacant possession of their properties. This situation did more than anything else to reduce the traditional supply of well-kept but cheap accommodation, which had been an important feature in the life of the town earlier in the century. This change also threatened the accumulated aesthetic values and patterns of urban behaviour of the preceding 80 years, which had enabled people on fixed incomes but with genteel pretensions to constrain the more crass materialist influences that were an inevitable aspect of 'popular' holiday resorts.

This was the era of the more ruthless building speculator and the beginning of the alteration of the relatively unchanging skyline of Bournemouth that had been temporarily frozen by building controls after 1945. Large houses in some of the smarter residential neighbourhoods such as the West Cliff had previously been rented out as integrated apartments or 'rooms'. Now they were either converted into expensive self-contained flats or replaced by modern, but extremely bland, apartment blocks in which there was little attempt to ensure that the harmonious appearance of the adjacent townscape was respected. Huge tower blocks over ten storeys high such as Admiral's Walk and the Albany appeared on the cliff tops between 1959 and 1964, and for the first time in living memory the horizontal silhouette of Bournemouth as seen from the pier was dramatically changed.

Restructuring after the Sixties

In a desperate move to try and preserve the decaying infrastructure and traditional social ambience of the resort, the town council almost made a disastrous mistake by seriously considering a gigantic American-backed redevelopment scheme (Bournemouth International Group) for the town centre, with plans for huge convention hotels and a 6000-seat convention centre with over 14,000 square metres of exhibition space. The fact that

the Council realized at the eleventh hour that the scheme would destroy the unique linear townscape of coastal Bournemouth helped to jolt the town out of its lethargy, and slowly and painfully, during the 1970s and 1980s, more practical solutions, better related to the particular needs of the resort, gradually emerged and were carried out.

The first achievement was the creation of a more modest, but still extensive, International Conference Centre on the West Cliff, which saved the middle-market hotel industry from collapse. The second followed the relaxation of regional planning restrictions on office building in the South East Region, and in order to create a more balanced year-round economy for the resort encouraged large service institutions to relocate from London, mainly to a specially designated office redevelopment area between the Lansdowne and Bournemouth. The most spectacular result of this initiative, however, was the establishment of the European Administrative Headquarters of the Chase Manhattan Bank at Littledown, the former home of one of the original ground freeholders of Bournemouth, the Cooper-Deans.

As modernist architectural and planning influences declined from the mid-1970s, the general standard of urban design gradually improved. As a result more sensitive understanding of the need to sustain the existing visual appearance of the more architecturally significant residential neighbourhoods of Bournemouth has gradually taken root, except on parts of the Boscombe and Southbourne Overcliffs where a more flexible approach to architectural design is felt to be more appropriate. New blocks of flats are now usually constructed in a more traditional style which enables a reasonable degree of visual and social continuity to be maintained. However this compromise has sometimes been obtained at the sacrifice of entire sections of original townscape, as in

Richmond Park and Southbourne.

As a result of the general revival of building entrepreneurship across Britain in the 1980s and 1990s and because government wanted to provide an increasing number of houses for both the free and social markets, Bournemouth over the last 20 years has had to contend with one of the most serious threats to its built environment that it has ever faced. In an attempt to make the maximum use of development land in towns to fulfill housing policies, Government ministers not only laid down exceptionally high targets for Bournemouth, but they also allowed established houses and gardens to be designated as so-called 'brownfield sites'. Under existing planning laws, this allowed any building entrepreneur the absolute right of redevelopment, usually in the form of flats, and irrespective of other non-commercial considerations. Consequently many developers and property owners whose only desire was to make money rapidly could justify their actions on the grounds that they are only following government directives to build an increasing, and now an excessive, number of flats.

The result was a redevelopment free-for-all, especially across the wide central belt of medium-sized villa neighbourhoods from Boscombe and Southbourne, across Queen's Park and Charminster, to parts of Winton. Not only did it become almost impossible for Bournemouth Council to protect the built integrity of these neighbourhoods, but because of the fluctuating number of extra housing units demanded by the government, it became very difficult for the Planning Department to establish a stable policy of urban expansion. There was a fundamental contradiction in the Regional Spatial Strategy for the South West,[17] in which, with reference to Bournemouth, the attainment of a better quality of life style was considered compatible with a projected increase of 16,000 dwellings over the next two decades, including an extra 1500 units within

Replacement of individual villas by flats west of the Commodore, East Overcliff Drive, November 2009.

Detail of new apartments in 2009.

In this respect, it is quite significant that the decision to construct a very large shopping centre, Castlepoint, on the earlier site of the Hampshire Centre in the northern suburbs of Bournemouth, was perhaps an admission by the developers that the unique scale of the centre of the resort is incompatible with the huge scale of modern commercial undertakings.

Bournemouth Council commissioned in 2007 a characterisation study of the neighbourhoods of the town[18] to prevent the further erosion of the unique characteristics of the principal residential areas of the town. It suggested that these areas could be preserved by directing new development to areas which are less sensitive to change and make little contribution to the town's character. More controlled redevelopment of areas lacking in identity and quality would allow local character to be enhanced. New building activity would be directed away from more historic and sensitive areas currently experiencing a degree of unwanted change. Finally, aesthetic, social and economic criteria would be used to distinguish between areas worthy of general preservation and others more suitable for a permitted level of development.

In the 21st century, the efforts of the citizens of Bournemouth to preserve the integrity of their existing urban environment are a tribute to the very deep respect still felt for the revolutionary urban experiment which began in a remote valley surrounded by a barren heath in southern England 200 years ago. Whether or not the original ambience of the Marine Village on the Bourne influences the changing appearance of the resort in future, the continual effort to perfect the intangible symbols of 'the better life' still gives the modern conurbation of Bournemouth its exceptional and abiding Sense of Place.

the Green Belt beside the River Stour.

There is a general feeling that too little respect has been shown by government policy for the need to sustain the distinctive urban characteristics of the town. Similarly, proposals for the rehabilitation of some of Bournemouth's principal leisure and entertainment facilities along Exeter Road seem to want to encourage a high density, metropolitan-orientated townscape, which is the very opposite of the restrained planning conventions that were applied to the Bourne Valley for the previous 170 years. Moreover, much larger commercial, retail and residential schemes, as for example between the Lansdowne, St. Paul's Road and St. Swithun's Road, are likely to create a much greater polarity of architectural perspectives between older and newer concepts of Bournemouth as a built environment than has been experienced before.

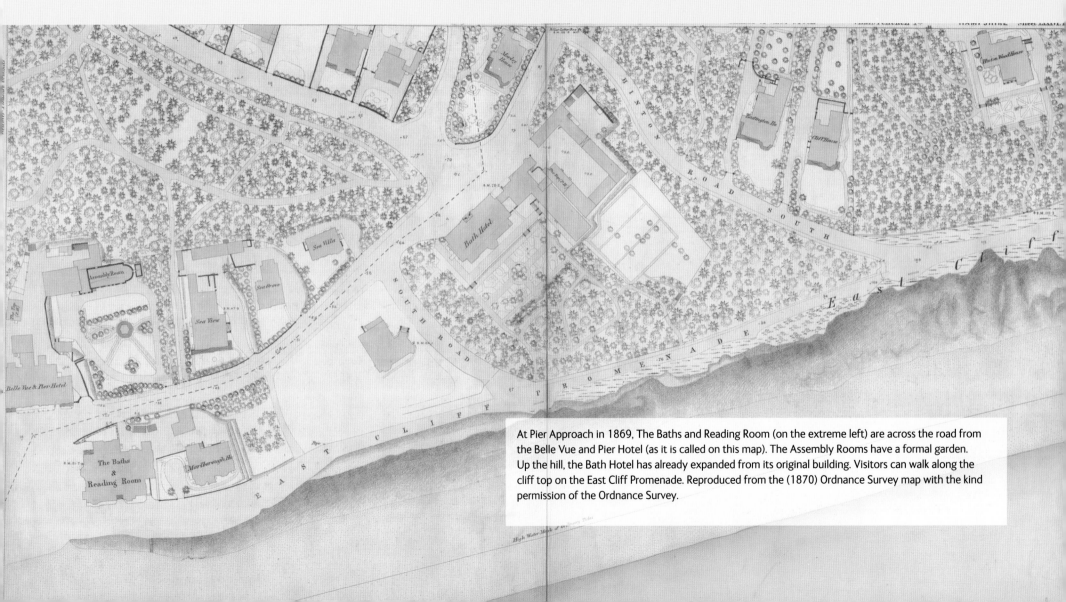

SIX
'NO AMUSEMENT OF ANY KIND'
John Cresswell

At Pier Approach in 1869, The Baths and Reading Room (on the extreme left) are across the road from the Belle Vue and Pier Hotel (as it is called on this map). The Assembly Rooms have a formal garden. Up the hill, the Bath Hotel has already expanded from its original building. Visitors can walk along the cliff top on the East Cliff Promenade. Reproduced from the (1870) Ordnance Survey map with the kind permission of the Ordnance Survey.

Chapter Six

WRITING IN THE MID-19TH CENTURY, Grantley Berkeley said: 'At Bournemouth, man has no amusement of any kind; and what is stranger still, when men and women meet at this watering-place, there is no association, no promenade, as at other places ; and not an opportunity sought in which to exchange an idea.'[1] Unlike many watering places at the time, Bournemouth had not sufficiently developed the infrastructure for collective entertainment. Tregonwell set up home here in 1810, and during the next 20 years he built five cottages as holiday homes with access to a near-private beach. Residents and visitors alike devised their own amusements. When not bathing, they walked through the wild heaths and pine woods, or along the sandy beach, took rides into the countryside or to nearby towns, or met socially in each other's homes.

The opening of the Bath Hotel in 1838 and the Belle Vue Boarding House the following year offered for the first time wider access to entertainments. The Belle Vue, standing close to the shore, was a pale imitation of the establishments that had been the focus of fashionable spas a century earlier. A Mrs. Slidle ran it and would cater for

Walking amongst the pines was one of the delights offered by the gardens and woods in the early town.

casual visitors and parties preferring to 'pic-nic'. A billiard table was offered, and an extension provided a Library and Reading Room supplied by David Sydenham. At a fee of 3/6d a week or 2 guineas a year, subscribers had access to a plentiful supply of books, magazines and newspapers, 'fit for the superior class of visitors'. Its immediate proximity to the beach gave a beautiful prospect and in the lounge one could partake of tea, coffee and ginger beer, and listen to new and fashionable music.

The hotels were the first respectable venues for entertainments. The earliest recorded chamber concert was held in the Bath Hotel on 3rd August 1838 before an audience of 150. Some 40 fashionable people from the local area attended the Regatta Ball at the Belle Vue Hotel in August 1849. There was a supper and dancing until 4.30 a.m. This was just before the Poole and Bournemouth Regatta held on Friday 16th August, during which there were numerous races for yachts in Poole Bay, attracting many spectators.

What was to become the Lower Gardens was described by Granville in 1841 as a 'narrow bed of peat earth lying over sand, on which a few miserable sheep are allowed to feed, or a scanty coarse grass is cut.' Westover Gardens ran alongside at a higher level. During the winter of 1848-9, this wilderness of fir plantation was cleared of undergrowth, new ornamental shrubs planted, and a path cut through the tall pines which was called Invalids' Walk, the scent of the trees, coupled with the ozone from the sea, conveying health-giving properties. During the First World War, its name was changed to Pine Walk in order not to draw attention to any wounded ex-servicemen.

Fortunately for the ladies, they could engage in the growing pastime of pressing wild flowers or collecting sea shells and seaweeds (guide books of 1840 and 1864, respectively, listed the many dozens to be found on the beaches). For the men, there was the prospect of shooting

the beach by 1840 with its suite of warm pools and every desirable accessory.

As new roads grew apace from the expanding centre, paths for walking were created. By 1855, several exploratory routes were recommended in the Guides, taking in the sights of Hengistbury Head and the outlying village of Wick in the east, or the chines in the west.

Besides promenading, such routes could be travelled on horseback or in carriages. Livery stables existed, and horses and brakes could be hired. Right from the start,

ABOVE The Clapcott Dean Harriers on the 28th January 1886.

RIGHT Strolling along the pier was in 1910, and still is in 2010, one of the normal leisure activities of Bournemouth's visitors and residents alike.

and fishing. A decoy pond was one of the earliest, even pre-Tregonwell, features at Bourne, although whether for sport or food is not clear. The Earls of Malmesbury at nearby Hurn Court and their guests had been shooting fowl out of the sky since the 1790s. Later guide books extolled the great variety of birds to be found in the area, and William Hart of Christchurch could supply already stuffed specimens as souvenirs for the home parlour, should the visitor be unable to bag his own.

From the start, sea bathing would have been a mixed pleasure and health-cure activity. Bathing machines are recorded by the 1830s, and the sexes were kept segregated either side of the Bourne stream as it flowed across the beach. These necessities of decorum were to persist for decades, but a letter of 1870 complained of males being less careful of their modesty, affronting the ladies walking the West Cliff paths. Mixed bathing did not occur until the beginning of the 20th century, and lying in bathing costumes to sunbathe was banned until the 1930s. An alternative to the sea was the Public Baths erected near

THE PIER TURNSTILE COMPETITION 1939

(20th YEAR)

Organised by Round Table No. 5, and supported by The Rotary Club

in aid of THE ROYAL VICTORIA AND WEST HANTS HOSPITAL and other Charities

For correctly estimating the number of persons
paying for admission to Bournemouth Pier

On REGATTA DAY – 12th AUG.

FIRST
PRIZE

VALUE
£145

FORD "PREFECT" 10 h.p. SALOON

Presented by Bournemouth Rotary Club

2nd Prize—Twenty-five National Savings Certificates
3rd Prize—Twelve National Savings Certificates

ABOUT 200 OTHER PRIZES

OPPOSITE PAGE TOP A small crowd has gathered on Bournemouth Pier in 1871, perhaps to watch the Bournemouth Regatta or simply queueing to board the paddle steamer.

OPPOSITE PAGE BOTTOM LEFT The Pier Turnstile Competition on Regatta Day 1939 was organised for the twentieth year by the local Rotary Club in aid of the Royal Victoria and West Hants Hospital and other charities. First prize for correctly guessing the number of people who paid to go on the pier was a Ford 'Prefect' saloon valued at £145.

OPPOSITE PAGE BOTTOM RIGHT An early hand-tinted photograph of Invalids' Walk.

Bournemouth guide books played on its central position for access to the beauties of the New Forest or the historic towns of Christchurch and Corfe Castle. The more adventurous would hire a fishing boat to row them around the bay (which, even then, was being termed 'Bournemouth Bay', despite its official name of Poole Bay). Excursions were recommended to places like Swanage. The small craft suffered by being hauled ashore to receive passengers, but the situation was improved in 1855 when a wooden landing jetty, 100 ft long by 6ft wide, was commissioned by local residents. It opened on 20th August 1856, but larger, deeper draught ships could not take passengers on pleasure trips until the first wooden pier was constructed in 1861. The first recorded excursion was a private one by the Shah of Persia in 1868, but it was not until 1871 that the 246-seater steamer *Heather Bell* started regular operations. Horse-drawn char-a-bancs were introduced in the summer of 1877 with four or five trips a week to places like the Rufus Stone, Corfe Castle, Lulworth and Bindon Abbey, with the Shaker encampment in the New Forest an especial attraction.

An Assembly Room was attached to the Belle Vue Hotel in the 1850s. For many years it was the focus of much activity, being used as a place of worship for various denominations, concerts and entertainments, public meetings and political assemblies and dances and many official and semi-official gatherings. In later years, many civic events were held there: indeed, the Improvement Commissioners deliberated there in 1856-57. Its Public Assembly and Lecture Rooms gave Bournemouthians a venue in which to enjoy concerts, entertainments,

ABOVE The Belle Vue Hotel and the Baths and Reading Room in 1864 with a good view of the villas along Westover Road in the background. The path along West Cliff was still very rough and untended.

BELOW Paddle steamers alongside Bournemouth Pier, bathing huts on the sands and a lady descending the East Cliff promenade armed with an umbrella to protect her from the sun.

Amateur Entertainment

Sir Percy Florence Shelley was born in Florence (hence his second name) in 1819 and died 70 years later. The son of Percy Bysshe and Mary Shelley (née Wollstonecraft), he bought Boscombe Lodge (later to become Boscombe Manor) in 1849.

For Victorians, entertainment began at home. No self-respecting household lacked a piano, which was the focus of Sunday evening recitals, sing-songs and recitations for family and guests. If you could not afford a piano, in Bournemouth one could be hired from local stores, and Professor Hartmann would instruct young ladies in playing and singing. This amateur activity spilled out into schools, church halls, pubs and hotels. One enthusiast was Sir Percy Florence Shelley. A man of many artistic tastes including drama, he built a theatre in the grounds of his new estate at Boscombe. Excited by its possibilities, Shelley had a larger theatre with proscenium arch and stage incorporated into his house where it remains today. He worked on much of

Athletics competitions were one of many events which took place in local parks.

The Shelley Theatre, Boscombe Manor.

the construction himself, to the disgust of his butler. The first performance took place in January 1856 with his own *He Whoops to Conquer*. Off and on throughout his tenure he put on many productions; some for friends, others for the public, when they were often for fund-raising.

political and evangelical rallies and balls. The Assembly Rooms saw the launch of many a local society and, from the late 1860s onwards, many intellectual groups were formed. Bournemouth soon had its own Meteorological Society, Natural History Society and Field Club.

Once the Bournemouth Improvement Act 1856 was given Royal Assent on 14th July, the Commissioners could begin one of their three top priorities: negotiations with the Gervis Estate regarding the Pleasure Grounds. The Commissioners also laid out cliff walks.

ABOVE The Westover Ice Rink in the 1930s.

RIGHT The Westover Ice Rink – Phil Taylor doing the Death Leap in 1934.

In contrast, whether for devotion to national security or the fun of 'playing soldiers', some of the earliest organized activities resulted with the formation of the Citizen Volunteers. A new threat from France, now under Louis Napoleon, caused a national call to armed readiness in 1859. Within months, Bournemouth raised some 35 men to form the Rifle Volunteer Corps (19th Hampshire Regiment). An Artillery Corps appeared in 1866. They met fortnightly for exercises at Hengistbury Head and elsewhere.

Churches were the centres of much simple social activity, especially in the outlying villages. Little is noted from the early days, although choirs from Bournemouth, Pokesdown, Moordown, Holdenhurst and elsewhere participated in the Vale of Avon Church Choral Society in the 1871 Festival at St. Peter's Church. An early feature was the mutual benefit societies, usually associated with the churches. Both the Congregational Church (1870) and the Presbyterian Church (1873) ran these, but the earliest was the Bournemouth Institute set up in 1865 at Branksome Place, Commercial Road. The concept was to occupy the youngsters usefully and increase their knowledge, especially amongst the journeymen artisans working on the burgeoning building sites. Their regular social gatherings shared recitations, readings and sing-alongs, with an occasional serious lecture. Similar meetings were held under the Temperance Movement banner, in an effort to stem an increasing wave of drunkenness during the late 1860s and early 1870s. Their early 'entertainments' with magic lantern slides included the Christian message.

Part of the Tregonwell estate under the shadow of Prospect Mount was tastefully laid out and called Cranborne Gardens, after Tregonwell's country residence. It was opened to the public with an archery meeting in August 1862. Known as the 'Archery Ground', it later became the site for the Winter Gardens.

With so much open ground available, there was probably much informal sporting activity going on, especially by the building workers. From the 1860s various sports clubs arose. An annual athletic competition started around March 1865, where amateur contestants engaged in races, jumping and throwing for prizes. In 1865, the Westover and YMCA Rowing Clubs were formed, followed in 1869 by the Bournemouth and Premier Rowing Clubs. At least one football club appeared, the St John's Lads' Institute from which Boscombe FC, now AFC Bournemouth, was formed in 1899. The Bournemouth Cricket Club started in 1869, eventually securing grounds two years later at Dean Park for their matches, with adjacent spaces for bowls and tennis.

Skating has proved an enduring activity in Bournemouth, with a first concrete-surfaced rink opening at Palmerston Gardens, Boscombe in 1875, later followed by the better-

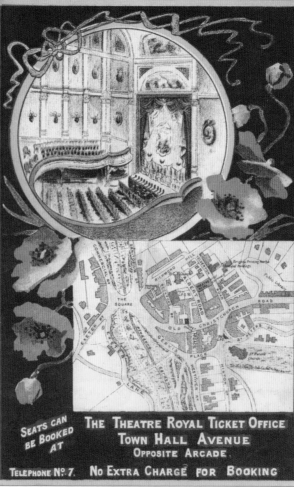

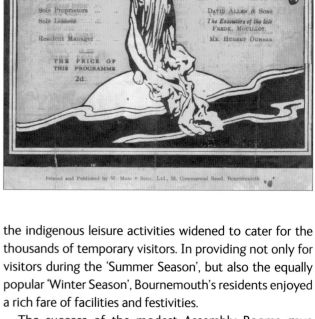

Three programmes for the Theatre Royal, the first two for 1899 and the third for 1910. Note the telephone number, 'No. 7'.

known rink in the grounds of the Winter Gardens. Until refrigeration could supply ice rinks, skating was done on roller skates, and later venues included Bournemouth Pier, and halls at Holdenhurst and Westover Roads, and the craze still persists today as skateboard parks.

Providing for the Tourists

The 1870s introduced new factors. In particular, with the arrival of the railway and the passing of the Bank Holiday Act 1871, Londoners could now take cheap day trips, spending up to 8 hours in 'sunny Bournemouth'. Many saw the financial benefits of the burgeoning holiday trade, and

the indigenous leisure activities widened to cater for the thousands of temporary visitors. In providing not only for visitors during the 'Summer Season', but also the equally popular 'Winter Season', Bournemouth's residents enjoyed a rich fare of facilities and festivities.

The success of the modest Assembly Rooms gave rise to other improved more central venues. The most important was the Town Hall which opened on 6th January 1875 in Old Christchurch Road. Although some civic activities took place there, it was used mainly for entertainment, especially in its larger 84ft long hall which held over 700 people. The proprietor, Harry Nash, expanded his horizons with a theatre, the Theatre Royal, in Albert Road. It had a 45ft proscenium-arched stage and a 600-seater auditorium, opening in December 1882. Three and half years later the YMCA opened two venues, the Shaftesbury Hall and the Cairns Memorial Hall, mainly for its own activities but also for outside hire. In Boscombe, the 3000-seater Grand Theatre opened in May 1895. Although it was visited by famous classical actors such as Beerbohm Tree and Henry Irving, it later catered for a wider clientele and was renamed the Boscombe Hippodrome in 1905.

After the 1851 Great Exhibition at Crystal Palace, large greenhouse-type public venues became fashionable assets for all-season resorts. Southbourne took the lead, transporting the Tedworth House glasshouse and opening it as the Winter Garden in 1874, mainly as a fernery supplying plants, but it held occasional concerts. In Exeter Road, the Winter Gardens Consortium eventually opened its grand hall in January 1877. Costing £12,000, the building covered 20,000 square feet and was chiefly of glass. It was domed with interior galleries and a balcony around the outside.

It failed twice before the Council took it over in 1893 for its latest artistic venture. Military-style brass bands were then commonplace. The Hampshire (Bournemouth) Volunteer Companies organized their own bands to accompany the pomp. Another popular band was the Bournemouth String Band. Less welcome were the itinerant musicians who descended on the town. The Royal Italian Band were better than most, but their seasonal nature displeased some until the Council

Two views of the Winter Gardens. The bottom one shows The Bournemouth Municipal Orchestra conducted by Sir Dan Godfrey.

ABOVE The starting line-up for a cycling race. The venue is uncertain but is probably Meyrick Park.

BELOW An Edwardian photograph of the fountain in the Lower Pleasure Gardens with a family strolling in the background.

ABOVE Childrens' Corner in the Lower Pleasure Gardens, 1905.

RIGHT One of the earliest airfields in Bournemouth, the Ensbury racecourse was a popular venue until it was offered for sale in 1928 and built on.

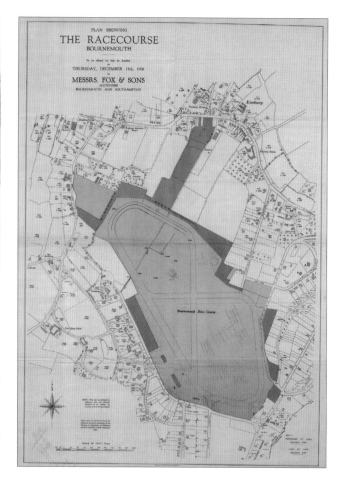

decided to retain them on a more formal basis, absorbing them in 1892 as the Corporation Military Band under a young son of a military bandsman, Dan Godfrey. It was an inspired choice, and under Godfrey the band divided its players between the end of the Pier and in various public gardens, with collective performances at symphonic concerts at the Winter Gardens.

Sir Dan Godfrey founded the Bournemouth Municipal Orchestra in 1893 and the Choir in 1911. He provided unrivalled opportunities for British music outside London making Bournemouth famous as the home of British music, where every composer could hope for a performance of his or her music. He promoted women composers at a time when this was not commonplace. 109 new works were performed in 1901-2, a typical season against a backcloth of funding problems, politics, and a

knife-edge existence for the orchestra. He was knighted in 1939 for his services to music. British music owes him a great debt. His legacy is the continued existence of the BSO and Choir, the only tangible memorials to his work in Bournemouth.

The Lower Pleasure Gardens were not opened until 1873. They were laid out as a beautiful promenading area flanked by the Bourne stream. They remain a major attraction. Boscombe Chine Gardens were formed by Drummond Wolff in 1883 and bought by the Council

The Lower Gardens.

The Second Annual Open Amateur Golf Tournament at Meyrick Park in 1932 was promoted by the Bournemouth Corporation.

in 1899. Parks were seen by the Victorians as vital to the well-being of the population, even the cemeteries were designed as places to visit. As the town grew and encroached upon and absorbed outlying villages, the Commissioners in their wisdom isolated plots of ground for leisure purposes and prevented their disappearance under bricks and mortar. In 1889, the Council secured the Five Parks Act, which provided that 425 acres of turbary commonland be laid out for general public use. The

first park to open was Meyrick Park on 28th November 1894. On the following day the 18-hole golf course was inaugurated, the first municipally planned links in the country. The other commons became King's Park, Queen's Park, Redhill Common and Seafield Gardens. Queen's Park was to contain another 18-hole golf course, whilst King's Park became the home of football. Both opened in 1902 and were named after the new monarchs. The provision of these and subsequent large open spaces gave the population a freedom to engage in both formal and informal activities – or none, just sitting around amongst beautiful surroundings.

The late Victorian period saw various innovations in entertainment. Vast painted panoramas depicting scenes around the world would be revealed to recitations and musical accompaniment. The magic lantern developed from a mere toy to having brighter lighting, extra lenses and mechanically-operated slides to produce 20ft diameter images that moved or dissolved into each other. Newly-discovered X-rays would produce amazement and suspicion as they penetrated bags and clothing. Most important was the showing of the Lumière Cinématographe for the first time at Shaftesbury Hall on 14th October 1896. These minute-long reels of moving pictures were to suffer for many years as a mere novelty programme supporting singers and magicians until their length and content sustained more narrative. Films were shown at many venues around the town in halls, churches and converted buildings until the first purpose-built cinema was opened in 1911 at Springbourne, aptly named The Coronation.

Booths showing cinematograph were present for a time at fairgrounds and circuses, along with freak shows and coconut shies. These ephemeral visitations are rarely recorded, even today. Poole and Christchurch were on the itinerary of fairground companies long before Bournemouth became a profitable site. Travelling circuses were more a Victorian phenomenon with Lord John Sanger, Barnum & Bailey and others bringing their acts from their winter bases. Some of these are recorded in the local press with details of the animals and acts. Billy Smart's Circus was a regular visitor to King's Park as late as the 1960s. East Common, near where Bournemouth Central Station is today, was a favourite site. It was here that 'Buffalo Bill' Cody brought his company in 1903 with all the American brouhaha and associated publicity.

Prior to the projection of moving images, there were Mutoscopes and Kinetoscopes, which are more widely known as *What the Butler Saw* penny-in-the-slot machines. A prerequisite of any seafront, Bournemouth gave licences for them as early as 1896. Licences were also given for fruit, sweets and ice-cream-sellers, especially close to the prime sites near the piers. Donkey rides were available at 6d for ½ mile. More interestingly, entertainment licences were also required for the Punch and Judy puppet shows and the concert parties, several of which existed, from the early black-face minstrels to the fashionable Pierrots of the 1900s onwards. These were typified by the Gay Cadets who built their own performing platform and provided songs and comic sketches to the

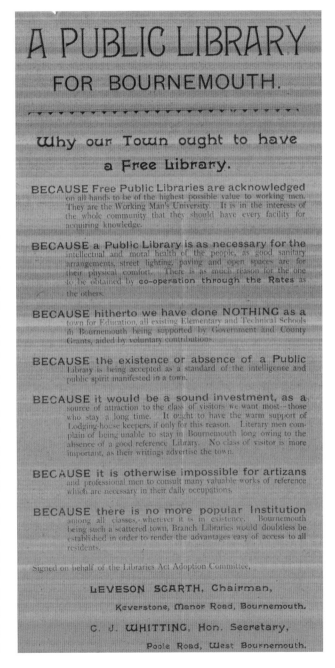

LEFT The Public Libraries Act 1892 allowed towns to use their funds to open public libraries. Like many Bournemouth projects, it met with both strong support and vehement opposition. The leaflet printed for the 1893 campaign supporting a public library set out very strongly the case why 'our Town ought to have a Free Library'.

summer visitors. Early troupes were required to be all male with drag acts.

Sydenham's Reading Rooms were an early attempt at supplying information, as were other subscription libraries. Some book stores operated lending libraries. The Commissioners' ratepayers' poll in 1885 opposed public libraries, but intellectual improvement of the general public came with the Public Libraries Act 1892, which aided their provision. The first Library opened at 6 Cumnor Terrace in Old Christchurch Road in 1895. A reading room opened in Boscombe at the same time, followed by others across the borough. Today, a fine new central library and a network of local libraries show how these first hesitant municipal steps formed the foundations for a long-standing and continuing contribution to leisure in the town.

Public access to the fine arts was spasmodic. The main provider was the Gallery of Fine Arts in Old Christchurch Road which would occasionally display a contemporary painting or two for public viewing. The Museum Act 1906 allowed Bournemouth to raise a ½d levy for the formation of a local museum. Such a repository had been suggested as early as 1868, as local fossils were carried off to the larger national institutions. The Bournemouth Natural Science Society, already custodians of earlier collections, feeling it had sufficient material for a nucleus of a local museum, offered it to the Council in 1912. The Council refused it. Meanwhile, Merton and Annie Russell-Cotes donated their collection of art treasures and paintings, and their East Cliff home to house it, to Bournemouth. The

In the 1960s, Ensbury Park Library on the corner of Keswick Road was only a small but well-used corner shop.

In 1938, as now, libraries provided for children's wider education and Winton Library published regular notes and news for children.

Russell-Cotes Art Gallery and Museum officially opened in 1922.

Despite the virtuous attempts to provide youth clubs, reading rooms and coffee taverns, loutish behaviour was a normal leisure activity of bored youngsters. A death by excessive drinking was recorded in 1868, as was the

The opening of the Old Kinson Library in the 1950s.

craze for throwing stones at visitors in the Gardens. Lads careering down the steep roads on velocipedes came to light following a serious accident on Poole Hill.

Again, the churches attempted to channel youthful energies. The first Bournemouth branch of the Boys Brigade was formed in 1894, and the first base, at Winton, was provided in 1896. The Boys Brigade played a major role in helping with Robert Baden-Powell's experimental camp on Brownsea Island in 1907. Those 20 boys at the camp were the forerunners of the world-wide Scouting movement. It is not surprising that Bournemouth was amongst the first towns to form Boy Scout groups, and by 1909 there were several across the borough. The movement was extended to younger boys and later to girls. Usually associated with churches, it focussed on self-reliance, skills-acquisition and public duty amongst the young, especially the less privileged, unhindered by Health & Safety and other modern regulations (the carrying of a 6 inch sheath knife was de rigueur). Scouting became, and remains, a valuable leisure occupation for generations of youngsters in the town.

The young could join adults within the Red Cross and St. John Ambulance to learn and practice first aid. All these uniformed groups were to play vital roles during the Second World War, which was also a period when the various Armed Forces formed Training Corps for youngsters to prepare for combat.

The growth of mechanical vehicles added to the leisure scene of responsible adults. Cycles of various types became available, aided by better quality roads, and a Bicycle and Tricycle Club regularly held events during the last years of the 19th century. The motor car appeared just before 1900. Trams are introduced, replacing the horse-drawn omnibuses, with routes from Poole to Christchurch. Both private and public transport gave the opportunity for greater access to the surrounding countryside. In 1910, the first international airshow heralded the arrival of yet another leisure attraction.

Public Entertainment after the First World War

The post-war years were times for expansion, despite the Depression. The Cinematograph Act 1909 introduced safety requirements which meant that building new cinemas was preferable to modifying old sheds. Also, cinema had come of age. Unhindered by the war, Hollywood dominated the world with spectacular films and glamourous stars. Going to the cinema was as fashionable as the theatre. The introduction of sound in 1927 increased its popularity. Larger and more prestigious picture palaces were built, capable of audiences of 2000 and more: the Regent in 1929, the Westover and the Lansdowne Odeon both in 1937. Across the borough, 16 cinemas in all served the local communities.

A feature of the inter-war cinemas was the provision of variety acts as a subsidiary to the films. This was known as

LEFT Contrast this photograph of spectators at a football match between Boscombe v. Bournemouth in April 1914 with a football crowd today!

RIGHT AFC Bournemouth team photo in 1986 with their manager Harry Redknapp.

BELOW AFC Bournemouth's greatest triumph. The programme for their FA Cup 3rd Round victory over Manchester United in January 1984.

F. A. CUP Round Three
AFC BOURNEMOUTH
v
MANCHESTER UNITED
Saturday, 7th January 1984
Kick off 3.00pm   Match Magazine Price 50p

AFC BOURNEMOUTH

cine-variety. The stage was large and often well-equipped to take the many visiting bands, singers and comedians. In addition, there was the mighty organ console to entertain between films.

Meanwhile, a new phenomenon occurred in the 1920s. Bournemouth had played a part in its history, when in December 1897 Guglielmo Marconi transmitted experimental telegraphic signals from a West Cliff house to the Isle of Wight. Some 20 years later the British Broadcasting Company was formed and started daily broadcasting in November 1922. A year later, station 6BM opened – on 17th October 1923. It was one of seven regional stations. With a studio at 72 Holdenhurst Road and a transmitting station at Bushey Road, Charminster, it relayed the main London programmes with a slot for local input. The nature of the receiving apparatus, and the novelty of free entertainment, brought the family together each evening to listen to sounds from across Europe on their 'wireless'. Of especial interest was the dance music, with band leaders achieving large followings. Radio was to persist as a popular home-entertainment medium for

decades: indeed, local boy Tony Hancock's *Hancock's Half Hour* used to empty the pubs when it was broadcast in the 1950s. However, the Bournemouth station soon went into decline after it was launched, with the plug pulled in 1939. However, when pirate radio stations challenged the BBC's monopoly in the early 1960s, one of its first Disc Jockeys on Radio Caroline was local boy Tony Blackburn, who then became the first DJ on BBC Radio 1 in September 1967.

Spectator sports were well served in Bournemouth. Boscombe Football Club was elected to the Football League in 1923 and renamed Bournemouth and Boscombe Athletic FC, better known as the Cherries. It vacillated between the Third and Fourth Divisions until 1987. Its greatest moment was when, under the management of Harry Redknapp, it defeated Manchester United in the F.A. Cup in January 1984.

Dean Park was the home of local cricket and was the venue of Hampshire Cricket Club when it played in Bournemouth. For many years, the

ABOVE Parasols and Boaters surround an early tennis match. The ladies on the courts in the background play in full-length skirts.

BELOW Bowls was another outdoor activity which was provided both privately and on municipal greens.

BELOW RIGHT The tennis courts in Boscombe Gardens in the 1930s.

British Hard Courts Tennis Championships were held at Melville Park, the home of the West Hants Lawn Tennis Club, founded in 1926 and recognized in 2009 as one of the top six tennis locations in Britain. But the town's oldest existing tennis club is the Victoria Avenue Lawn Tennis Club set up in 1910. Winton Pleasure Ground (better known today as Winton Rec.) had been opened by the Council in 1906 with a cricket pitch, tennis courts, bowling greens and 'the only quoits court in town'.[2] A group of the regular tennis players formed Richmond Park Tennis Club in 1910. At the time, it was on the edge of the town, but as Winton expanded, it moved to its Victoria Avenue location close to Boundary Road in 1921.

Other structures added to the landscape. The Pavilion, envisaged by Ferrey as early as 1836, finally emerged in 1929 as a brick Art Deco theatre and concert hall for the Bournemouth Municipal Orchestra. For its first decade, it provided a mixture of music and theatre, with touring companies bringing in the stars. The building also housed a fine large ballroom and a restaurant. During the Second World War, the Pavilion had hosted the less extravagant fare of comedians, dance bands and Variety acts, with occasional revivals of veteran musicians with veteran artists. The transfer of the Municipal Orchestra freed the stage for touring companies for visits of a whole week or sometimes more. Some plays were direct from London's West End. Increasingly well patronised seasons of ballet and opera companies came, especially the D'Oyly Carte with its Gilbert and Sullivan repertoire. Big names visiting the Pavilion included Michael Caine and Dirk Bogarde. By the 1970s it was losing money with poor attendances, a trend which has continued to threaten its existence. As a theatre, it lost out to Poole's Lighthouse, but a proposed Pavilion Dance was expected to revive its fortunes as a cultural centre.

The opening of the Pavilion created problems for the ageing Theatre Royal. In the 1930s, it was a venue for the several repertory companies that toured the country. Short seasons were provided, their great advantage being able to produce current West End plays without incurring royalties. Around the same period, came the realisation of a project started in 1919 of creating a playhouse for the growing interest in amateur dramatics. The Bournemouth Dramatic and Orchestral Club decided in June 1928 to investigate building their own theatre for their productions. A company under the name of the Little Theatre Club Ltd was registered and A. J. Seal was instructed to draw up plans. On 15th June 1931, the Little Theatre in Hinton Road was formally opened by St. John Ervine with George Stone's production of *The Merry Wives of Windsor*. In 1938, the Bournemouth Little Theatre Club beat 200 similar organisations in winning the *News Chronicle* Amateur Dramatic Contest. During the late 1930s, the theatre adopted the name of Palace Court Theatre.

Opposite the Pavilion, on the site of the earlier roller rink, another addition was the Westover Ice Rink which opened in 1930 (see page 91). It was the eleventh in a nationwide spate of building 33 such rinks, after the invention of providing ice surfaces. As well as individual skating, there were the spectator aspects of the famous ice-shows which started in 1933, and later ice-hockey. It

was also the venue for boxing promotions, and it was here that Freddie Mills, who became World Light Heavyweight Champion in 1948, won his first fight in 1936. The Rink closed in 1991. On Pier Approach, a typically municipal building was opened in 1937. Its main purpose was as a public baths, but it was an arena for swimming races, including the English Schools National Championships, and later became famous for its summer aquatic shows.

Formal dining-out was the preserve of the establishment, with annual banquets at the finer hotels replete with after-dinner speeches. Less well-off people might enjoy a Sunday-school party. Both are recorded in the Victorian period. Dining-out was often an accompaniment to a night at the theatre or cinema and these had their own restaurants. Even department stores had restaurants complete with palm court orchestras in the 1930s. Eating out as a main leisure activity was not really possible for most people, or so it was claimed when Vincent Forte opened his American-style Ice Cream Parlour in the Square on 14th May 1937. Although there were some 70 restaurants and numerous cafes and snack-bars in 1939, the war was to curb such extravagance.

By the late 1930s Bournemouth could boast of a full complement of entertainment houses, some modest like church halls, others palatial. However, when war was declared on 3rd September 1939, all places of entertainment were ordered to close for the duration of hostilities. It was feared that a direct hit of a bomb on a crowded hall would be too demoralising. When the German bombing onslaught failed to materialise, it was decided that public distraction would be far more beneficial. First the cinemas opened, then the theatres and other places not requisitioned for Air Raid Precaution or wartime service. The cinemas became extremely popular, with attendances reaching all-time records with mostly escapist films and newsreels which gave the families at

home glimpses of the terrors of their menfolk at war.

Activities connected to the war effort were all-embracing and created a great camaraderie amongst communities, whether knitting comforts for the troops in each others' homes, attending beetle-drives in church halls, doing fire watching at night or, ultimately, organizing street victory parties.

During the war, much of the beach was barricaded off and the piers breached to prevent enemy landings. This did not stop some enjoying a few of the free areas. Bournemouth was within a restriction zone which meant - coupled with pleas not to travel - that the tourism industry declined. However, the presence of Allied troops in the town meant a fair amount of activity at the many venues – especially ballrooms – and initiating the locals into the mysteries of baseball.

In November 1937, a nondescript brick building opened in Exeter Road on the former Winter Gardens site as an indoor bowling green, claimed to be the finest in the world. Its activities were curtailed by the war when the building was used for storage and as a mess hall for Allied servicemen. When hostilities were over, the Pavilion felt a need to concentrate on modern stage shows by capitalising on the touring circuit. The Municipal Orchestra moved to the former bowling venue which was renamed after the illustrious Winter Gardens. Although visually less impressive than the former 'cucumber frame', it happened to have superb acoustics. It re-opened on 18th October 1947 with Rudolph Schwartz as its new chief conductor. The Winter Gardens remained the base of the orchestra, whose name was changed to the Bournemouth Symphony Orchestra in 1954, until they closed in 2000. The BSO attracted a loyal audience with seasons of Sunday afternoon and Thursday evening concerts.

Both piers had been breached during the war and it took some time to rebuild them. A Pier Theatre was finally constructed at Bournemouth, opening in 1960. The decorative designs reflect the Festival of Britain of a decade earlier. It is one of only a few pier theatres remaining in Britain. Born of Music Hall, then Variety, the end-of-pier shows were enjoyed by a relaxed, easy-to-

please, undemanding audience. Song and comedy, with an occasional novelty act, was the format for a weekly-changing clientele. Bournemouth's intended policy was to provide something different. Impresario Harold Fielding was brought in, together with Peter Myers and Ronald Cass.

The first production was 'Carry On Laughing', an urbane and slick revue using six girls and six men. In recent years, Bournemouth Pier Theatre has had 'one night stands' of big-name acts travelling round the country. These shows are greater attractions than the usual summer show, and being at weekends, are perhaps aimed at the resident audiences.

Boscombe Pier also had a structure built on it. It was promisingly called the Mermaid Theatre, but when it opened in June 1962 it was as a roller-skating rink, and it later became an amusement arcade.

The Bournemouth Municipal Choir in 1932-3.

The Television Age

On 2nd June 1953, millions of people crowded in front rooms across the country to witness the televised Coronation of Queen Elizabeth II. For many, this was their first exposure to television. More sets were bought, and with the introduction of Independent companies later in the decade, people remained at home glued to their TV sets, whilst the high street entertainment venues languished. 'Can't revolution tonight, Brother: there's something good on telly.' ran the *TV-Times* commercial. The 1960s/70s saw a sharp decline in cinema-going, especially in the suburbs. Many closed, but some venues were revived by the Bingo craze, taking advantage of the declining audiences. Some half-dozen Bournemouth cinemas were converted. Those cinemas with a large stage were able to capitalise with one-night gigs by pop stars, the most notable was in 1963 when the Beatles appeared at the Gaumont. By 1974, only two major cinemas remained, the Odeon and the Westover. In another attempt to remain commercial, they both split their auditoria, first twinning, then adding more.

In 1995, an ambitious trial of drive-in cinema took place at Honeycombe Chine with space for nearly 200

The Pavilion from Westover Road in the 1930s.

Lord Mountbatten at the opening of Pokesdown Youth Club in 1965 being greeted by Mayor and Mayoress Morris.

cars looking on to a huge 20 metre by 5 metre screen. *Wild River* was screened on 25th May to 130 cars. It was regarded as being the first drive-in cinema event in this country. It was tried again in King's Park later that year but never repeated.

The same period saw innovation in eating habits, as it became stylish to eat out in the evenings and tastes widened to include food from many different cultures. By 1959, the Nanking Chinese Restaurant had opened in Albert Road, and within another four years, the Taj Mahal Indian restaurant opened in Poole Road. By 1961, another food-form appeared, the hamburger. The first Wimpy bar was part of a German company, but named after the Popeye character. This company was to be eclipsed by the McDonald chain which opened at 35 Old Christchurch Road in 1984. In recent decades, Bournemouth has been swamped with restaurants and pubs providing for leisured meals, catering in exotic cuisines or just traditional 'pub-grub'. A contemporary scan through the 'lonely hearts' section of newspapers reveals some 50% of hopefuls include eating out as a prime leisure activity.

As the 1950s advanced, cars brought in new leisure activities, unfettered by the limitations in public transport. The growing numbers of car-owners would potter around country roads of a Sunday: it was the new 'promenading'. With their cars, they explored the British countryside and visited the many booming attractions. Caravans added to the freedom, less dependent on dubious B & B's. Although many seaside resorts had caravan camps, Bournemouth stayed aloof. Holiday camps, too, were not countenanced, the nearest being the camp, later Pontin's, in Christchurch opposite Wick. Butlin had planned to open a large holiday camp similar to his first in Clacton-on-Sea in Bournemouth in 1940, but the onset of war prevented this.[3]

In 1978, the Arts Council reorganised distribution of arts provision and its funding with potentially serious consequences for Bournemouth. The Bournemouth Symphony Orchestra was required to use the new Poole Arts Centre as its main base. The Winter Gardens had lost its purpose, and summer shows were using the BIC, Pavilion and Pier Theatre. Successive Councils vacillated on the closure of the Winter Gardens, which by now had gained a great popular affection. Reneging on a referendum and an election promise, both main local political parties rode out the storms of protest. The final concert by the BSO was played in 2000, and the demolition of the Winter Gardens started on 24th April 2006. Despite acquiring an international reputation, the orchestra was by then almost a stranger to its home of origin, with occasional concerts at the Pavilion and BIC, and firework-festooned extravaganzas in parks. Classical music was left in the hands of amateur orchestras like the Westbourne Orchestra and various choirs who used churches as venues. A brave offshoot of the BSO, Kokoro, provided rare glimpses of contemporary music, never really appreciated by Bournemouth audiences.

The site of the former Pier Approach Baths was replaced

The Zig-Zag Path.

by a wet-weather venue intended for beach-users. The IMAX cinema opened in March 2002 providing a stunning visual experience on a vast screen measuring 19 metres by 25 metres. Only a few films were shot using the full apparatus, and such cinemas could only be sustained by showing feature films - especially those of the prevalent dynamic action films. This was successful elsewhere but the Bournemouth IMAX seems to have been denied this provision. Vilified for being in the wrong place, hindered by delays, disliked by those hating modern architecture and abandoned by its owners, the venue was regarded as a total disaster after just a few years.

Many people have become increasingly health-conscious as their life styles of car travel, lounging in front

Boats moored at Wick.

of TVs, indulgent eating and drinking habits, plus stressful jobs, have created the need to rectify the damage. Jogging started life as a semi-eccentric lone activity in the 1970s, but it is now manifested in frequent marathons for charitable causes. Some 6500 female runners raised £400,000 at Bournemouth events during 2008. Yoga and Pilates sessions are held in modest church halls, but leisure centres are a growth industry, with their serried ranks of walking machines and body-toning equipment, after which, a quick drink or two, a bite to eat, and a drive home in the car. The Littledown Centre is the largest in Bournemouth, and one of the most successful in the UK. It

opened in 1989 at a cost of £7 million, its main sports hall and swimming pool enclosed by a 48m span timber frame vault. Activities include badminton, bowls and martial arts. In contrast, the leisure pool in the Bournemouth International Centre has closed, as have other facilities elsewhere in the town, including some school pools.

There was liberation from the formal ballroom with the faster rhythm Jazz-influenced music which had expressed itself in the Jitterbug during the War, with American troops demonstrating their skills on the Pavilion dance floor. It was Rock'n'Roll, encapsulated in the 1956 film *Rock Around the Clock*, which sent teenagers literally dancing in the aisles to the trepidation of cinema managers. Music, too, became more available. Guitar playing was discovered

to need only a few chords to render a gratifying sound. Skiffle allowed a sprouting up of many a local group, and, in the mid-60s, equally many a sub-Mersey Beat combo. By the late 1970s, young music needed only to be loud with a dominant beat. Dance halls dispensed with live musicians and used gramophone records, straight or mixed, with darkened ambience and flashing lights. Discos, by their underground nature, are difficult to trace in the historic record. An early contender was the former Boscombe Hippodrome, since turned into a ballroom by Mecca, which opened as The Academy in 1982. It was successful enough to win the 'Discotheque of the South' award at least twice. It had guest groups like the Three Degrees, Hawkwind and the Eurythmics. It closed in June 1993 with losses of £400,000, with the clientele being attracted by Richard Carr's new club, The Cage. It is now a banqueting hall restored to its original Victorian interior.

Early contenders for nightclubs would have been the Village and Le Cardinal, both in Glenfern Road, and Whiskys in Old Christchurch Road. The beginnings of the present dominance of the evening/night activities which must be classed as leisure is perhaps difficult to define. Sex, drugs (and/or drink) and Rock'n'Roll is often regarded as the result of a moral decline in the late 1960s. A more likely watershed would have been the relaxing of drinking laws paving the growth of bars and night clubs driven by the sale of alcohol, with additional attractions. Bournemouth was happy to embrace this new night culture, with hoteliers, businessmen and club owners claiming it gave a vibrant new image to the town. In 1996 Richard Carr of The Academy nightclub said that the industry generated some £15m.

For two centuries, Bournemouth has experienced a rich variety of activities. Many still exist or could be revived, but fashions change and new ones are promoted, often re-using former leisure facilities.

SEVEN

TRACKS, TRAMS, TRAINS AND PLANES
Peter Kazmierczak and Mike Phipp

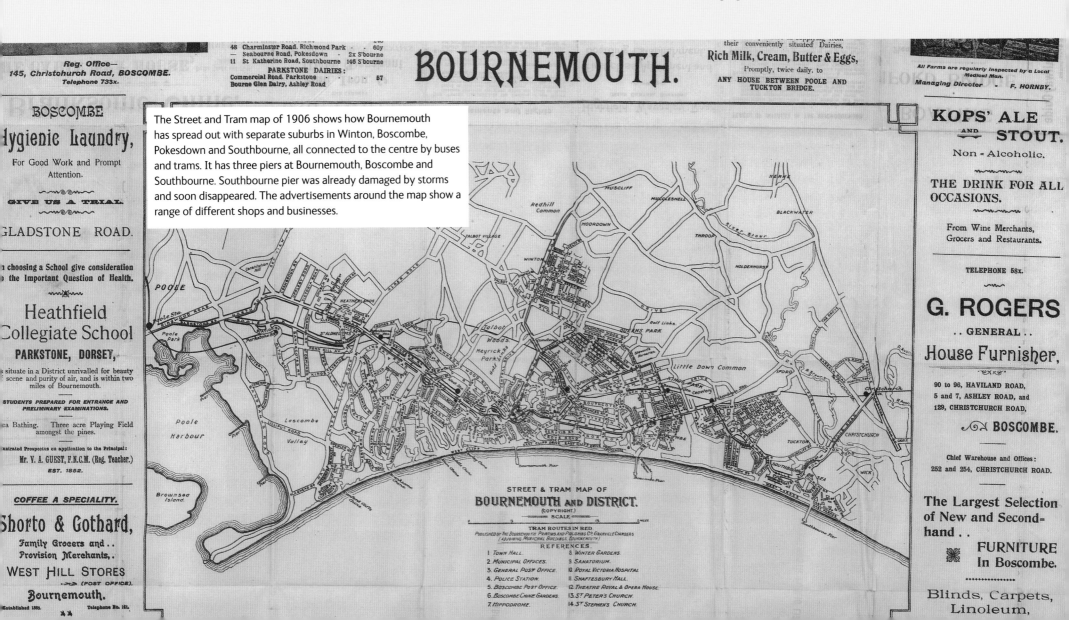

The Street and Tram map of 1906 shows how Bournemouth has spread out with separate suburbs in Winton, Boscombe, Pokesdown and Southbourne, all connected to the centre by buses and trams. It has three piers at Bournemouth, Boscombe and Southbourne. Southbourne pier was already damaged by storms and soon disappeared. The advertisements around the map show a range of different shops and businesses.

STREET & TRAM MAP OF
BOURNEMOUTH and DISTRICT.
(COPYRIGHT.)
SCALE

TRAM ROUTES IN RED.
PUBLISHED BY THE BOURNEMOUTH PRINTING AND PUBLISHING CO. GRANVILLE CHAMBERS
(ADJOINING MUNICIPAL BUILDINGS, BOURNEMOUTH.)

REFERENCES
1. TOWN HALL.
2. MUNICIPAL OFFICES.
3. GENERAL POST OFFICE.
4. POLICE STATION.
5. BOSCOMBE POST OFFICE.
6. BOSCOMBE CHINE GARDENS.
7. HIPPODROME.
8. WINTER GARDENS.
9. SANATORIUM.
10. ROYAL VICTORIA HOSPITAL.
11. SHAFTESBURY HALL.
12. THEATRE ROYAL & OPERA HOUSE.
13. ST PETER'S CHURCH.
14. ST STEPHEN'S CHURCH.

Chapter Seven

BOURNEMOUTH depended for its development and growth as a resort and its continued prosperity on transport for tourists and residents alike. From roads via railways and back to roads, the vitality of its day-to-day activities depends on movement to school, work, shops, hospitals and the airport. This chapter looks at the history of transport in Bournemouth from the earliest tracks to the modern networks of interlinked roads, railways and air transport.

Roads around Bournemouth

Long before Henrietta Tregonwell took a journey across the heath in July 1810 and fell in love with the area, people had been walking or riding across the lands between Christchurch and Poole for centuries. Sometimes they came in peace, to bury their dead: sometimes in anger at the onset of invasion. Others came to exploit minerals or for more illicit trade. Some came out of curiosity, others for a definite need. Many just wanted to get from A to B by the easiest route.

Ancient Britons knew the area. From settlements along the banks of the Stour, they climbed up on to Littledown, Wallisdown and Canford Heath to lay their dead in barrows

In the early days of Bournemouth the only bridge across the River Stour was at Iford, linking Christchurch with the villages further up the valley.

and other burial grounds. Romans landing at Hengistbury Head in 43 AD, though preferring to penetrate inland via the meanderous Stour, nevertheless established a way across the district. They took the high ground over Stourfield Heath, Moordown and High Howe, crossing the Roman Road from Badbury Rings to Hamworthy, before heading for Wareham. There is a possibility that this was part of a Roman road coming across the New Forest from Winchester and the rest of their road network.

The Saxon villages strung along the south bank of the Stour were interlinked by narrow trackways. Roads at that period were more a permission to cross someone's land, than a definite fixed line. The growth of crops or vegetation would cause the route to veer somewhat from one year to the next. What is now Castle Lane, that notoriously busy road running across the northern part of Bournemouth, was an early form of by-pass to avoid Holdenhurst and Throop, thus providing a more direct route linking Wimborne and Christchurch.

By the early 16th century, a coastal route between Poole and Lymington had been established. It came down Poole Hill, through what was later The Square and Lansdowne, then along Christchurch Road to Iford and beyond. From this road other tracks led northeast to Holdenhurst (later Holdenhurst Road), north across the heathland (Wimborne and Charminster roads) and south to the coast at Boscombe and Alum Chines.

A third east to west track led across Wallisdown, then followed the line of the present day Talbot, Alma and Richmond Park roads. This might have been an attempt to avoid the Poole to Ringwood turnpike and its tolls, which was established in 1759. Turnpikes were the first real improvement in the road system since Roman times, but not everyone was happy to pay the charges. However, this route over Stourfield Heath appears to have fallen out of use by the beginning of the 19th century.

Smugglers also established their own more surreptitious tracks from the seashore to the inland villages such as Kinson, where they stashed their contraband. These tracks were not publicised for obvious reasons, hence seldom appear on printed maps. The Christchurch Inclosure Act of 1802 fixed the general road pattern that had been built up over many centuries. The Act, for the enclosure of common and waste land, required those administrating it to lay out roads and make provision for their upkeep. Some 25 roads in all, together with six gravel or clay pits for their maintenance, were provided for. In the ensuing Award of 1805, five principal roads of 40 ft width were suggested:

Road No.1 - Christchurch Road and Poole Road

Road No.2 - Holdenhurst Road

Road No.3 - Richmond Hill, part of Wimborne Road and Charminster Road

Road No.4 – Wimborne Road from Cemetery Junction

Road No.5 – Redhill Lane

The work of Benjamin Ferrey on the 'Marine Village' of the 1830s, Christopher Crabbe Creeke as the Bournemouth Commissioners' Surveyor from the mid 1850s, and the expansion of the town with the coming of the railways in the 1870s all built upon this basic framework of roads.

Sweeping roads and crescents appeared in the more affluent areas. Further out from the town centre, housing development in the Victorian and Edwardian period was very much on a formal rectangular pattern, with roads running at right angles and parallel to the main thoroughfares. Winton, Malmesbury Park, Springbourne

This early photograph of Wick Ferry in the 1860s shows the simple transport available against the background of Christchurch Priory.

The *Marie Therese* aground off Hengistbury Head in 1898 is a reminder of the hazards of travel a little over a century ago.

Old Tuckton Bridge about 1900 and its toll house.

The old toll bridge was replaced by the present Tuckton Bridge, seen here under construction in 1905.

Tuckton Bridge in 2009, with a Yellow Bus travelling towards Christchurch.

and Pokesdown exemplify this.

During the 1930s, tree-lined avenues and drives were popular in residential districts. After the Second World War, on new housing estates such as at West Howe, straight roads were noticeable by their absence. This was taken to the extreme in many developments during the 1980s and 1990s, particularly at Townsend, Muscliffe and Littledown, with their numerous short closes and gardens leading off a curvaceous spine road through each area.

The one new major road through the area has been the dual-carriageway A338, completed in stages between the late 1960s and early 1980s. It follows the western side of the Avon Valley as the Bournemouth Spur Road, past Holdenhurst and Littledown. It then cuts through the residential areas of Springbourne, where properties were purchased compulsorily to make way for it. It passes the centre of the town in cuttings and on viaducts as the Wessex Way to end as a single carriageway at a traffic-clogged gyratory system beyond Westbourne. A route not defined by previous historical connections, it was built to serve the needs of the motor vehicle, bringing in tourists and commuters from surrounding areas.

Bournemouth's road network of today basically derives from the tracks and pathways established by people living many centuries ago. There was no grand scheme of things, no overall design. However there were opportunities to alter radically the pattern of roads and neither were taken up. First, the Inclosure Act of 1802 largely confirmed the existing pattern of tracks and lanes. Second, the Abercrombie Plan of 1946 proposed a central tripartite loop road system: only echoes of which appeared 25 years later in part of the Wessex Way. Finally, in the 1960s a network of roads was proposed which would have provided routes by-passing the centre of Christchurch and much of Castle Lane. It would have taken a road along the Bourne valley from Canford Heath into Bournemouth to connect with the Wessex Way. This transport plan for the whole conurbation provided an opportunity to provide easy movement into the town centre, but objections from many different groups stopped it.

So what we have today, with daily traffic jams, bottlenecks and parking difficulties has evolved rather than been planned. Whether the next hundred years will bring a radical change to the road network, only time will tell.

LEFT Wessex Way under construction in 1967.

ABOVE Wessex Way approaching Bournemouth past Holdenhurst in October 2009.

Trams and Trolleys, Buses Too –

Internal transport links are vitally important to the economic well-being of any town. The coming of the railways to Bournemouth in the 1870s stirred private enterprise into action, with horse buses connecting the stations with the town centre and surrounding hotels; even out into the developing suburbs. By the end of the 19th century, there were around 100 licensed horse buses in the town. The service was of a rather cavalier nature though, with overloaded buses, lax timekeeping and the occasional fight between rival firms in order to capture a fare.

Some saw an opportunity to provide a better, more reliable service. In 1881 a meeting was held in support of a firm of London engineers who wanted to construct a tramway linking Bournemouth with Poole. Along with

other schemes in that decade, it failed due largely to a lack of finance and specific local backing.

In 1897 the dynamic British Electric Traction Company (BET) arrived in town. With energy and vigour they proposed a tramway running between Poole and Bournemouth. Local public opinion was divided over this scheme. Many thought the tramway would afford a very convenient means of getting from place to place, certainly more reliable than the horse buses. Others were less sure, citing narrow streets unable to accommodate the tramcars, together with a feeling that they would be a detriment rather than an advantage to the town. Poole Council was in favour, Bournemouth was not.

In April 1901, a 3 ft 6 in gauge electric tramway opened between the railway station in Poole and County Gates, on the Bournemouth boundary near Westbourne. Whilst this was being constructed, BET applied for an eastwards

extension through Bournemouth to Christchurch. This forced Bournemouth Corporation's hand into developing, rather reluctantly, their own scheme. If anyone was to build and operate a tramway through Bournemouth, it would be the Council. However, the Council dallied and BET fought back with the threat of litigation and injunctions. The Council retaliated with the possibility of an appeal to the House of Lords over the matter. Common sense finally prevailed, with BET selling out their interests in the area. Bournemouth and Poole came to an agreement, in which the latter agreed to lease their tramway to Bournemouth Corporation for 30 years, to be worked as part of their new system.

The first trams began running in Bournemouth on 23rd July 1902, between the Lansdowne and Pokesdown. By the year's end, further routes had opened along Holdenhurst Road and out to Westbourne. Bournemouth's tramway

A tram arriving at the Lansdowne after coming up Old Christchurch Road. There was no overhead cable, but a power supply between the tracks.

system was complete by autumn 1905, save for a loop through Lower Parkstone in Poole which was opened in 1906. Tram tracks radiated out to Winton and Moordown, through Southbourne and on to Christchurch.

Standard overhead wiring was used, except for the central section from the Lansdowne to Poole Hill, where for aesthetic reasons, unsightly wiring was replaced by current collection from a conduit beneath the tracks. Due to unreliability and rising maintenance costs, this conduit

was replaced in 1911 by the normal overhead wiring.

Although a very short-lived bus service operated between The Square and Pokesdown in 1899, the first Corporation buses appeared in April 1906 linking Boscombe and Boscombe Pier. Other services followed, for instance from Westbourne to Alum Chine. These routes, though, were regarded as feeders to the main tram network. The hilly routes down to the seafront put a considerable strain on the transmissions of the petrol buses and further planned routes, such as between the Central Station and Bournemouth Pier, were abandoned due to the steepness of the roads, especially Bath Hill.

The Council did not have it all its own way regarding

bus services, for in 1916 Bournemouth & District Motor Services was formed. By 1919 it was operating services out of the town to Lymington and Ringwood. Changing its name to Hants & Dorset the following year to reflect better its sphere of operation, it established a large network of routes to the surrounding towns of Poole, Wimborne and further afield. The Salisbury-based Wilts & Dorset firm also began operating a route into Bournemouth. Thomas Elliott had been working horse buses around the town under the name of Royal Blue for many years. His stables were in Royal Blue Mews in Avenue Lane, Bournemouth. He died in 1911 and his two sons, John and William, took over the business, purchasing the first motor char-a-bancs in 1913, using them to take visitors on day trips. After the end of the First World War, more vehicles were obtained, many of which were on chassis that had been built for military use, and the range of excursions increased, including a trip to the Isle of Wight via Lymington, added in 1919. A railway strike in 1911 gave the Elliotts an opportunity to start a weekend service from Bournemouth to London. In 1924, the Elliott brothers agreed not to operate stage services in return for Hants & Dorset's assurance that they would not operate any tours, excursions or long distance services from Bournemouth.

In 1928, the London service became 3 times daily all year round, and picked up in various towns along the route (Elliott Brothers being one of the pioneers of this form of travel). The journey took 5 hours, and cost 12 shillings and six pence single or one pound return from London to Bournemouth. The express services were quickly expanded to include destinations such as Torquay, Plymouth, Ilfracombe, Bristol, Birmingham and Margate. On Sunday 8th March 1931, Elliott Brothers opened a new bus station in Bournemouth, jointly with Hants & Dorset. It was a two-tier building with an entrance on to Exeter Road, with Royal Blue coaches using the lower tier and

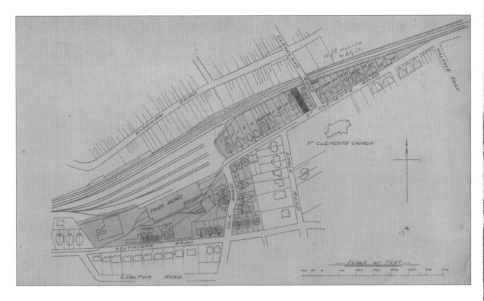

A plan showing the tram depot at Southcote Road alongside the tracks of the railway line into Bournemouth Central in 1903. The site is used today by the Borough's waste collection services.

Original drawing of the Corporation Tramways engine house at Southcote Road.

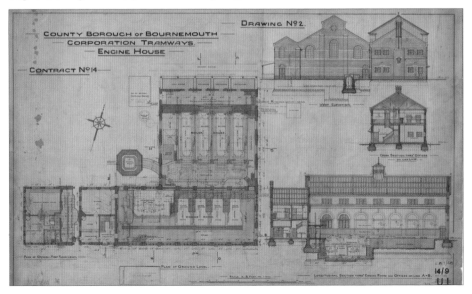

One of Royal Blue's earliest services in The Square in 1905.

Hants & Dorset buses the upper tier.

Elliott Brothers sold out in early 1935. The tours and excursions part of the business was taken over by Hants and Dorset, and the express services passed to the Southern National and Western National companies. Their express services were incorporated into the Royal Blue network, which continued to be run from Bournemouth as a subsidiary of these companies. The Royal Blue routes now ran from London to Bristol, London to Bournemouth, and the area between as far west as Penzance. They also provided a South Coast Express from Bournemouth to Margate, and with associated motorways connected Bournemouth to Cheltenham, Birmingham, Northampton and Liverpool. The Royal Blue services were a distinctive feature of Bournemouth's tourism until they were incorporated into National Express in 1973.

Back in Bournemouth itself, with the enlargement of the Borough to include areas previously in Dorset, the Corporation instituted a series of express limited-stop services in 1930 to its suburbs beyond the reach of the

The cover of the 1930
map of Royal Blue Motor services.

ABOVE Winton Peters Hill looking south with a tram approaching in 1905.   BELOW Winton Banks looking north in 1905.

trams. Trams were now seen as old fashioned and uncomfortable. As a reflection on their unpopularity, the cumbersome title of 'Bournemouth Corporation Tramways & Motor Services' was changed in 1931 to 'Bournemouth Corporation Transport Services'. In 1932 Bournemouth received its first covered-top double-deckers for use on routes from The Square to Iford, Southbourne, Castle Lane and Malvern Road.

The Bournemouth Corporation Act (1930) gave powers for trolleybuses to operate those services currently worked by trams, as well as along new routes. Trolleybuses were seen as the ideal solution for most of Bournemouth's transport needs, being clean, quiet and having good hill-climbing ability. An experimental service between Westbourne and The Square began on 13th May 1933 and was quickly pronounced as a success. Regular services began on 22nd June 1934 and within two years trams in Bournemouth were but a memory. The final tramcar made its last journey back to the depot from Christchurch on 8th April 1936. The former tram route along Capstone Road was the only one never converted to trolleybus operation.

Routes that had never had trams fell under the spell of the new trolleys. Barrack Road in Christchurch, Beaufort Road and Cranleigh Road received the new overhead wiring, as did Charminster Road towards the centre, and Wallisdown Road and Columbia Avenue on the north-western side of the town. The final trolleybus route opened along Castle Lane on 15th October 1951. New trolleybuses were introduced, an elegant new depot was built at Mallard Road and passengers reached record numbers. The future looked very promising.

However, the very cold winter of 1962-63 hit the trolleybus network hard, with total suspension of the service just before the New Year. Early in 1963, the decision was made to replace the much-loved trolleys with conventional diesel-engined buses. Declining passenger numbers, the impossibility of obtaining new vehicles as manufacturers pulled out of the trolleybus business and the lack of flexibility that trolleys had with regard to new road layouts all contributed to their demise. Westbourne lost its trolleybus service in 1965, as did Holdenhurst Road and Ashley Road. Over the next four years the network was progressively cut back until the final scheduled services ran on 19th April 1969. No more would be heard the characteristic swish as a trolley bus passed. Gone were the sparks from the trolley heads on a frosty morning and the excitement when the trolley poles came off the overhead wires, stopping the traffic.

The Borough buses lost their 'Corporation' status in

1973 and, after a marketing campaign, became known as 'Yellow Buses' in 1982. With deregulation of buses following the Transport Act of 1985, they became a private limited company wholly owned by the Council. In 2005 the Council sold Yellow Buses to Transdev, but retained a 10% stake in the business. Earlier, the Transport Act of 1968 led to the formation of the National Bus Company which

Two souvenir trolley bus tickets issued to mark the Coronation of King George VI in 1937. @ The Estate of the Late Eustace Nash.

now controlled Hants & Dorset and Wilts & Dorset. A new corporate image was introduced and the Wilts & Dorset name disappeared. When deregulation of bus services in the 1980s led to a management buyout, the Wilts & Dorset name reappeared in 1983. In 2003 it became part of the Go-Ahead Group, providing a comprehensive service in Bournemouth and beyond, including a very frequent service across the conurbation linking Christchurch with Poole.

Today there are principally two competing firms operating buses within Bournemouth: Yellow Buses owned by Transdev and Wilts & Dorset, part of the Go-Ahead Group. Other firms thrive too, notably Shamrock which operates many of the school services around Bournemouth.

So the wheel has turned full circle in the past century, from an almost free-for-all with horse buses, through a very regulated system with Corporation control of trams and trolleybuses, to the deregulation and privatisation towards the end of the century.

Railways of Bournemouth

Today, standing on the platform of Bournemouth station, each train looks much the same as any other. The white-liveried Class 444 electric express units glide effortlessly on their way up to London or down to Poole and Weymouth. The Cross-Country diesel trains take passengers further afield to Birmingham and the cities beyond. Occasionally a blue Class 450 suburban unit appears, but otherwise conformity reigns. Efficient? Yes. Romantic? Well not as much as if the date was 1910 rather than 2010. An Edwardian traveller from that earlier period would certainly recognise the station, with its refurbished roof

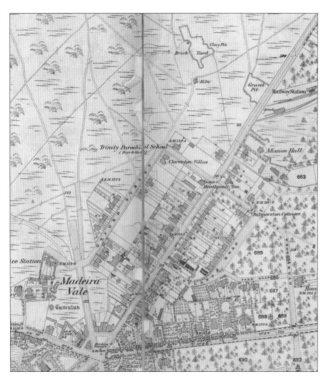

In 1869, the railway had arrived at the border of the Improvement Commissioners' area. The station had a single platform. Reproduced from (1870) Ordnance Survey map with the kind permission of the Ordnance Survey.

and pair of long platforms. However, they would stand bemused at the coaches that would whisk them away to their destination.

Bournemouth and railways have had an interesting relationship with each other. Initially the town seemed hostile, later welcoming and now probably indifferent. Down the years, Bournemouth has been served by three principal named trains. Each, in its own way, has typified the relationship the town has had with the railways. It also illustrates changes in society and general mobility within the population.

The Named Expresses

The *Bournemouth Belle*, formed of luxurious Pullman cars, brought the fashionable and well-heeled down from London and the Home Counties. There were well-sprung seats, all tables laid out for a three-course meal and porters on hand to carry the luggage. Bournemouth prided itself as a two-season resort, with those seeking warmer climes and clear air making the winter season of no inconsequential value. Leaving the capital around mid-morning it reached Bournemouth in a little over two hours. The return trip left late in the afternoon to facilitate an arrival in London after the evening rush hour. Because of these timings, it was not a train for Bournemouthians: very few residents would have travelled by it. Rather it was a train bringing visitors who were coming to stay in the town for a week or a season.

The *Pines Express* had an entirely different clientele. This train, originating in Manchester, with portions from Liverpool and Sheffield, brought in the summer holidaymakers from the industrial Midlands and North. Buckets and spades were to the fore. Pale ale and packed lunches might have been on the family's menu, though a restaurant car was provided. Again, this was a train bringing in visitors, rather than used by local residents themselves, and it came into Bournemouth West.

The third named train, the *Bournemouth Limited*, was the service that local residents would use. Leaving around 8.30am, it reached London non-stop in two hours. The return train left at 4.30pm, enabling a full day to be spent for work or leisure in London. Post-war, this train became known as *The Royal Wessex*, but with stops en route and so taking longer.

So there was a train for the affluent from London, a train for holidaymakers from the north, and a train for Bournemouth residents to visit London for the day. This was the basic pattern that existed for much of the 20th century. So how did Bournemouth's railway network develop?

Development of the Network

The first railway in the area, the Southampton and Dorchester, opened on 1st June 1847. It gave the area that was to become Bournemouth a wide berth simply because the district was so sparsely inhabited. It was deemed better for the line to take a circuitous route through the market towns of Ringwood and Wimborne, rather than over desolate heathland by the coast. There was a real possibility that a more coastal route would have been chosen at the time. How might Bournemouth have developed if that, rather than the more inland path, had been taken? In the event, the nearest station to Bournemouth was at Hamworthy, at the end of a branch line serving Poole and a doubtless bumpy carriage ride across the heath.

There the situation rested throughout the 1850s, with no railway development in the area. Bournemouth's population languished, even declining slightly. Come the 1860s, railway construction was on the agenda. 1st November 1860 saw the Dorset Central open its line from Wimborne to Blandford. This later became part of the Somerset & Dorset Joint Railway (S&DJR): a through line to Bath connecting with the Midland Railway to the north. Another route to the north, though of less importance, went to Salisbury, and opened on 20th December 1866. Between these two dates, the name 'Bournemouth' appears for the first time on the railway map in the title of the Ringwood, Christchurch and Bournemouth Railway. This line reached Christchurch on 13th November 1862, though there was no further progress for almost eight years.

The first passenger train steamed into Bournemouth station at 8.29am on Monday 14th March 1870. For the record, it arrived right on time. There was some interest from the local populace: flags were strung across Holdenhurst Road, a band was playing and the station was crowded. However, because of a lack of a positive opening date, no great ceremonies were held to mark the event. The local newspaper, the *Bournemouth Visitors' Directory*, prophetically noted that the station would not be adequate for the requirements of the town for very long. It also said that the line opened to the great satisfaction of the inhabitants generally. There were dissenting voices who did not want the iron monster in their neighbourhood, bringing in the hoi polloi.

In 1872, another railway, the Poole & Bournemouth, approached the town from the west. The first section from Broadstone to Poole opened on 2nd December, and was extended to Bournemouth West station on 15th June 1874, situated on Queen's Road. On the same day, the earlier one on Holdenhurst Road became known as Bournemouth East.

Both these termini belonged to the London & South Western Railway (L&SWR) which, during the 1880s, reinforced its hold on Bournemouth. There was some competition for the growing traffic from the town. The local townsfolk and Bournemouth Improvement Commissioners were unhappy at the town's treatment by the L&SWR. The Great Western Railway had eyes on Bournemouth, planning a line from the east as an extension of a line from Didcot and Winchester. The L&SWR stood to lose considerable trade. So, in 1883 they set out their plans for a line connecting the two town stations, together with a grand new central passenger terminus near Branksome Wood Road. Their route would have cut through Talbot Woods: the Commissioners wanted a line much further

An aerial photograph of Bournemouth Central Station in 1933. At top left is the Hampshire County Cricket ground at Dean Park. The area to the left of the station is almost entirely now offices, as well as the ASDA supermarket and the Bus Station.

north. In the end, a compromise was reached with a route taken mid-way between the two and the idea of a central terminus was scrapped.

The original East station, inadequate almost from the day it opened, was replaced by a fine new station on the west side of Holdenhurst Road on 20th July 1885. Now the main station in Bournemouth, it was renamed 'Bournemouth Central' on 1st May 1899. To avoid reversal of S&DJR trains, which the LSWR owned jointly with the Midland Railway, a cut-off was built avoiding Wimborne. This opened to passenger trains on 1st November 1886, enabling a freer flow of traffic from the north. Indeed, the late 1880s was one of great hopes and expansion, with the Bournemouth Direct Line from Brockenhurst through the New Forest via Sway, and the Bournemouth Junction Railway, connecting the town's two stations, opening on the same day, 6th March 1888. At last the town had a fast direct service to London, without the rather tortuous ride via Ringwood.

The final part of this jigsaw occurred on 1st June 1893, with the opening of the northern side of the Branksome triangle to passenger traffic (though the actual viaduct over the Bourne had been completed some five years earlier) and the Holes Bay Curve. Bournemouth now had direct links with Dorchester and Weymouth.

In addition to the main termini in Bournemouth, three other stations were built to serve the needs of the local populace. The first was Pokesdown, though it was originally named Boscombe. There had been much support for a station in this district, although it only opened down in a deep cutting on 1st July 1886. Boscombe received its own station in 1897, situated off the Ashley Road. The third place where one could board a train was Meyrick Park Halt, set on an embankment in the woods, and opened on 1st March 1906. One of the casualties of the First World War, it had only a short life of some eleven years.

Boscombe Station in about 1900.

Steam's Golden Years

The golden age of railways in Bournemouth matched that of the steam locomotive. The Pullman cars, the non-stop expresses, the holiday trains packed with excited tourists, the busyness of the whole system. Gleaming green express engines, fussy little tank engines and black freight locomotives.

The main engine shed was alongside Bournemouth Central station which was not the ideal location, being cramped and adjacent to residential streets. Plans were made to relocate it to Branksome, out of the borough altogether, but these came to nought. Life was hard on the footplate, but the enginemen had an affinity with the machines they drove. And what locomotives they were. In the 1920s *King Arthurs* ruled the main expresses. The larger *Lord Nelsons* appeared in the 1930s, whilst post-war it was the *West Country* and *Merchant Navy* classes that dominated. Local trains were usually in the hands of small M7 tank engines.

Passenger numbers were ever increasing, particularly when holidays with pay were introduced. They reached a peak in the 1950s. Few people owned a car so everyone came either by train or coach to the seaside, invariably on a Saturday if staying for a week or more. A procession of overnight trains brought visitors into the town from the northern industrial cities, dumping them at the West station in the very early hours to find a café before they could get past the stern landlady into their holiday accommodation.

Retrenchment and Closures

The closure of the Ringwood to Christchurch line on 30th September 1935 came as no real surprise. Its mainline aspirations had long gone with the opening of the Bournemouth Direct line in 1888 and its services were of a purely local nature. The cuts of the mid 1960s had a more lasting influence on the rail network around Bournemouth.

From 4th May 1964, the Brockenhurst to Hamworthy route via Wimborne, along with the West Moors to

Salisbury line, lost their passenger trains. Bournemouth West and Boscombe stations officially closed from 4th October 1965, though the West station had not seen any trains since the 5th September, the service having been replaced by buses. Finally the Somerset & Dorset shut from 7th March 1966. Freight services lingered on for a few more years, into the 1970s as far as Wimborne was concerned, but elsewhere the rusting rails were soon removed. Through Bournemouth, all that remained was the pattern of services concentrating on the mainline running via Christchurch and Poole which exists today.

Electrification and Beyond

The final steam trains ran on 9th July 1967, replaced by electrification on the Southern's well-established third rail principle. The steam shed was demolished, with tarmac providing an extension to the station car park. The centre lines through Bournemouth Central were removed and replaced by reversing sidings near to Beechey Road so that Class 33/1 diesel locomotives could haul electric units over the final leg of their journey to Poole and Weymouth. 4-REP and 4-TC units worked the mainline services to Waterloo, with 4-VEPs on the stopping trains. The 4-REPs gave an exhilarating ride, well able to achieve 100 mph, though the official limit was 90 mph.

On 16th May 1988 electrification was extended to Weymouth and stylish modern 5-WES units replaced the earlier electric units. These in turn were withdrawn from the route at the beginning of 2007 in favour of German-built Class 444 Desiro units, to the chagrin of many passengers who enjoyed the comfort of the 5-WES trains which were considered by many to have been Britain's best express electric units.

Freight traffic still rumbles through Bournemouth station: stone from Somerset to Hamworthy and sand from Wool to the London suburbs, but nothing calls at the long removed sidings. Plans to 'modernise' Bournemouth station, by demolition and replacement with an anonymous structure, were cancelled. In 2000, the glass roof was refurbished back to its Victorian splendour.

The future of the passenger traffic through Bournemouth seems secure. The station is alive from before dawn every weekday morning with commuters heading up to

William McArdle – the first man to fly at Bournemouth – 16th October 1910.

Southampton and London. The car park is well filled, whilst others arrive by bus. Trains, motor traffic and travellers are in perfect harmony. However, the petrol will not last forever. Doubtless a future generation of electric cars will bring customers to Bournemouth station in the next hundred years.

Of those who currently drive to Southampton, few will realise that as they ride at 70 mph along the A338 dual-carriageway, better known as the 'Spur Road', they are actually travelling along the route of the first railway to serve the town. 'Railways to roads' was the cry in the 1960s and 1970s. Perhaps the future will see this trend reversed, with past routes reopened. A prime candidate would be the route from Poole to Wimborne, together with the line down to Bournemouth West. A fleet of modern tramcars bringing in commuters to the centre of Bournemouth: who knows?

Bournemouth Air

At the beginning of the 20th century, Bournemouth made sure it kept up-to-date with the emerging aviation scene. Less than six months after Bleriot had crossed the English Channel, local businessmen William McArdle and Armstrong Drexel were building their own Bleriot style aircraft. They put on the town's first flying display at Talbot Village (now the site of Bournemouth University) during Whitsun 1910. Such was the novelty that townspeople travelled to Winton by tram and then walked the rest of the way. However in July 1910 the town hosted the Bournemouth International Aviation

Bournemouth Aviation meeting in 1910. Mayor Lipton Grahame-White taking part in the Centenary celebrations.

The programme for the International Aviation Meeting in 1910.

ABOVE Charles Rolls competing at the Bournemouth International Aviation Meeting in 1910.

BELOW The first seaplane on display at Bournemouth Pier in 1912.

For several years afterwards, demonstrations were given from flat green areas around Bournemouth. Even Father Christmas arrived by plane in 1912 before travelling in more traditional coach and horses through the streets to Beales.

The Bournemouth Aviation Company set up a flying school at Talbot Woods prior to the outbreak of the First World War, moving the short distance to Ensbury Park at the end of 1916. Pilots were trained for the Royal Flying Corps but, more surprisingly, 'Joy Flights' were offered to the public despite there being a war on! After the war there were attempts to establish airline services to Bournemouth, but they proved unsuccessful and so Ensbury Park was used for air races in the late 1920s. The site was unsatisfactory and Sir Alan Cobham visited Bournemouth in the spring of 1930 to offer his advice on

Meeting at Southbourne as part of the town's centenary celebrations. This was regarded as a prestigious event, with over twenty pilots from Britain and Europe attending. Again the townspeople travelled in their thousands to see the daring aviators, but the event was marred by the fatal crash of Charles Rolls, the co-founder of Rolls-Royce. Bournemouth was on the aviation map.

a suitable location for a municipal airport. Nothing further happened at the time and it was down to neighbouring Christchurch to put Bournemouth on the airline network. A small airfield at Christchurch was expanded in the spring of 1935 and airline services began to Cardiff, Croydon, Plymouth and Portsmouth. However the operators of the airfield declared themselves as 'Bournemouth Airport'. This did not go down well with the people of either Bournemouth or Christchurch. In the summer of 1935 Bournemouth and Poole Councils joined forces to buy land in Magna Road, Canford for the development of an airport, but gave up in 1938 due to escalating construction costs. Sir Alan Cobham was also well known for his Flying Circus which visited Bournemouth on a number of occasions between 1932 and 1935. As well as stunt flying and parachuting, the Circus enabled many people to have a flight around the town (5 shillings for a four minute flight, 10 shillings for a normal flight and £1 for aerobatics).

The outbreak of the Second World War saw the construction of an aircraft factory at Christchurch airfield. Operated by Airspeed, it went on to produce Oxford trainers, *Horsa* gliders and *Mosquito* fighter-bombers for the RAF. The airfield was also used by a trials unit involved in the early development of aircraft radar. The national airline, BOAC, moved its flying boat base to Poole Harbour in 1939, trying to maintain air links with the Empire. Their services were for government officials and military VIP's. RAF Hurn opened in August 1941 on land at East Parley which Sir Alan Cobham had recommended as an airport site in 1930. Hurn's main involvement in the war effort was the training of *Horsa* assault glider pilots and paratroops during 1943. It was then the home of a number of fighter-bomber squadrons for D-Day operations. There were six *Typhoon* squadrons and two *Mosquito* squadrons — a total of 150 aircraft. After D-Day the Americans used Hurn for a few weeks.

BOAC Lancastrian passenger aircraft in 1945.

In November 1944, Hurn took on a new role as Britain's Civil Air Terminal with services operated by BOAC to Africa, the Far East and, from May 1945, Australia. At the time there was no London Heathrow and so the world's major airlines all flew into Hurn. Services from the United States by American Airlines and Pan American started in October 1945. American Export became the world's first airline to offer regularly scheduled landplane (as opposed to seaplane) commercial flights across the North Atlantic. Using the reliable Douglas DC-4 aircraft, it began passenger services from New York to Hurn Airport (with stops at Gander, Newfoundland, and Shannon, Ireland) in October 1945. Each one-way flight lasted about 14 hours. Pan American also used the DC-4 for its own flights a few days later. Eventually, the company began using the new Lockheed *Constellation* and *Super Constellation* aircraft.

After the war, the Airspeed factory at Christchurch (it became part of De Havilland Aircraft in 1952) continued with the production of the *Ambassador* airliner and then a range of *Vampire, Venom* and *Sea Vixen* fighters for the

RAF and RN. Many of these aircraft were for the export market and work continued until closure of the factory in June 1962. When BOAC moved to London Heathrow, their hangars at Hurn were taken over by Vickers-Armstrongs for aircraft production. From 1951 they produced *Varsity* trainers for the RAF, followed from the end of 1953 by the very successful *Viscount* turbo-prop airliner. Initially selling to airlines within Europe, it soon broke into the lucrative North American market. The *Viscount* was also built by Vickers at their Weybridge site, but the majority of the 444 produced were built at Hurn. It was replaced by the BAC One-Eleven airliner which was built from 1963 until 1984: another export success. Large numbers of local people were employed at both Christchurch and Hurn, carried to work by a convoy of Hants & Dorset or Corporation buses. Bournemouth and Christchurch both played an important part in Britain's aircraft industry; a point that is often unknown or else ignored.

Air services from Bournemouth grew gradually from the 1950s, its title officially changing from Hurn Airport to

Seeing the Bournemouth Symphony Orchestra off on a Continental tour at Bournemouth Airport in 1965.

Bournemouth (Hurn) Airport in the spring of 1953. Jersey Airlines operated to the Channel Islands and Manchester and Cambrian to Paris and Cardiff. Silver City flew car ferry services to Cherbourg and the Channel Islands and Dan-Air flew to the Channel Islands and northwards to Aberdeen. Local travel firm Palmair have operated holiday flight to Majorca and the Mediterranean since 1958. Recently it has frequently been voted one of the top airlines by *Holiday Which* magazine, despite only having one Boeing! Originally in the hands of the Ministry of Aviation, the airport was purchased by Bournemouth and Dorset Councils for £750,000 in April 1969.

The first Air Pageant was held at Bournemouth Airport in the summer of 1977. These proved very popular with the public, but ended in 1991 due to air services at the airport expanding. The RAF Red Arrows have been visitors to Bournemouth seafront during most summers since 1971. Again their displays have brought large numbers of visitors to the town. This resulted in Bournemouth staging its first annual seafront Air Festival in 2008, harking back to the times of Cobham's Flying Circus and a prelude to major events in 2010.

Bournemouth Airport is currently owned by the Manchester Airports Group. Recent years have seen the

Palmair Boeing 737 at Bournemouth International Airport.

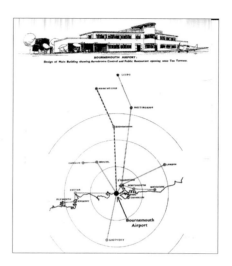

Bournemouth Airport map stressing the central importance of the airport.

development of low cost airlines operating services within Europe. Ryanair included Bournemouth in their network from the spring of 1996, later being joined by Thomsonfly. Expansion into longer distance services had always been hampered by runway length, so this was extended in 1996 to cater for the majority of airliners in service at the time. It enabled *Concorde* to visit the airport on a number of occasions, including supersonic flights around the Bay of Biscay and a joint *QE2/Concorde* holiday to/from New York. Passenger numbers reached one million during 2008 and a much needed new terminal was built during 2009 to cater for the increasing passenger numbers. A major employer at the airport is Cobham Aviation Services – so maintaining a family name link from the 1930s.

Having been involved in Bournemouth's first centenary celebrations, aviation continues to play a major role on the occasion of the town's bicentenary.

EIGHT

'A MEDITERRANEAN LOUNGING PLACE'
or 'ENGLAND'S MIAMI'

Vincent May and Keith Wilkes

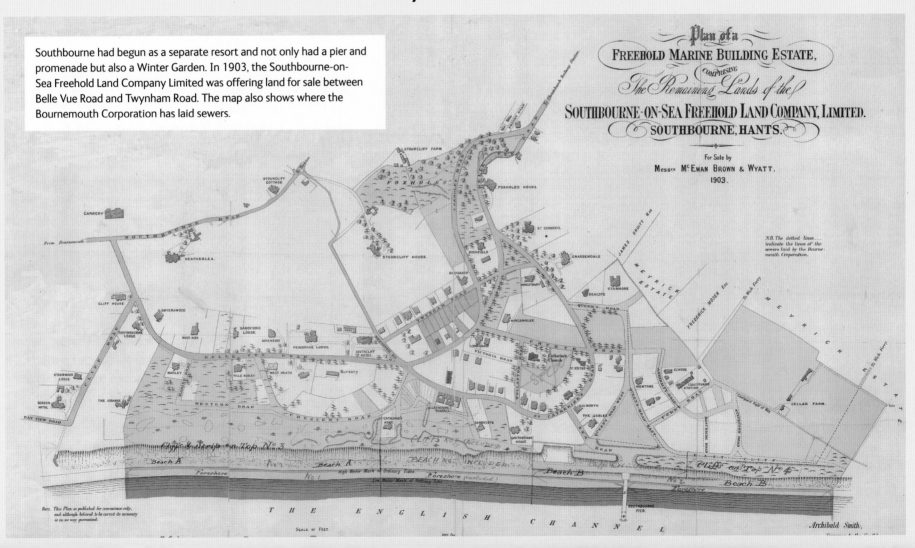

Southbourne had begun as a separate resort and not only had a pier and promenade but also a Winter Garden. In 1903, the Southbourne-on-Sea Freehold Land Company Limited was offering land for sale between Belle Vue Road and Twynham Road. The map also shows where the Bournemouth Corporation has laid sewers.

Chapter Eight

TOURISM CONTRIBUTES £670 million to the Bournemouth economy today. It attracts every social and economic group and like a small number of large resorts has a very important conference market. Throughout its history, the town has adapted to changing fashions whilst attempting to become and then remain the premier resort in Britain.

Tourism in large numbers owes its origins in Britain very largely to the development of the railway network and the provision of organised holidays for workers in the country's growing industrial cities. The image of Bournemouth was initially as a place for winter visits and for its healthy climate. You came to Bournemouth if you were escaping cold northern winters and/or were ill. For some visitors to the town, the overpowering image was that it was dominated by invalids. As late as 1912, D. H. Lawrence wrote to Jessie Chambers advising her 'never to come here for a holiday. The place exists for the sick. They hide the fact as far as possible, but it's like a huge hospital. At every turn you come across invalids being pushed or pulled along. Quite a nice place of course, everything arranged for the comfort of the invalid, sunny sheltered corners and the like, but pah – I shall be glad to get away.'

The way in which the resort was publicised in its early days and the later marketing of the town reflect in many respects the fashions of the time, but it is also fair to say that because Bournemouth had little history at the time it was able to establish itself as different and argue that it was better than anywhere else. Not everyone agreed with that view. For example, Matthew Arnold wrote to his youngest sister in 1849 that 'Bournemouth on the Sea is a very stupid place; a great moorland covered with furze and low pine woods comes down to the sea-shore, and breaks down towards it in a long sweep of cliff, half sand, half mud,' and Arnold Bennett wrote in his Journal for 29th December 1909, 'I decided absolutely against Bournemouth. It was symbolic that I couldn't even get China tea there'.

In its earliest days, the town attracted small numbers of visitors, initially as an exclusive sea-bathing resort, then for the importance of its climate for health. Once the railways arrived, the market expanded rapidly with links to the northwest via the Somerset and Dorset Joint Railway. Hotels were built mainly close to the cliffs and many houses became bed and breakfast establishments.

Tourism in Bournemouth falls into several distinct phases, according to Roberts.[1] From its beginnings to the 1870s, it was known not only as a select location to visit, but more importantly it was a health resort for upper-class invalids and their families, especially during winter. They came to Bournemouth not to take the waters but to breathe its clear winter air. After the Improvement Commissioners were set up, they worked very hard to ensure that people would come to an attractive and healthy town. The beautiful landscape and ambience of walks, wooded valleys and its beaches and an image of healthiness with clean air, sewage-free streets and beaches were the key to its image. That did not mean all and sundry would be welcome or that everyone would like the convalescent character of the town. It did mean that its entertainment facilities provided visitors with a range and quality which befitted a resort which would be able to rival not merely the English resorts but also those of the Continent, especially the Riviera. Thomas Hardy described the town as 'A Mediterranean lounging place on the English Channel'.

Brookside and bridge near Pier Approach in 1865.

The enduring attraction – calm blue sea, clean sandy beaches, wide promenades, cliff-top walks, beach huts and the pier.

ABOVE Boscombe Spa Hotel in 1878. It opened in 1874 and offered suites of apartments, a Coffee room with commanding views of the Channel, the Isle of Wight and the Dorsetshire coast and a Smoking Room. It also provided 'Good Saddle Horses and Carriages with Careful Drivers'. A bus met all trains. It closed in 1880 and became a boarding school for boys, called Bournemouth College. This closed in 1885 and became the Boscombe Chine Hotel.

BELOW Lansdowne Crescent c.1870.

ABOVE The Bath Hotel in 1862.

ABOVE LEFT The South Western Hotel, the nearest hotel to the Central Station, in Holdenhurst Road: 1920s.

BELOW Lansdowne House at the corner of Lansdowne Road and Madiera Road.

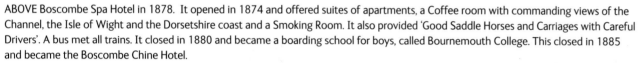

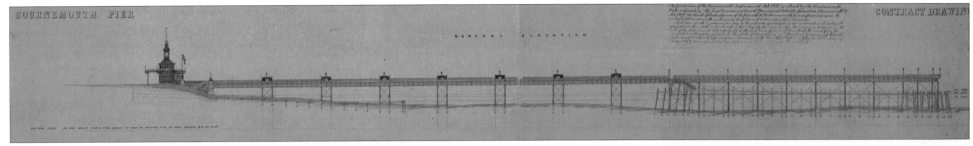

The Market Expands

Once the railway arrived in 1870, the second phase began with middle-class summer visitors. This not only encouraged the expansion of hotels and boarding houses, as well as extending the seasons when the town was busy, but increased the needs for a wider range of leisure activities for the visitors. The third phase, according to Roberts, was from the 1890s to 1914. 'Bournemouth £1 1s from London; 110 miles; three hours; is also well known as a winter station. Winter mean temperature 41 degrees F. It has good villas built in the midst of pine trees. The sea-bathing is good. Beautiful pleasure gardens in the valley along the course of the Bourne. Sanitation excellent.'[2]

Excursionists and middle-class tourists arrived in larger numbers, but the town was also becoming more attractive as a retirement place. This gave impetus to additional house building, but also increased the markets for both the leisure facilities and shops.

Throughout these Victorian and Edwardian periods, the town invested both time and funds in developing the facilities, the pier, the walks, and the promenades along the foot of the cliffs. Although the first design for a pier was drafted in 1849, a short wooden jetty was only completed in 1856. George Rennie, a renowned engineer, designed a longer pier also of wood. Opened on 17th September 1861, its wooden piles were attacked by Teredo worm and

ABOVE The original drawing of the Pier dated 1878.

RIGHT The Pier toll house buildings: detailed design 1878.

BELOW RIGHT A detailed drawing of the Bournemouth Municipal Bathing Huts, 1910.

replaced in 1866 by cast iron piles. Just over a year later, the T-shaped landing stage was swept away in a gale. The pier was repaired and remained in use until November 1876 when it collapsed during another severe storm. It was now too short for the pleasure steamers, so it was demolished. A new pier designed by Eugenius Birch was completed in 1880 at a cost of £2,600 and opened by the Lord Mayor of London on 11th August 1880. Initially 838 ft in length, it was extended in 1894 and 1909 to over 1000 ft.

Former chairman of the Bournemouth Commissioners, Capt James Hartley, said that the Undercliff promenade was 'about all that was necessary to place Bournemouth in the very front rank of English health resorts, and enable us to compete with the attractions of the Riviera and other places abroad'. Like many of the projects intended to add to Bournemouth's prestige, there was considerable local debate for and against the proposal.

The Commissioners also worked hard to ensure that the quality of the bathing waters and the general environmental quality of the resort was the highest possible. Much effort went into building a promenade

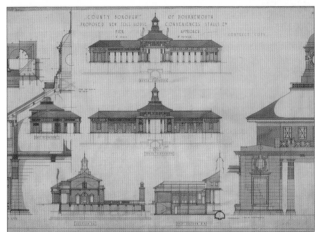

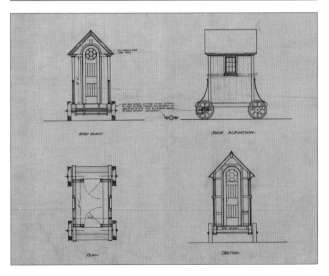

Working on the Undercliff Drive in 1907.

along the seafront, a pier, and sewers. Clean air was essential: as Walton commented, 'For Bournemouth, the tourism product was not simply the hotels and leisure facilities but the environment characterised by pine woods, winding gardens and babbling streams, parks and clean safe bathing.'[3] The Medical Officer of Health, A.D. Edwards, was able to write in 1914 that '... the town has attained a standard of health and a comparative freedom from [infectious] diseases which give it a remarkable place among the large towns of the kingdom. Nature has been lavish in her gifts' and 'The makers of modern Bournemouth have been careful of these gifts, for they have built a city with fair broad roads, tree-lined.'[4]

Indeed they had done more because the promenade had been extended, cliff railways constructed (in 1908) and the pier rebuilt and extended. The fact that visitors could leave their hotel and walk through attractive and sheltered gardens, or walk along the cliff-top with its exceptional views to the Isle of Wight and the Purebck coast, then

stroll along the sea front, owed a great deal to the gradual extension of the Promenade. The piers, at Bournemouth, Boscombe and for a short time at Southbourne, provided an opportunity to view the town from seawards. Although the history of the piers is well documented and Andrew Emery's *History of Bournemouth Seafront* describes in detail the way the seafront came to be one of the town's most valued features, the role of the promenades in both threatening and safeguarding its qualities is, like the sewers, often overlooked. The early Bournemouth had beaches, both sandy and gravelly, which depended on the steady erosion of the cliffs by gullies and by waves. Once the promenades began to be built, this regular supply of beaches was gradually cut off. Promenades with their well built seawalls allowed the cliffs to become stabilised and

vegetated, and this meant that the cliff paths, such as the Zig-Zag, could be permanent. However, the beaches began to diminish and in places the cliffs cut back into the cliff top removing, especially at Southbourne, roads and properties. One of the town's most important tourism products began to disappear. Fortunately, many of the hotels had been built well back from the cliffs with wide areas for the Overcliff Drives and open spaces which still characterise the cliffs.

Seawalls were in place at Alum Chine, and from Bournemouth to Boscombe by the end of 1911. Some gaps were filled between the World Wars, but the seawall only extended eastwards to Southbourne in the 1950s, mainly funded through the Coast Protection Act

RIGHT Mayor Alderman Charles Hunt opening the Undercliff Drive on 29th June 1911.

BELOW The Undercliff Drive in 1912.

1949. At Southbourne, there were extended discussions between Bournemouth Council and the Southbourne Cliffs Association (SCA). Nine properties on Southbourne Overcliff Drive were in danger of collapsing over the cliffs, but the SCA members argued vehemently against having to pay coast protection charges. By February 1954 the cost of various Works Schemes exceeded £1.5 million. As late as 1972, cliff face erosion was still occurring and the council decided to grade and drain the cliffs with further losses of cliff top land. Of the nine houses at risk in 1949, six disappeared and three remain close to the edge of the cliff.

Bournemouth's beach and seafront form an artificial landscape. A regularly replenished beach[5] lies between wooden and rock groynes and is backed by a stone or concrete sea wall. The promenade above this used by walkers, cyclists and vehicles for access. There is then a wide variety of structures housing toilets, cafes, beach managers' offices and first aid, separated by beach huts. The cliffs behind these structures are drained, graded and planted (sometimes with non-native species). This is all regarded by the town as a product and yet the beach itself continues to respond to the waves as all beaches do. The beach behaves naturally, is regarded as natural and yet is not.[6] Between 1970 and 2006, over 6 million cubic metres of sand and shingle was added to the beach. Without the promenade and the beach, Bournemouth would quickly lose probably its most important asset as a resort.

Holidays with Pay

The First World War meant that although visitors continued to come to the town, more attention was given to coping with the growing numbers of convalescing soldiers as well as the wider impact of the human losses in Flanders. With the war over, the town resumed its growth and despite the Depression, tourists continued to come to the town. The war had interrupted normal life for many families, but holidays continued to grow especially during the 1920s and 1930s. Although most professional and white-collar workers had paid holidays, many workers had no such entitlement. Nevertheless between 1925 and 1937, the proportion of workers who had some sort of paid holiday rose from 17 per cent to 47 per cent in 1937.[7] The Holidays with Pay Act 1938 increased that to 60 per cent. By the time war broke out again in 1939, family holidays longer than a week were well established as part of many families' annual calendar.[8]

One distinctive feature of the period was the way in which advertising used images of the coast. Typical posters depicted women as 'bathing belles - a

RIGHT Southbourne-on-Sea, poster describing the attractions in 1880.

BELOW Southbourne pier collapsed.

ABOVE The beach at Southbourne: a place to enjoy the "natural" but artificial beach.

LEFT Southbourne in the 1970s and (BELOW) the same area today, with Hengistbury Head in the far distance.

young woman clad in revealing swimwear, disporting herself upon the beach and among the waves.'[9] Many resorts, however, wanted to do more than simply appeal to potential visitors who sought merely sun, sand and fun. To establish a more genteel image, they used the seaside as a background for a woman, usually not in swimwear, whose social and recreational activities were not necessarily centred on the sea itself. For example, a Great Western Railway poster entitled 'Bournemouth for health and pleasure', published about 1937, shows an elegant and fashionably dressed woman looking over an equally elegant and restrained Bournemouth, an image of refined leisure. In both examples, the woman forms part of the landscape, but in the first case she symbolises the natural elements of sun and sea. In contrast, her poise and the ways she is depicted gazing across the almost entirely artificial environment of Bournemouth emphasizes that here the natural elements have been channelled entirely to serve the visitor.

Tourists were also always encouraged to take excursions

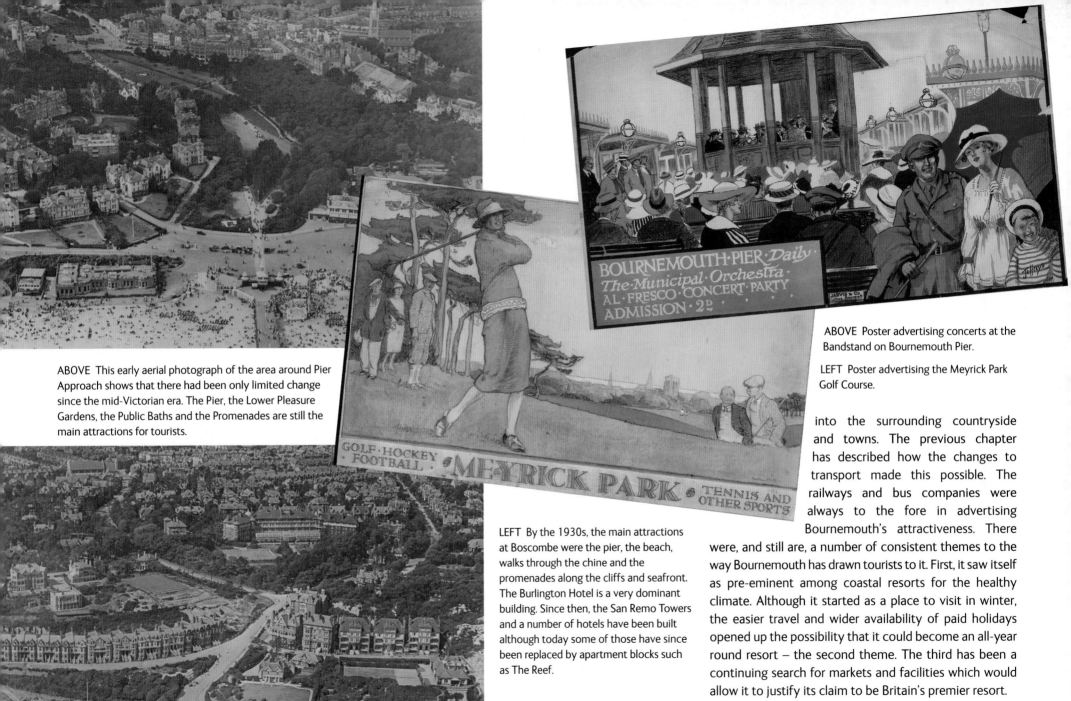

ABOVE This early aerial photograph of the area around Pier Approach shows that there had been only limited change since the mid-Victorian era. The Pier, the Lower Pleasure Gardens, the Public Baths and the Promenades are still the main attractions for tourists.

ABOVE Poster advertising concerts at the Bandstand on Bournemouth Pier.

LEFT Poster advertising the Meyrick Park Golf Course.

LEFT By the 1930s, the main attractions at Boscombe were the pier, the beach, walks through the chine and the promenades along the cliffs and seafront. The Burlington Hotel is a very dominant building. Since then, the San Remo Towers and a number of hotels have been built although today some of those have since been replaced by apartment blocks such as The Reef.

into the surrounding countryside and towns. The previous chapter has described how the changes to transport made this possible. The railways and bus companies were always to the fore in advertising Bournemouth's attractiveness. There were, and still are, a number of consistent themes to the way Bournemouth has drawn tourists to it. First, it saw itself as pre-eminent among coastal resorts for the healthy climate. Although it started as a place to visit in winter, the easier travel and wider availability of paid holidays opened up the possibility that it could become an all-year round resort – the second theme. The third has been a continuing search for markets and facilities which would allow it to justify its claim to be Britain's premier resort.

Three early 20th century posters advertising the town's pleasures.

Wartime Tourism

Up to the beginning of the Second World War in 1939, hotels, promenades and cliff lifts continued to be built and the range of attractions expanded. Despite the impact of the war, with the chines mined and the beach fronted by anti-invasion scaffolding, Bournemouth continued to fulfil a role as a place of relaxation. Despite the wartime restrictions, Bournemouth remained in the early war years much as it always had been. As J.B.Priestley put it in 1941 'Nobody could call it a bad war in Bournemouth. Its front line aspect is negligible. The shops still look opulent, and thousands of well-dressed women seemed to be flitting in and out of them: in short, a good time can be had by all.'[10] As the war progressed, and D-Day approached, conditions changed.

In particular, as in the First World War, the town played an important role as a convalescent place for wounded personnel. At the same time, for many families who had run bed and breakfast accommodation, as well as other households, incomes were replaced by payments for

billeting both military and government personnel serving or re-located to the town. Providing accommodation was not tourism in the normal sense, but it did ensure that many small establishments were able to continue to function throughout the war. Payments were not generous. For example, for six airmen based at RAF Station Bournemouth the total payment was £6 17 shillings 8 pence. The first airman's lodging payment was 10 pence: additional airmen were worth 8 pence. Breakfast was 9 pence, dinner one shilling, tea 3 pence and supper 5 pence.

Bournemouth was also a very important location for rest and recreation of the American Forces. *Furlough in Bournemouth*, published by the American Red Cross (ARC), sets out the facilities which the town offered. The town is described as 'unique in that it combines the sophistication of a city with the gaiety of a beach town and the quiet charm of country club life'. 'Exclusive civilian hotels' had become 'luxuriously furnished Red Cross Clubs high on the cliffs above the ever-fascinating waters of the Channel'. The Marsham Court and Carlton hotels were for Enlisted

ABOVE Mayflower Coaches of Hambledon Road, one of many companies providing excursions in the 1920s.

RIGHT The Miramar Hotel was the place for female personnel from the American forces in 1944. Courtesy of American Red Cross.

Men, the Ambassador was for Officers and the Miramar provided breakfast in bed, a complete beauty salon and single rooms for nurses, Womens' Army Corps (WACs) and ARC girls. Sightseeing included Lulworth Cove, Corfe Castle – described as 'once the most impregnable fortress in all England' – and the Isle of Wight. One photograph of the breached pier and beaches is captioned 'Miami Beach? Atlantic City? Santa Monica? No . . .! Bournemouth.' Similarly the *Combat Journal* of the 311th Timberwolf Regiment of the 78th Lightning Division of the American infantry describes Bournemouth as England's peacetime Miami, where they could find 'pubs, theaters (sic) or the Pavillon (sic) dance hall . . . a very popular and elaborate rendezvous.'[11] There is an interesting contrast between the ARC description combining sophistication, gaiety,

charm and country life and the suggestion that it might be another Miami, Atlantic City or Santa Monica. Bournemouth's Founding Fathers would certainly have agreed with the former, but hardly with the second.

The Square and Lower Gardens – throughout the year, sheltered sunny places to stroll, sit and shop – just as the Victorian founders expected.

Post-War Tourism

Once the war was over, the town could begin to return to its more normal pattern of summer visitors. Summer visitors came regularly from the northern industrial towns by rail and for some time the town's image and marketing did not change. Changes were happening nevertheless, and overseas holidays began to become more common, even if it was only taking the family camping in France or further afield. As the ferries and then the airlines developed and package holidays became cheaper, the attractions of the Mediterranean resorts, much more akin to Miami than Bournemouth ever was, captured more and more of the British tourist market. In the 1960s, small guesthouses and bed and breakfast establishments supported their income through the winter months by taking in students attending in gradually larger numbers the degree and diploma courses at the Municipal College. The language schools also needed accommodation for their students. Many of the hotels closed at the end of September, and apart from opening briefly for Christmas and New Year, remained closed until Easter.

Bournemouth had begun to falter as a resort. It needed to change what it offered. The biggest and, it turns out, most successful response was the establishment of the Bournemouth International Centre (the BIC) in 1984: an investment of £17million. Further investment in the BIC took place in 1990 when the Purbeck Hall was opened at a cost of £9 million, and in 2005 when the much larger Windsor Hall and the Solent Hall opened at a cost of £22 million. By 2009, the BIC and the Pavilion together added about £115 million directly and indirectly to local economy. Peter Gunn, their Managing Director was reported in 2009 as saying 'Were it not for those insightful civic leaders more than three decades ago, we may never have had such an internationally renowned venue,'[12] a view supported by the results of a guest poll which reported that hotels in Bournemouth were ranked higher than destinations like Paris, Milan and Barcelona.[13] Large enough to accommodate some of the country's largest and most publicised conferences, including the annual party political conferences, the BIC provides a strong attraction all year round. Conference/exhibition tourism is worth in the region of £71.7 million and helps to sustain tourism generally throughout the year.

In earlier phases of the resort's development, there had been first the strength of the winter health market, and then the transition to the summer holiday. The BIC provided a stimulus to the town becoming an all-year resort. Although the lowest occupancy rates in the late 2000s were during the winter months of January and February, the previous tendency for some establishments to close down or reduce staff began to alter. Some smaller hotels did close to become residential or care homes, or were replaced by blocks of flats, sometimes providing a second home for those working in other parts of the country.

Tourism in the 21st Century

By the end of its first 200 years, Bournemouth still has many of the same characteristics which marked it through much of its tourism history. London, the South East, the South West and the East and West Midlands generated 77% of all visitors in 2008. The majority of holidays were additional (32%) to people's main holiday (21%) and 28% of all holidays were short-breaks. The distance travelled by all visitors to Bournemouth has declined from 259

Bournemouth's brighly-coloured 1930s beach huts on West Beach are amongst its attractions.

miles in 2006 to 169 in 2008, indicative of the increasing importance of the additional holiday/short-break market. Why do people come to Bournemouth? 'Seaside, beaches, coast' 93%, were the main attraction/motivator in 2009, followed by 'visited before' (75%), 'countryside/natural history' (66%), 'easy to get to' (58%).[14]

The official website at the end of August 2009 said 'With seven miles of golden sands and sparkling sea, the vibrant cosmopolitan town of Bournemouth has it all – a vast variety of shops, restaurants and holiday accommodation, buzzing nightlife and endless countryside with beautiful award-winning gardens and water sports galore.'[15]

It went on to say 'Enjoy the sophistication, where the Continent blends effortlessly with contemporary, traditional and everything British'. It recommended six things which any visitor should do: '1. Visit the Russell-Cotes Art Gallery & Museum. 2. Do the Pier -to -Pier walk. 3. Whatever the season, enjoy an expert-guided walk through Bournemouth's many parks and gardens. 4. Enjoy high tea: the ultimate British tradition! 5. Hire a beach hut, another great British tradition and 6. Get in the water!'[16] All very much what visitors have been doing for the previous

200 years as the resort developed.

August 2009 saw the official announcement that the final stages were occurring of construction of Europe's first artificial surf reef, near Boscombe Pier, a project expected to put the resort firmly on the UK surf map. Part of the £11 million Boscombe Spa Regeneration Project to revitalise the area of Boscombe around its chines, it was funded through the sale of a seafront car park to Barratt Homes for development of 169 apartments at Honeycombe Chine. This part of Bournemouth had increasingly lacked modern facilities and there had been a number of proposals to regenerate the area.

The decision to construct a surf reef also provided a stimulus for reconstruction of the 1950s Overstrand. This included new changing rooms, toilets and warm showers, the Sorted Surf Shop providing surf lessons, surfboard and kayak hire, the Urban Reef Restaurant, overlooking the reef, and 'beach pods', the modern equivalent of beach huts, to buy 'a little bit of luxury' on what the Borough was now

ABOVE The new accommodation above the traditional accommodation on Undercliffe Road overlooking Boscombe Pier.

LEFT Development of Honeycombe Chine, Boscombe November 2009.

describing as the most innovative seafront in the UK.[17]

The reef at Boscombe was designed to provide what surfers describe as a Grade Five wave on a day with good swell. In contrast, the world-renowned Hawaii Pipeline is a Grade Eight. In calm weather, it would provide safe, flat conditions for families and beach users. According to Bournemouth Tourism the main market would be the short, mid-week break. The reef was expected to attract an extra 200,000 people every year and add £3m (0.12%) to annual tourism income. Concerns had been expressed, as

had happened with most earlier projects dating back to the first promenade, about changing the town's clientele, even driving some of its traditional market away and the effects upon its environment. Despite the doubts, the surf reef was finally opened on 2nd November 2009.

Bournemouth has been adept at adjusting to changing markets, although it was sometimes slow to do so. By 2009, the resort had grown into a major seaside resort, still relying on its traditional offer of sea, beaches, cliffs and gardens. However, it had diversified by adding the

conference market, attracting more visitors all year round and stimulating major events such as an International Air Festival which in 2009 attracted about 1.34 million visitors over four days. Completing the surf reef would further diversify the market and continue to strengthen the town's claim to be Britain's Premier Resort. Dr Granville in 1841 saw the town becoming that, but he could not have imagined the way in which the town now makes the claim.

NINE

BOURNEMOUTH GOES TO WAR

John Cresswell

During the 1930s, German visitors and the Luftwaffe had gradually surveyed most towns along the south coast of England. The Stadtplan von Bournemouth shows every bridge, the proposed parachute dropping area at the present-day Townsend and facilities which would need to be secured as soon as possible after the invasion began.

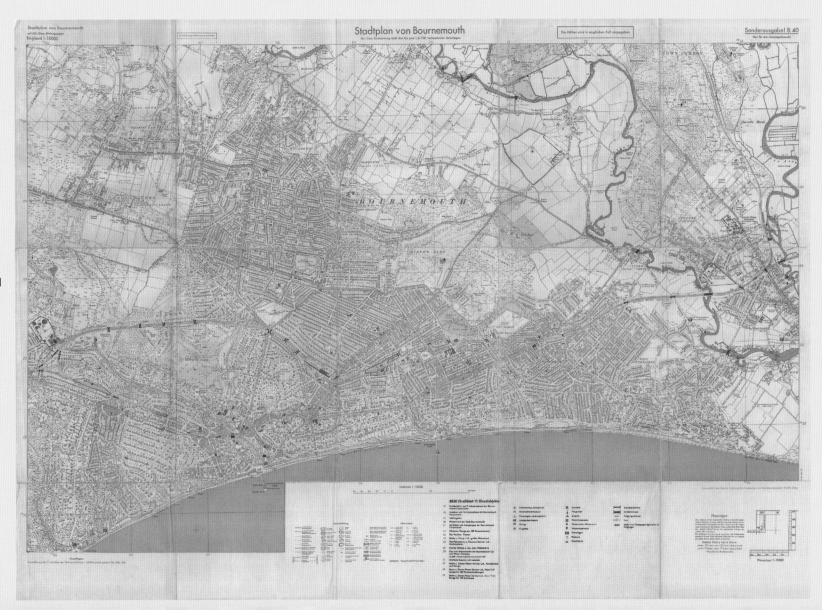

Chapter Nine

IF 'YATTINGAFORD' could be positively identified as Iford, then the battle there in AD 901 between the Saxons Edward the Elder and Ethelwald marks the earliest known recourse to arms in Bournemouth.

Prior to this date, Hengistbury Head had protective defences thrown up during the Iron Age, and there are other bank-and-ditch enclosures scattered across the present borough, yet this border between the Durotriges and the Atrebates remains mute on any conflict between those Celtic tribes. The Romans and Normans both bypassed the wastes of the Bournemouth area and concentrated on the harbours of Poole and Christchurch. The names of Hengist and Horsa, as well as Viking names, have been applied to various roads in east Southbourne, yet these Jutish warriors and the other Norsemen almost certainly made no raids on this coast. For most of history the undeveloped Bournemouth area was a place of peace.

However, the wide sandy shore of Poole Bay invited good beachheads for invaders. In 1574 the Earl of Southampton regarded it as 'a place very easy for the ennemye to lande there conteyning by estimacion oon quarter of a myle in length, being voyde of all inhabiting'. A map of the following year shows a beacon at Bournemouth (presumably on Hengistbury Head), perhaps lit when the Armada moved up the Channel in 1588.

A portrait of Volunteer Frederick Dacombe in his uniform in 1863. Mr. Dacombe was the first Bournemouth Inspector of Weights and Measures to be appointed. Apart from being a portrait of a town official, the photograph gives a good idea of the appearance of a Volunteer in uniform in the earliest days of the Movement.

Volunteer Forces

The Volunteer Act of 1794 encouraged the establishment of 'Corps and Companies of Men as shall voluntarily enrol themselves for the defence of their Counties, Towns, Coasts, or for the general Defence of the Kingdom' as a response to threats of invasion from France. On the coast, these volunteer corps not only had a role as defenders of the realm but also acted in support of the Revenue. Lewis Tregonwell, a captain of the Dorset Volunteer Rangers, patrolled the coastal areas of eastern Dorset and western Hampshire.

With the Peace of Amiens in 1802, many of the Volunteers were stood down. However, the peace was short-lived. By 1803, the 20th Light Dragoons based at Christchurch Barracks were guarding the Bournemouth coast and ships patrolled the Solent. Some 400 Volunteers also stood ready and for their night vigils were presented with greatcoats by Sir George Tapps and Thomas Wilson of Stourfield. French preparations for a cross-Channel invasion were finally thwarted when the Battle of Trafalgar gave Great Britain dominion over the seas, with Waterloo being the *coup de grâce* in 1815.

Fears brewed again when Louis Napoleon, nephew of the former Emperor, returned and assumed the title of Napoleon III after a *coup d'état* in 1852. At this time, Britain viewed both France and Russia with equal alarm. The crisis in Turkey tipped the balance, and Britain allied with France against Russia. This short war of 1853-56 is generally named after the Crimea, but there were other successful actions in the Baltic. The unsung hero of these northern campaigns, Captain (later Rear-Admiral Sir) Bartholomew Sullivan, who had earlier served as 2nd Lieutenant on Darwin's voyage on HMS *Beagle*, came to live in Bournemouth in 1865.

One of the first Bournemouth Artillery Volunteers, Bombardier Ridout, was in later years Sergeant-Major. He was described as a good, thorough, humble citizen of the town. This is what a volunteer artilleryman looked like on the formation of his Battery in the year 1868.

As the threat of war with the 'Old Enemy' France grew, General Peel, Secretary of State for War, issued a letter on 12th May 1859 to the Lords Lieutenant of the Counties requesting the raising of local Volunteer Forces: originally the brainchild of Admiral Sullivan, as far back as 1851. A year later, 35 men took the oath of allegiance at the Belle Vue Assembly Rooms on 4th September to become the 19th Hampshire (Bournemouth) Rifle Corps. Charles King was commanding officer initially, but was later succeeded by Christopher Crabbe Creeke, a post he held for 20 years. They threw themselves into their role, buying their own uniforms and rifles and paying their own expenses. Shooting practice was a favourite pastime as well as a requirement. The Volunteers had several ranges across the borough. They took part in many ceremonies and displays, and for such occasions it was felt they should have a band, so various ladies collected funds for this. The musicians were still fighting men. One of their first parades was at the opening of Bournemouth Pier. The Bournemouth Volunteers held many a mock battle with their Poole counterparts in what is now the Lower Pleasure Gardens. The 19th joined other independent units in 1864 to make up the 4th Administrative Battalion of the Hampshire Volunteer Corps.

Although Lord Malmesbury proposed an Artillery Corps from the start, it was not until November 1866 that enrolment began. Sixty volunteers made up the 4th Corps Hampshire Artillery Volunteers, with J. Haggard in command. Again it was mainly funded from the men's pockets. The uniforms cost £3 10s for men, and £20 for officers. The four big guns, which were smooth bore muzzle-loaders firing 24 lb shot, did not arrive until 1867. Two were taken to the headquarters in Old Christchurch Road, and the other two to the Southbourne cliffs, aimed at moored targets out at sea.

Hostility towards the French ameliorated with the

Private John Watts of the 19th Hants Rifles Corps was a small man who stood only 5 feet tall and whose intelligence was of poor quality. He was described at the time as the laughing stock of the place and the wonder is how he became enrolled. Very keen to serve, he was with difficulty discharged from the Corps. He is holding an Enfield muzzle-loading rifle, the arm of the period. The cup on the floor had been presented to him.

MILITARY TOURNAMENT IN MEYRICK PARK.
"Tent Pegging in Sections."   Bordon R.F.A. secure 3 pegs.

MILITARY TOURNAMENT IN MEYRICK PARK.
Throwing horses and shooting from behind them by Sergeants of the R.H.A.

Two sketches showing a military tournament in Meyrick Park in July 1910.

Prussians laying siege to Paris in 1870 and the deposition of Napoleon III. However, the Bournemouth Volunteers continued and by the mid-1880s they had nearly 200 men. During the more peaceful times of the late 19th century, there were rationalisations of the various companies in the area. After a time, the Artillery Volunteers emerged as the 6th Hampshire Battery of the Royal Field Artillery under the Territorial scheme.

Drill halls were provided for the men. Field Marshal the Right Honourable Viscount Wolseley opened one in Holdenhurst Road on 23rd May 1896. It was the gift of a Miss Mitchell of Alum Chine Road. The earlier Victoria Hall, Portman Road, Boscombe Drill Hall, opened in 1891.

The Boer War (1899 – 1902)

Although the struggle with the Boers in South Africa had no direct effect on Bournemouth, the loyal residents, buoyed up after the patriotic fervour of the Queen's Diamond Jubilee, regarded it with interest. Home defence commitments meant that the Artillery Volunteers, as a Corps, could not join the fighting, but many Volunteers offered their services. Initially, these were spurned by the Regular Army, but after many reverses in the field, they were allowed to join.

Two strong detachments of Rifles were sent from Bournemouth in 1901 under Lieutenant W. R. Thomson. Their activities in South Africa were connected with communications, and their only major action was an occasion when they were

The cover of a programme printed to mark a visit of the Home Fleet in 1910, Bournemouth's Centenary Year.

ambushed, but unable to see the enemy they could not return the fire. One member of the force was seriously injured in the Barberton railway accident in 1902. In all, nine local Volunteers were killed in South Africa; 4 more died from disease.

On their return home in May 1902, they were given an official welcome by the Mayor and Council. News that the war had ended was received on Sunday 1st June 1902. The following day the town was decked with bunting and a service of thanksgiving was held in the Square. By 1903, the Volunteers numbered 1100 men of all ranks. In 1908, under the reorganisation of the Army by Richard Haldane, Secretary of State for War, the Volunteers joined with the Hampshire Yeomanry to become the Territorial Force.

The First World War (1914 – 1918)

The European Powers had been jockeying for supremacy for many years when the assassination of the Austrian

Archduke Ferdinand and his wife at Sarajevo on 28th June 1914 lit the tinderbox of war. The German-speaking nations started declaring war on their neighbours. Germany declared war on France on 3rd August and, to avoid the fortifications along their joint border, swept through neutral Belgium to the north. To stem this aggression, Britain declared war on the Germans on 4th August. It was to be the first truly international war involving countries from all continents. Subsequent history called it the First World War, but it was termed the Great War at the time – the 'war to end all wars'.

Earlier in 1914, Bournemouth was looking forward to a bright summer season which had already started well at Easter. The Bank Holiday weekend of 1st to 3rd August was more subdued, and despite some reduction of excursion trains and pleasure steamers, there were still promising numbers of visitors. However, the news of the Belgian invasion sent them scurrying back home, and those booked to come later cancelled their lodgings.

The nation was now on a war footing. Many able-bodied men willing to fight had already joined the Reservists or Territorials, waiting for possible emergencies. On Tuesday 4th August, they were called out to guard strategic places like the railway stations and the cliffs. Gold coinage was replaced by banknotes, people panicked to hoard food, and the price of staples increased. Non-nationals were to register, and Germans only remained with a special permit. However, xenophobia and hostility grew to the extent of complaining about the playing of Wagner's music at the Winter Gardens.

Rumours of restrictions had to be quashed, and by the late summer some normality had resumed. The war was expected to be 'over by Christmas'. Many men joined up voluntarily, but the increasing death toll demanded yet more. The war years were marked by recruitment campaigns. At one recruiting rally, the Rev. E. J. Kennedy

ABOVE The 1910 Centenary Fete in Meyrick Park, with the Artillery preparing a display.

RIGHT By 1917, food was scarce and the German U-boats had severely restricted iimports. Only 3 to 4 weeks food supply was in stock. Local people signed this pledge to reduce their consumption of bread.

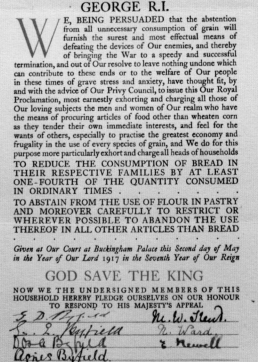

'encouraged' volunteers with the report that some 20,000 men from nearby Lyndhurst had been reduced in battle to a mere quarter! Later the pleas for volunteers ended with compulsory national conscription. Not all troops were destined for Flanders. For example, units of the 7th Battalion of the Hampshire Regiment and the 6th Hants Artillery Battery billeted in Bournemouth were sent to India in 1914, before serving in Mesopotamia (present-day Iraq).

Bournemouth, with its recuperative reputation, was

one of many coastal towns asked to receive wounded and sick soldiers. A Military Hospital in the form of a large marquee was erected in the grounds of the Royal Victoria and West Hants Hospital in Shelley Road, Boscombe. Crag Head, a large house in Manor Road, was also offered. The first wounded soldiers started arriving in October. As the war dragged on, many other places were given over, such as the Mont Dore Hotel (the present Town Hall) especially for Indian troops.

Many thousands of troops, awaiting transport to the battlefronts, were billeted around the town, some in family homes, and others at campsites. They became part of the local scene and were usually feted by residents. They were given special treatment with visits to the theatres, and shows, but some residents complained about their monopolizing seats in parks: others were complaining of the hasty marriages carrying off their womenfolk! A 'Women's Patrol' of volunteer vigilantes walked the streets to protect young girls from unwanted attention. A more positive result was the formation of three Empire Clubs around the town where girls could be distracted with physical training, singing and dressmaking.

Belgian civilian refugees and soldiers received special treatment after the exaggerated details of German atrocities. Wounded soldiers at the Grata Quies Hospital in Branksome Park earned their keep by making wooden toys. This activity was transferred to the Tachbrook Toy Factory in Bath Road, which opened in February 1916.

As the war drained the male population, many occupations were filled by women. They proved themselves equal to the work and received some national recognition when in January 1918 the vote was given to some, but not all, women, although it was not until 1923 that women first became MPs. A major employer of women was the Horton Heath Factory, just a short train ride away beyond Poole, which made cordite explosives.

Other more local civilian light industrial factories turned their hands to the war effort, mainly supplying the demand for shells for the muddy battlefronts of France. Even home workshops became organised under the Amateur Ordnance Volunteers to supply munitions parts at their own expense. Lathe courses were offered at the Municipal College at ten shillings for 12 lessons to encourage others to join the work. In January 1915, all lights were required to be extinguished so as not to be visible to enemy gunships out at sea. Coastal towns were being shelled along the North Sea. A later order called for all public lighting to be switched off since air raids had begun. Zeppelins and *Gotha* aircraft were bombing London, but fortunately Bournemouth was spared any attacks.

Fund-raising harnessed the energy and generosity of the people of Bournemouth. Flag days were regular occurrences, ranging in causes from whole allied nations to wounded army horses. Sums collected ranged from £500 to £700. In total 36 flag days raised £28,000. Other means of raising money included the tried methods of bazaars, displays and entertainments. These needed to be properly authorised, and the Corporation became the local registration authority, to which an assortment of eleven charities signed up immediately. Later, War Bonds were introduced promising a good return. The Corporation invested, and encouraged their wide support.

For those less able to give money, there were opportunities for knitting comforts and balaclavas and making other clothing for the troops abroad. Items were also made for the Hospital Supplies Depot in Southbourne.

Economy in life styles was encouraged for the war effort. An Imperial War Economy Exhibition was held at the Grand Hotel in October 1916 demonstrating how cookery, housecraft, even poultry-keeping, can prove less wasteful. An added attraction was a display of German military equipment including machine guns and an

aeroplane. This event was in aid of War Savings Week. At one of the last such occasions to raise money for British armaments, some £250,000 was collected, sufficient to buy a Monitor gun for the Navy, although it was later noted that the only time the Bournemouth people ever saw a British weapon was after the Armistice.

At the beginning of 1916, Bournemouth had between 2000 and 3000 billeted soldiers en route to the war zones. Drill halls, parks, football grounds and even a cemetery were used for drilling. Other sites were used for the necessary training in digging trenches and firing. The aerodrome at Talbot Village took on a more military role as a flying school for both the Royal and Belgian Flying Corps. A number of crashes around the town occurred, not least that of a Major Laycock in 1918 who took his Bristol fighter too low whilst impressing his girlfriend.

Despite this ever-growing military background, the newly formed Bournemouth Chamber of Trade in February 1916 claimed visitor-attractions should be the town's main priority. Visitors continued to come during the holiday periods, undeterred by the restrictions on lighting, and later on alcohol licensing. All the entertainment venues continued to do reasonable business, even the Pierrot shows on the beach. Shops also did well, especially the new Bobby's, Plummer's, and even Woolworth's, challenging the longer-established Beale's. The larger stores had their own tearoom with palm court orchestras.

Sport on a small scale presumably continued, but Dean Court had no organised football since the end of the 1913/14 season. Similarly, first-class cricket at Dean Park was interrupted in August 1914, and the game did not resume until a charity match in 1918. However, the locals were introduced to baseball in 1917 when a crowd of several thousand saw an American team beat the Canadians at Meyrick Park.

Paddle steamers had ceased their excursions, and

venturing out on the water was limited to rowing boats, and then no further than the length of the piers, not least because of the rough seas. Motor coaches (then called charabancs) offered trips to the surrounding countryside. However, petrol was restricted, and companies were often fined for transgressions. By 1917, the use of coal gas meant the charabancs could venture into the New Forest, each carrying its own explosive mixture in a gasbag attached to the vehicles. Fewer trams created crowds scrambling to board and so to reduce these unseemly melees, queueing was introduced in 1918. Little of this is unfortunately not well recorded visually. Taking of photographs or making sketches within four miles of the coastline was prohibited for security reasons. Holidaymakers and locals alike were fined for carrying cameras.

One unwelcome 'growth industry' was the increase in ambulance trains coming to Bournemouth. The bloody battles of the Somme started in mid-1916. The local St. John Ambulance Brigade had by then adopted standard procedures in dealing with the casualties: the majority were taken off at Boscombe Station in Ashley Road, but those destined for Mont Dore or Grata Quies went to Bournemouth Central or Bournemouth West Stations. The walking wounded disembarked first, then the stretcher cases were carried out. This was quite demanding where lifts were not available at some of the hospitals. Often the streets were crowded with well-wishers. By the time the war was finished, the Brigade had dealt with 10,206 wounded men.

These reluctant visitors to the town were well catered for. Their blue uniforms made them distinctive. Seats were provided for them in the Square and deck chairs on the beach at Boscombe. In the cloisters of the Undercliff Drive by Bournemouth Pier, a canteen was established supplying all kinds of beverages, cakes and cigarettes, free of charge. It was run by volunteers and proved popular,

The Mont Dore on Remembrance Day 11th November 1921.

the costs being defrayed by donations. There was also a bathing tent supplied for those wanting to swim.

Whilst newspapers gave full coverage from the battlefronts, there was an audience for information about the war. Many speakers lectured at the various halls. The Bournemouth Natural Science Society held a series of talks on the war efforts of the Empire nations. The immediacy of the cinematic image made such films depicting the battles of the Somme, Jutland and Ancre (the final battle of the Somme) very popular at the local cinemas.

With the shortages of food, many waste areas were turned over to allotments to encourage growing vegetables. At West Howe, the YMCA created a Red Triangle Farm Colony for ex-servicemen invalided out of the Army. It was the first of its kind in the country. In February 1917, the Ministry of Food attempted voluntary rationing of staple foods, but it was necessary to impose a Rationing Scheme twelve months later. To alleviate the hardships, National Food Kitchens were opened in Winton

and Springbourne where wholesome cooked meals could be had at reasonable prices. Especially useful to working mothers, they served over 170,000 meals in their first five months.

During late 1918, the enemy nations sued for peace, with Germany finally signing an Armistice on 11th November. In those days without radio or television, the news of this was proclaimed by the Mayor outside the Municipal Offices in Yelverton Road. Offices, shops and schools closed, and large crowds thronged the streets rejoicing. The bells of St. Peter's Church rang out, car horns sounded, and flags were waved. More seriously, a service of thanksgiving was held in the Square in the afternoon with the Mayor and the visiting Bishop of Winchester presiding. There was another service at St. Peter's in the evening. Outside, the blackout screens were removed, fireworks lit and cheerful people strolled late into the night.

It took well into 1919 to return the town to anything resembling normality. In truth, there could never be a return to the pre-war days. Very few families escaped a loss. The official Book of Remembrance contains the names of 650 dead: no doubt there were more, and many more again were wounded and maimed. Some of the dead were interred in the various local cemeteries where special plots were created, each with a simple standardised headstone, and with the War Cross alongside the plot. For example, 120 British and Belgians are buried in Boscombe Cemetery in Gloucester Road, 75 of the graves in the war plot.

Recognition of Bournemouth's loss was marked with a war memorial designed by E. A. Shervey, the Deputy Borough Architect. It was made of Portland Stone, and officially dedicated on 8th November 1922. Around the town, factories, churches and offices erected their own memorials. Bournemouth's Great War holders of the Victoria Cross, Corporal Cecil Noble and Sergeant Frederick

Riggs, together with Lieutenant Colonel Derek Seagrim VC from the Second World War, are commemorated on a scroll held by Lewis Tregonwell on his statue outside the BIC. At St. Peter's Church, a Chapel of Resurrection was built in 1925/6 for its parishioners.

The Second World War (1939 – 1945)

The election of Herr Adolf Hitler as Chancellor of Weimar Germany in 1933, and the subsequent rise of his National Socialist Party, brought fear to many observers in Western Europe. Some were more sympathetic, and the local activities of the Fascists have still to be researched. The local authorities, however, were obliged to follow Government directives. In 1935 a committee was set up across the conurbation to activate Air Raid Precautions (ARP). It was felt that if war were to break out between Germany and Britain, the Luftwaffe would immediately seek to bomb this country into submission. Spending ratepayers' money on such a surmise was not popular with many, but begrudgingly plans were slowly put into action.

When war was finally declared on 3rd September 1939, Bournemouth was placed on a war footing. Immediately, all places of entertainment were closed since it was felt a direct bomb hit on a large gathering would create public dismay. After days of anti-climax when nothing happened, this decision was reversed, and throughout the rest of the war, places like cinemas, dance halls and sports arenas were to provide the populace with distraction from the privations

of war. For the cinemas, with their often-escapist fare and newsreels, the wartime proved its most popular period ,generating audiences never equalled before or since.

In the early stages of the war, Bournemouth was not regarded as a military target and a number of Government offices moved from London. It became a safe haven for children evacuated from London, Southampton and Portsmouth, although as the months of non-engagement dragged on through the 'Phoney War', some individual evacuees returned home. When the hostilities began in earnest, the children were replaced by French and British soldiers snatched from the beaches of Dunkirk. Soon after, all the local beaches were heavily protected

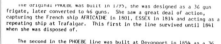

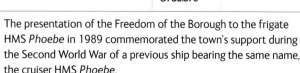

The presentation of the Freedom of the Borough to the frigate HMS *Phoebe* in 1989 commemorated the town's support during the Second World War of a previous ship bearing the same name, the cruiser HMS *Phoebe*.

by mines, barbed wire, anti-tank blocks, and both piers were breached to prevent landings by enemy ships. The usual seaside activities were cordoned off for residents. Visitors were dissuaded from coming to the town by the whole south coast coming under an exclusion zone. With many hotels in the area experiencing poor business, several were requisitioned by the Government to billet soldiers, especially those from the Commonwealth. The visit in 1941 by King George VI and Queen Elizabeth to address Dominion airmen at the Pavilion was the first visit to Bournemouth by a reigning monarch.

Possibly the most important decision of the war was made at Bournemouth. When the Labour Party held their conference here in 1940, the delegates passed a resolution to join a coalition government as long as there was a change of leader. This led to Winston Churchill being invited to become Prime Minister throughout the war.

Individuals, local communities and organisations joined in the massive war effort. There were almost weekly flag days in aid of countless charities: but the main thrust was in National Savings. Eventful War Weeks would raise millions of pounds for patriotic causes like buying *Spitfires* (of which Bournemouth could claim two) and subsidising a cruiser such as *HMS Phoebe*. These weeks would incorporate marches and displays by the respective armed forces, and at every meeting place from schools to cinemas there would be requests for donations.

Knitting 'comforts' for the troops was a popular activity: whole neighbourhoods would come together in each other's homes to knit and gossip, and save heating and lighting costs by sharing hospitality. Recycling was in vogue, even then. Boy Scouts gathered scrap paper, not to save the environment but for the manufacture of bullets. Even the Council assisted with the donation of past minutes papers. The public were asked to sacrifice their pots and pans for aircraft parts, and iron railings were removed and turned into tanks after the authorities persuaded people that privet hedges were more 'natural-looking' than metal.

Luxuries were the temptations of the swastika-emblazoned 'Squander Bug', a cartoon character used to discourage wasteful spending. Rationing of food staples was not started until 1940, but was gradually increased. The various British Restaurants, one of which opened at the Pavilion in 1942, provided nourishing meals without ration coupons.

Local authorities and the public were encouraged to 'Dig for Victory' by ploughing up open spaces and allotments to grow crops, or to keep chickens, rabbits, and even pigs in back gardens to supplement the diet. Land Girls were mobilised, Rabbit Clubs formed. 'Make do and mend' was another Government slogan to encourage people to wear their clothing for as long as possible, by darning or altering. 'Utility' was introduced in 1941 and applied to clothes and furnishing. The quality was basic, but not always tasteless.

Whilst all these activities were voluntary, compulsory National Service was introduced for the armed forces. Those remaining, the under-aged and over-aged, were persuaded (later enforced) to join the Home Guard, or ARP, or engage in fire watching. In addition, there were places in the Auxiliary Fire Brigade, the Special Constabulary, St. John Ambulance Brigade or Red Cross, and the Women's Voluntary Service: housewives were strongly encouraged to take an active part in war effort work.

The young were encouraged through the Scouting and other uniformed movements to play their part, and on reaching their teens, to join the army, air force or navy training corps to prepare themselves for active service.

The first ARP Circular came from the Government on 9th July 1935. A month later, Bournemouth councillors met with those from Poole and Christchurch to form a joint Committee to serve the conurbation. Proportional to their respective sizes, Bournemouth was to fund 70% of the costs, Poole 25%, and Christchurch 5%. An ARP Controller for the three towns was appointed in 1937 and based at Fairlight Glen, Avenue Road in October. The ARP Bill was approved by the Government in November 1937 and became an Act commencing on 1st January 1938.

Later called Civil Defence, the ARP was an overarching organization. It was the efficiency with which this was organized that saved so many lives when the bombing eventually arrived. The major driving forces in Bournemouth were Councillor Harry Mears, who became Chairman of the ARP Committee in 1939, and Alderman Sir Charles Cartwright who was Controller. The Borough of Bournemouth was divided into three sectors: Central, Eastern and Northern, with headquarters at Fairlight Glen, Grovely Manor, and the Embassy Club, Brassey Road respectively. The control room was in the basement of the Town Hall. These sectors were then subdivided into a total of 31 Posts, each with its own level of command. The ARP commandeered local halls for these nerve centres. The personnel were drawn from their own areas, and were called upon to keep their post manned at all times.

At times of alert, signalled by air raid sirens, the Wardens would leave their homes or places of work to assemble at their Post. Their role was to act only when a bomb was dropped in their allotted zone. Trained Incident Officers would rush to the place where the bomb(s) fell, referred to as an 'incident', assess the problems and report back to their Post with requests for the necessary assistance. At the main headquarters, each incident was given a

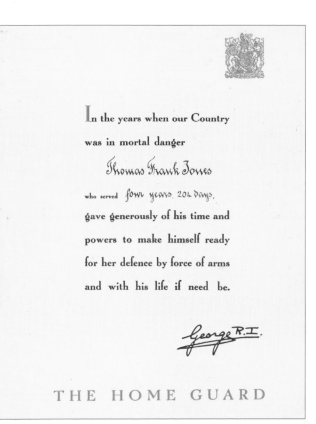

The Home Guard certificate awarded to Thomas Jones, who served in the Home Guard from its formation in May 1940.

unique number and the recovery progress monitored. The Incident Officer took charge of his situation and guided all the operations necessary to rescue survivors, remove the dangers of escaping gas and water, control traffic in the site area, and later to clear the debris and ensure the site is safe and secure. The whole episode involved directing the various services, over which the Incident Officer had total command.

In Bournemouth, 1500 men registered within 48 hours following calls in May 1940 for a Home Guard as an initial line of defence against an invading enemy.

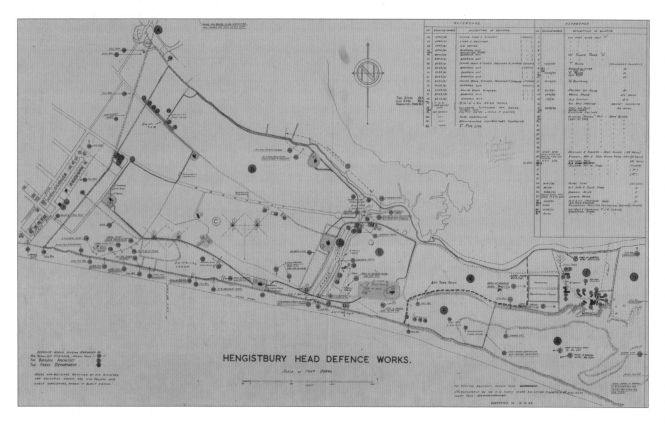

HENGISTBURY HEAD DEFENCE WORKS.

A plan showing the radar station and defences on Hengistbury Head. Reproduced from the 1932 Ordnance Survey map.

Although ineligible for National Service because of their age or being in reserved occupations, many had wartime experience from the First World War. Bournemouth raised two major battalions, 6th and 7th Hants, totalling 5000 men, and various service industries formed smaller units to defend the railways, gas and electricity supplies. The Home Guard trained like regular soldiers in readiness and also manned the coastal defences. Less glorious was their required presence at bombed buildings to prevent looting.

For the most part, Bournemouth was spared much of the bombing that was meted out to the industrial towns and airfields during the Battle of Britain of 1940-41. The enemy aircraft that did fly overhead were on their way to or returning from bombing raids on the Midlands. They were following radio directional beams from France, but a radar station at Hengistbury Head deflected them in an effort to misguide the navigators. Any early bombing was mainly from aircraft ditching their bombs on the last area of British soil before returning over the English Channel.

The first local bomb fell just after midnight on 3rd July 1940 on a house at Cellars Farm Road, Southbourne. The house was destroyed but there were no casualties. The ARP centre at Grovely Manor attracted some attention during

1940, and scatterings of incendiaries were also a menace, but otherwise the bombing was spasmodic until November when six parachute mines caused 53 casualties.

Most of the bombing was at night. The town was clothed in darkness in a universal 'Black-out'. Light from buildings was forbidden, streetlights were switched off and vehicle headlights dimmed. More fatalities resulted from accidents than enemy action. Normal activities were curtailed by the hours of darkness: evening church services were held in the afternoons and shopping and theatre-going times were brought forward to allow earlier home going.

Protection of the populace was an early consideration. The fear of poison gas attacks prompted a distribution of gas masks in 1939, before war was declared. Public air raid shelters were constructed in parks, but some were soon dismantled as seemingly unnecessary and dangerous. Many buildings built in 1939 incorporated air raid shelters in their basements. The Odeon Cinema, San Remo Towers, and the Saxon King public house all boasted having adequate shelters. All homes were offered Anderson and/or Morrison shelters, but the Education Department dithered about provision at schools.

The Allied Air Force reception and training unit run by the Canadians was based in the town throughout the war. With the entry of the United States into the war after the bombing of Pearl Harbour in December 1941, American armed personnel were stationed locally. Many hotels were requisitioned for senior staff, whilst to the north of Bournemouth and in the New Forest airfields sprang up from which many missions were flown against occupied France. The Americans joined the increasingly numerous Commonwealth troops as common sights in Bournemouth and they were welcomed at servicemen's clubs and especially the dance halls. The sports fields were well used and baseball was played in Bournemouth again.

Bournemouth's worst raid of the war took place at lunchtime on Sunday 23rd May 1943. A total of 77 civilians and 131 servicemen lost their lives. The number of servicemen, many of them Canadians, was so high because some of the bombs fell on to two hotels, the Central and Metropole, in which they were temporarily based. Beale's store was completely destroyed, as was the Punshon Memorial Church.

ABOVE LEFT The Hotel Metropole at the Lansdowne.

LEFT Beale's seen from Old Christchurch Road.

ABOVE RIGHT The fire brigade at Beale's.

RIGHT The Central Hotel and Punshon Memorial Church on Richmond Hill.

The presence of these Allied forces attracted the attention of the Germans. A number of bombing raids during 1943 were serious, but none more than the raid by 25 FW190s on the quiet Sunday morning of 23rd May, during which the Metropole and Central Hotels were hit causing hundreds of casualties amongst the stationed troops.

The Germans had cause for concern since Bournemouth was one of many south coast centres preparing for the D-Day invasion. For the Americans, it was this western distribution of their troops on English soil which determined that they would be allotted the more heavily defended Omaha and Utah Normandy beaches. On 5th June 1944, Poole Bay was full of troop-carrying ships which quietly slipped away during the night.

The advance by the Allies into northern France distracted German attention away from Britain, and the

LEFT Soldiers and ARP wardens at a mobile canteen after the bombing of the Hotel Metropole in 1943.

BELOW The crew of a Typhoon fighter/bomber at RAF Hurn in 1944.

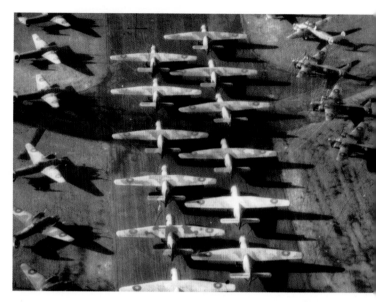

ABOVE This rare but poor quality photograph shows Horsa assault gliders lined up at Hurn in 1943.

BELOW The breached Bournemouth Pier and anti-invasion scaffolding in 1944 and the beach and promenades crowded with soldiers, mainly from the United States infantry. Courtesy of American Red Cross.

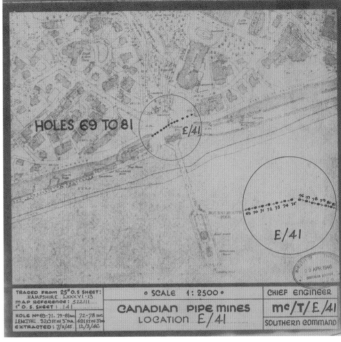

ABOVE Landmines were laid across the chines and the Bourne valley. After the war their removal was recorded. Reproduced from the 1932 Ordnance Survey map.

LEFT Crew of 'Innocents Abroad' and a 1000 lb bomb in front of United States Auxiliary Air Force at RAF Hurn in 1944.

people of Bournemouth felt less involvement with the war. Many restrictions were lifted. However, another reminder came with a new influx of refugees from London which was being bombarded by V-weapons, which fortunately did not target Bournemouth.

The battle for Berlin ended on 2nd May 1945, and finally VE-Day (Victory in Europe) was celebrated on 8th May. There was rejoicing across Bournemouth, but most revellers congregated around the Square. Bonfires were lit in the streets and there was dancing and singing (especially the 'Hokey-Cokey'). Later in the month, street parties were celebrated with communities collectively contributing saved-up food rations.

The war continued against Japan for another three months until its surrender on 15th August. Again, there were celebrations but with less exuberance. For many families, being reunited with their loved-ones from the European theatre of war, some of whom had been prisoners, had eased anxieties.

As the troops gradually returned home, there was still much to do to remove the scars of war, both physical and economic. Fortunately for Bournemouth there were only 51 air raids, dropping some 2271 bombs (mostly incendiaries). It had fared better than many large towns. The bombing resulted in 168 civilian deaths and 507 injured. 182 servicemen were killed and 401 people had been made homeless, according to official figures published by *The Bournemouth Times* on 8th December 1944. The magnificent action of the Civil Defence teams helped prevent many more. Damage to buildings was also relatively slight with 246 properties being totally destroyed or needing to be demolished. However, just over 13,000 buildings were damaged, most only slightly. The only major buildings destroyed were Beales department store, the Punshon Memorial Church and West's Cinema, as well as the Central and Metropole Hotels.

Many local people had also played a critical role during the war working in the Airspeed aircraft factory at Christchurch airfield which produced *Oxford* trainers, *Horsa* gliders and *Mosquito* fighter-bombers for the RAF. The airfield was also used by a trials unit involved in the early development of aircraft radar.

The Post-War Period

In 1944 Sir Patrick Abercrombie was invited to draw up post-war plans for Bournemouth, but building programmes were delayed by shortage of materials. 371 prefabricated homes (known as prefabs) were built as temporary shelter. The first 185 two-bedroom prefabs went up at Strouden Farm in 1946, and were not replaced until twenty years later. Many residents came to love these homes and were reluctant to leave. By way of a living memorial to those who fought in the war, the Council sought to erect a home for disabled ex-servicemen. Thanks to the kindness of the Misses Cooper Dean, a site in Castle Lane was secured and the Memorial Homes were occupied in 1948.

For several years afterwards, beach-goers were warned against washed-up mines. The piers had to wait until the 1950s before being eventually rebuilt. Just an occasional air raid shelter or pillbox now remains in the Bournemouth landscape. The airfield at Hurn has become an international airport. As the scars heal, commemorations continue to mark the bloodiest war in the hope it will never be repeated.

In the post-war period, the break-up of the British Empire brought conflict with independence groups. On the world stage, the Soviet Union and China assumed the role of possible aggressors. In the east, British National Service soldiers engaged in battle against the Communists in Malaya and Korea. Nearer home, *Vampire*, *Venom* and *Sea Vixen* fighters were built by De Havilland at Christchurch. For many years the local Civil Defence continued, still under the command of Harry Mears. Fear of nuclear war gave rise to the Campaign for Nuclear Disarmament, of which a Bournemouth branch was formed in 1959, run jointly by the Principal of the Municipal College and a newsagent. They sent contingents to the annual Aldermaston to London marches, and harried CD exercises, set in the New Forest after a supposed nuclear attack on Bournemouth.

A new form of insidious warfare now concentrates vigilance: terrorism. The first series of attacks came with renewed Republican demands from Northern Ireland, mainly on civilian London. A bold venture during the Conservative Party Conference at Brighton in 1984 came close to killing Prime Minister Margaret Thatcher. When the Party Conference came the following year to Bournemouth, the possibility of a repeated attempt triggered great security searches beforehand. All manholes across the town centre were inspected, which were then sealed. Ironically, it was on such a seal that Mrs Thatcher tripped and injured her ankle!

The Provisional IRA was accused of bombing Bournemouth on Friday 13th August 1993. Six incendiary devices went off in four stores in the centre of town, and two explosive bombs – fortunately only one detonating – at the Pier Theatre. Damage was estimated at £1 million. As ever, the British put a brave face on it.

TEN
EDUCATION– BRINGING LEARNING TO ALL
Vincent May

This 1898 map shows the growing working class areas of Boscombe and Pokesdown with their schools (St James and Pokesdown, Holy Cross and the Convent), the Sanitary (Isolation) Hospital and the Boscombe Arcade. There are some larger properties south of Boscombe, but the Hotel Burlington, Boscombe Manor and Wentworth Lodge are separated from the rest of the area by large grounds. Reproduced from the (1898) Ordnance Survey map with the kind permission of the Ordnance Survey.

Chapter Ten

PART ONE

Village Schools[1]

During the past 200 years the role of education has changed significantly, but few would have expected it to be one of the most important employers and sources of income for Bournemouth in the 21st century. The history of education in Bournemouth is about the growth of many different schools (Part 1), internationally recognized language schools (Part 2, written by Mike Francis, Dan Ferris and Simon Freeman) and a large university (Part 3). It is also about the importance of individual benefactors, the churches, private schools and the increased role of the State in providing the funds.

In 1810 few children went to school. They attended Sunday School if there was a church or chapel near their home. Some villages had 'Dame's Schools', where one of the women taught small groups of young children, usually in a private house or cottage. Paid a small weekly sum, sometimes supplemented by the clergy or a local landowner, the 'Dame' was rarely trained and often had no education. One vicar of Kinson wrote that the villagers were unhappy with these arrangements and 'were desirous of more efficient means of education'. In 1818,

a Parliamentary Select Committee reported that there were no schools (despite its population of 517) in Kinson. Christchurch had 'a school on the National System' with 220 children, but this was a Sunday School rather than a day school. Holdenhurst parish, which by 1818 included the new Bourne settlement, had 191 people but no schools.

As the new Bourne grew, it attracted working people to build and service its houses, hotels and businesses. They could not afford to pay for their children to go to school, but some of the wealthier residents felt strongly that provision should be made for the children of the town's poorer residents. However, there was a wider debate in the country about who should provide schools – the state or the religious bodies.

Little happened until 1833 when a Parliamentary Bill proposed a system of 'universal and national education of the whole people'. The House of Commons rejected the Bill, but the Government agreed to make £20,000 available as grants 'in aid of private subscriptions for the erection of school houses for the education of the poorer classes in Great Britain'. The vicar of Kinson requested £56, and £40 was granted in response to a Memorial (see opposite page).

This application itself is historically important because it was rewarded by the first Government funding of any school in the area of today's Bournemouth. So in 1835, with the population of the parish at 775, the Kinson school was built with two rooms one each for 40 boys and 40 girls. The rooms were 16 feet square. The total costs of construction were £160, of which £104 had been collected. The annual expenses of running the schools were £35 and were paid by subscriptions

The land was leased for 99 years at an annual payment of 2 shillings and 6 pence, with the requirement that it should 'be for ever appropriated and used solely for a

ABOVE This faded 1930s photograph is all that survives of Kinson Village School

BELOW The original site of the Kinson Village School at Millhams junction with Wimborne Road.

To the Right Honourable the Lords of His Majesty's Treasury.

Memorial of the Vicar and other promoters of the Daily and Sunday school on the National System, for the education of the children of the Poor belonging to the Chapelry of Kinson in the Parish of Great Canford in the County of Dorset.

Showeth – That a Daily School had been for some time past carried on in union with ne established in an adjoining Parish, but in consequence of the distance which has prevented the children from paying a regular attendance, the inhabitants have requested that the School should in future be conducted in their own Parish;- That the school has accordingly been removed to Kinson; - That in consequence the number of children now belonging to it, and from the increase in the number of scholars being anticipated, it is found absolutely essential that a schoolhouse be erected for their accommodation;- That the house now rented is totally inadequate for the purpose and has rendered it unavoidable to separate the scholars by removal of a portion of them to the vestry room of the church which is some way distant from the present school, thereby causing such impediment to the proper management and regulation of the School; - That your Memorialists finding it impossible to raise by subscription a fund sufficient for the erection of a school house, from the owners of the land and the inhabitants of the Parish, have considered it expedient to apply to the National Society for a grant towards this desirable object, to the correspondence with which Society your Memorialists beg to refer your lordships for any information that may be required on the subject; That your Memorialists will be ready to submit any audit of their building accounts which your lordships may be pleased to direct, and to make such periodical reports respecting the state of their School, and the number of scholars admitted, as may be demanded.

Your Memorialists declare that there are no charitable funds, or public or private endowments in the place, which might render inexpedient or unnecessary any further grant for promoting the education of the children of the poor in the Parish

Dated: Kinson, 10th March 1835

Signed W.D.Bartlett, Vicar, J.W.Pyman, Jn. Way, Christr. Hill, Wm. Footner*. Edward Elliot

* Churchwarden, Kinson

A copy of the Memorial sent by the vicar of Kinson in 1835 requesting funding from the Treasury to build and run a school in the village.

school for the instruction of children only, of the labouring, manufacturing and other poorer classes in the parish of Kinson'. The school building was used until 1936 (just 100 years) and was demolished in the 1950s.

The Hampshire parishes were slower to react, although the *Victoria County History* for Hampshire says that a Day School for Dissenters had opened in 1825 in a cottage at Muscliffe. In 1833 Holdenhurst had a Sunday School run by the Established Church with 39 boys and 25 girls, and a Day School for up to 101 children

Pokesdown in 1870 with its National School (for both boys and girls) next to St. James's Church. The village also had a Mechanics Institute and a Reading Room. At the same time, there were two pubs, a smithy and an Independent Chapel. Reproduced from the (1870) Ordnance Survey map.

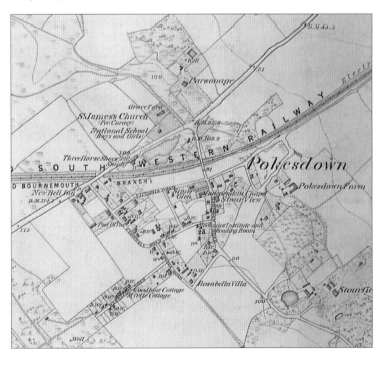

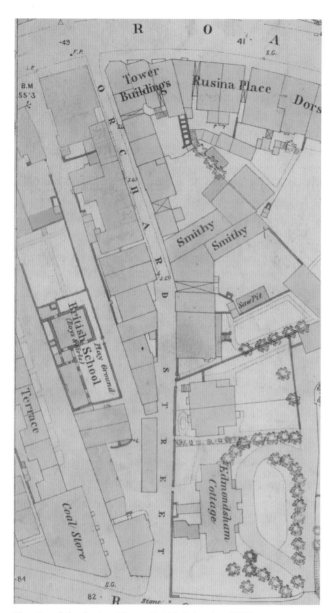

The site of the Orchard Street British School in 1870.
Reproduced with the kind permission of the Ordnance Survey.

Talbot Village School was founded by the Talbot sisters in 1862.

St. Peter's School in the centre of Bournemouth in 1900.

opened there in 1846 on the road between the village and Throop. To the east, at Pokesdown, a Day School opened in 1835 and a Day School at Bourne had 9 boys and 9 girls. By 1838, in the Marine Village of Bourne, there were many poorer families with children living in cottages at the lower end of the present-day Commercial Road. Two cottages, made available by Sir George Tapps-Gervis at his expense, were knocked into one to form a temporary church that was also used as a school.

So by the beginning of the 1840s, there were schools at Kinson, Pokesdown, Bourne and the Throop School in the then settlement of Winton. A Congregational Chapel built in 1849 in Orchard Lane became, in due course, the Bournemouth British School. British Schools were usually supported by the Nonconformist (or Independent) churches and the British and Foreign Schools Society. However, in 1845 the Reverend Morden Bennett was appointed to the District Chapelry of Bournemouth. He had a major impact on the future pattern of what eventually became the town's primary schools. The Gervis Estate provided land for a school which opened in 1850, alongside the new St. Peter's Church. By 1857, there

were 87 children. In 1854, Bennett became chairman of the committee which persuaded Parliament to pass the Bournemouth Improvement Act 1856. Bennett's next task was providing much improved school buildings in Moordown. He had already collected a good proportion of the cost of the building before announcing its construction. So in 1853, St. John's Moordown came into being to serve a population of about 300 people. By 1865, it had 50 children. St. James at Pokesdown followed in 1857. Sir George Tapps-Gervis provided land in Orchard Street where Bennett opened a mission room and an infants' school with 40 children in 1865, which became St. Michael's School. In Springbourne, Bennett bought four acres of land in 1867 for the site of St. Clement's Church and School, although a temporary school only started in 1871.

Others also set up schools, most notably in Talbot Village where St. Mark's was built in 1862 as part of the village established by the Talbot sisters, and in Winton (the Winton British School) in 1866. As a result of differences over the nature of the religious education, Holy Trinity School was set up in 1869 on a site provided by Robert

Kerley. Nevertheless, by 1870 Bennett had largely set the pattern of what became the denominational (CE) schools in Bournemouth, interspersed between schools set up in the older villages. This was about to change.

There was a strong feeling in many parts of the country that there was still a serious absence of education for children whose parents did not belong to the churches. There were also concerns about child labour, a major political issue, especially in rural areas. Where schools existed, there was often considerable absenteeism during harvest and other periods when extra hands were needed. This was a sufficiently serious problem that the Agricultural Children's Act (1873) stated that a child between the ages of 8 and 10 years could only be employed in agriculture if it had completed 250 school attendances in the preceding 12 months. Children over ten only needed 150 attendances. A parent, not the school, had to provide a certificate confirming the attendance.

The Elementary Education Act of 1870

The Elementary Education Act of 1870 established a national system of state education that rested on the principles that there should be efficient schools in reach of all and where such provision did not exist it should be compulsorily provided. Elementary schools that did exist were financed by voluntary bodies of a religious nature. Schools could be identified as 'Infant Schools' (St. Michael's), 'Day Schools' (Muscliffe, Pokesdown), 'Evening Schools' (none locally at the time) and 'Sunday Schools' (Holdenhurst).

The Act also perpetuated a dual system - voluntary denominational schools and nondenominational state schools.[2] Elementary schools were to be provided

	Elementary Education Act 1870 Revised Code of Regulations, 1872 Standards of Education		
STANDARD	Reading	Writing	Arithmetic
I	One of the narratives next in order after monosyllables in an elementary reading book used in the school.	Copy in manuscript character a line of print, and write from dictation a few common words.	Simple addition and subtraction of numbers of not more than four figures, and the multiplication table to multiplication by six.
II	A short paragraph from an elementary reading book.	.	The multiplication table, and any simple rule as far as short division (inclusive).
III	A short paragraph from a more advanced reading book.	A sentence slowly dictated once by a few words at a time, from the same book.	Long division and compound rules (money).
IV	A few lines of poetry or prose, at the choice of the inspector.	A sentence slowly dictated once, by a few words at a time, from a reading book, such as is used in the first class of the school.	Compound rules (common weights and measures).
V	A short ordinary paragraph in a newspaper, or other modern narrative.	Another short ordinary paragraph in a newspaper, or other modern narrative, slowly dictated once by a few words at a time.	Practice and bills of parcels.
VI	To read with fluency and expression.	A short theme or letter, or an easy paraphrase.	Proportion and fractions (vulgar and decimal).

Children were expected to reach these standards in the 3Rs (reading, writing and arithmetic). If they reached Standard V by the age of ten, they could leave school. An interesting contrast with the 21st century National Curriculum.

ABOVE The Throop School teachers and children in 1888.

LEFT Lily and Pascoe Marshall in 1899 at Throop School with Kasmea and Baruta, orphans who had been rescued from slave traders by Hugh Marshall, a colonial magistrate in Northern Rhodesia who grew up in Bournemouth.

nationwide to supplement those provided already for over 2 million children by the churches, private individuals and guilds. Many needed improvements or additions to buildings before they could accept increased numbers. Inspectors appointed by the Education Department assessed the efficiency of schools and the deficiency of places. Holdenhurst and Christchurch were told that they were short of 680 places for children up to 13 years old.

Both School Districts appealed against the decision. Separate Local Inquiries were held on consecutive days in December 1873. The Managers of the Bournemouth British School, who had struggled to find a suitable site to replace their school in Orchard Lane, objected to the strong lobbying by the denominational schools for their own expansion. Their strongly worded memorandum to the Inquiry emphasised that such an expansion of the Church of England schools would prevent Nonconformists (by now about half the population) 'requiring elementary instruction' from receiving it. They also argued that 'compulsory education is urgently needed throughout the district and cannot be enforced where none but Church schools exist.'[3] As a result of the Inquiry, the number of deficiencies was revised to 504 places.

The 1870 Act did not make going to school compulsory, but School Boards were allowed to make attendance compulsory between the ages of five and ten. They could also keep children at school until they were thirteen, but children over ten years old could leave if they had attained Standard Five in each of three skills or made 250 attendances for each of five years (Dunce's Pass). Codes of Regulation (which included Schedules for the teaching of various subjects) could be seen as the National Curriculum of the day since grants to schools depended on outcomes of examination by Inspectors. In Mathematics, girls were to be judged more leniently than boys — sums set for them were to be easier than for boys.

1870 to 1903

The final three decades of the 19th century saw five main developments:

The further expansion of the Church of England schools

The establishment of Roman Catholic schools

The development of the small group of British Schools as non-denominational schools

A significant number of small private schools

The establishment of technical training Institutes (described in Part 3 of this Chapter)

Several more Church of England schools were built during the 1870s. Holy Trinity School leased a site in Oxford Lane (now Oxford Road) from Mr Clapcott Dean. By the standards of the time, it was a large school with separate classrooms for boys, girls and infants plus two additional classrooms and a master's house, in an area described as ' a good centre of working-class population.'[4] It was demolished in 1972 when Wessex Way was built. In 1877, the Reverend Bennett established a small school, St. Martin's, at the corner of Holdenhurst Road and Waverley Road. A year later, he set up St. Ambrose's School in Westbourne which became a mixed and infants school in 1892 in Middle Road (now R. L. Stevenson Avenue).

In 1878, separate boys' and girls' schools opened in Moordown, and St. Andrew's School opened in 1878 for 176 children as the Malmesbury Park area was developed. In the parish of Southbourne, Dr Compton provided a small chapel school in 1876 which became permanent in 1884 on a separate site from St. Katherine's Church. This was unusual because up until then the schools and churches throughout the new town and suburbs had occupied adjacent sites.

Parents were expected to pay towards their children's education until the 1891 Education Act effectively made elementary education free.

As the number of Roman Catholics in the town increased their children needed education, but no schools were set up until after the 1870 Act. With the help of Lady Georgiana Fullerton, a nursing order of nuns, the Religious of the Cross, opened a convent and a girls' boarding school with some day pupils in 1871 in Branksome Wood Road. Some volunteer ladies began classes in one of the Windsor Cottages on Richmond Hill, but as classes needed to be organised more formally, a teacher was employed, and in

autumn 1877 St. Joseph's School started at the junction of Lansdowne and Madeira Roads. In 1878 the school moved to Avenue Road and was renamed St. Walburga's. It continued with voluntary teachers, until the Religious of the Cross were asked to take charge and began teaching there in January 1880. By January 1884, the number of children was 44: 14 boys, 8 girls and 22 infants.

The premises were only temporary, and so at Lady Fullerton's suggestion, Yelverton House in Yelverton Road was obtained largely through the generous help of her husband who gave £1,000 towards the cost. The balance of the purchase price, amounting to another £3,000, was met by a mortgage and a bank loan. The total sum of £6,000 also covered the cost of furnishing the school. The debt was paid later by two donations. The new school opened at the beginning of 1886, with 51 children. In 1887 the nuns moved to Boscombe, but remained in charge at St. Walburga's School until the end of the summer term 1889. The Branksome Wood Road convent was taken over by Sisters of Mercy, from London, in August 1887 and they re-established St. Joseph's Home. They also took charge of St. Walburga's School, one of the nuns becoming Head Mistress. Once the Department of Education had recognised the school and approved building plans, the school re-opened in reconstructed buildings in June 1894, soon after the school fees were abolished. There were exactly 100 children, with a Head Mistress and two assistant teachers. The 1899 annual report praised the standard of teaching and the excellent organisation of the School.

In Boscombe, the number of Catholic children was also growing, so in 1886 the Religious of the Cross with the help of Baroness Pauline von Hugel, started a school in a large house named Trevone with six pupils - Mary Culverwell, William McArdle and Blanche, Lily, Ruth and Fred Lambert.[5] They also bought about four and half

acres of land between Parkwood Road and the boundary of the Wentworth Estate for their new convent and the foundation stone was laid on the 6th September 1888. In 1902, a boys' preparatory school was opened and extensions were undertaken in the girls' department. Trevone was used until 1889 when Holy Cross School was built for about 100 pupils on a half acre of land between the Convent and St. James Square given to the Sisters by Mrs James. The nuns ran it without any official assistance until the Education Act 1891 provided for an additional grant of ten shillings a year for each child between the ages of three to fifteen years of age.

The small group of British Schools supported by the Nonconformist communities also took advantage of the available grants to develop as non-denominational schools. The Bournemouth British School in Orchard Lane was struggling to provide adequate accommodation. The 1873 Inspector's report condemned the building as unsatisfactory and the lease was about to run out. Unless the Holdenhurst Road branch of the school was extended, according to the Inspector, the grant would be withdrawn in April 1874, leaving 250 children without school places. In the event, the school remained open and moved to a new site on Clapcott Dean's estate in Madeira Road. It opened in April 1875 with places for 500 children, although by 1878 it had only grown to 315.

There had been considerable friction between the Managers of the British School and the church authorities, the former seeing the church as interfering directly in their proposals to develop close to the Holy Trinity site. 'Feelings were obviously very warm, and no doubt in the heat of the moment some of the protagonists expressed themselves emphatically.'[6] Even with the new school, the Managers remained concerned that working class children could never be properly educated unless non-denominational education was available. They wrote to the Education Department saying: 'Parents will continue to prefer Dame schools, though inefficient, to church schools under clerical management, and the attendance of the children will be irregular, and of too short duration as the returns show, until compulsory powers are given to an efficient and unsectarian public body.'[7] They threatened to close the schools to force the Education Department to establish a School Board, but nothing more happened.

In Pokesdown, still not part of Bournemouth, the National School was extended in 1875 by adding two classrooms and doubling its numbers. By 1881, there were 141 children and parents paid one penny a week per child up to a maximum of four pence per family. As the costs of running the school rose, so did the fees. In 1886, parents

RIGHT Cartoon of Paul Verlaine the French poet who was a tutor at the small private St. Aloysius School in Westbourne in 1876.

BELOW Cliff House Preparatory School, Soutbourne-on-Sea, 1920s.

Map showing the location of the Boscombe Corpus Christi and Boscombe Convent Schools. Reproduced with the kind permission of the Ordnance Survey.

paid three pence per child with a maximum of eight pence per family.

Other surrounding areas also established British Schools, with partial grants supplemented by weekly fees: the first at Winton in 1877 next to the Congregational Chapel in Wimborne Road. The next opened at Westbourne in 1879 in rented accommodation in Shaftesbury Terrace Back Road off Seamoor Road. Always a small school, it had 126 places at a one penny fee in 1893. The Boscombe School opened in 1879 in Gladstone Road, on land provided by Mr Moser of Carbery House. By 1893, it had 537 places and charged fees between one and two pence. It had cost £624 10 shillings to build.

Small private schools had been set up early in the town's development and, by 1866, there were 32, many providing boarding accommodation. Started in privately owned houses, always as a school for either boys or girls, they took advantage of the large gardens and the availability of farmland for their grounds which provided play areas, such as the Saugeen School in Manor Road.

Preparatory schools for boys were common. Some are better recorded simply because they attracted individuals who later became renowned, such as John Galsworthy, or writers who taught for short periods, the most noteworthy being Paul Verlaine. Few have survived to today.

The education of girls lagged behind boys, even in the private sector, but boarding and day schools for girls began to appear. Wentworth College in College Road opened in 1871 and the present-day Talbot Heath School has grown from a school established as Bournemouth High School in 1886 'to provide a first-class liberal education, grounded in Christianity, equal to that of the great public schools but available at low fees to the daughters, among others, of the professional classes.'[8]

Southbourne-on-Sea had a number of private schools, for example, Cliff House Preparatory School. Pembroke Lodge Boys' School opened in 1880 in a large house off Belle Vue Road just west of Southbourne Cliffs Hotel and Mount Pleasant (for boys) was notable for having a large playing field at its house in Dalmeny Road. There was also a cluster of girls' schools in Southbourne. St. Cuthbert's Girls opened in 1895 in Polesworth, originally the parsonage of St.. Katherine's Church, and later known as The Lodge. Miss Tucker's Girls' School began over a shop in Boscombe in 1896 and then moved to 37 Belle Vue Road, Dr Compton's house, Locksley, which he let to Miss Tucker. She bought it later the same year and renamed it Grassendale.[9] In 1897, 7 acres of farmland were bought and a large extension built in 1909. During the late 1920s and early 1930s,

The Saugeen School seen from Manor Road. The bottom photograph shows what was called the 'Big School Room'.

numbers fell so that in 1936 it closed and moved into the former Portman Lodge Boys' School house to become St. Mary's Gate, closing finally in 1987.

At the same time, the Portsmouth RC Diocese was considering establishing a boys' day grammar school in Bournemouth. However, the Grassendale site was for sale and the Jesuits bought it for £8000. They soon found that there were insufficient Catholics living in the area to support a day school and so added a boys' preparatory section. The school opened as St. Peter's in 1936 with thirty four boys and is unusual in having remained and grown to its present size of over 1700 pupils within the state system.

Private schools had continued to appear throughout the new town and by 1914 there were more than fifty private secondary schools: the most important being Bournemouth School, Bournemouth Endowed High School for Girls (now Talbot Heath), Bournemouth Collegiate School for Girls, Boscombe Convent and Knole High School. Few remain today.

Bournemouth Local Education Authority (LEA)
1903 to 1974

In November 1901, the Urban Districts of Pokesdown and Winton and the Parish of Southbourne became part of Bournemouth which became responsible for their schools (four in Pokesdown, three in Winton and one in Southbourne) from 1st July 1903. Bournemouth now had 21 schools with 7752 children, 2502 in the six Council Schools and 5097 in the 15 Non-provided Church or Trust Schools. It also became responsible for the three science, art and technical schools (which were under voluntary management), the evening schools and a centre for training pupil teachers. Joint responsibility for Bournemouth School (which had opened in 1901) rested with the Borough and Hampshire County Council.

Under the Education Act 1902, Church Schools become known as Non-provided schools, which meant that the Church owning the school remained responsible for the building of the school and the maintenance of the outside. The LEA met the day-to-day running expenses. Before finally accepting responsibility for the upkeep of the inside of the buildings, the Borough Engineer and the Chief Sanitary Inspector had to report on their condition. For example, they reported that St. Walburga's had defects to the stucco on the outer walls, repairs necessary to the roof, dampness in some of the interior walls and an unsurfaced playground. The School Managers stated at the end of March 1905 that the building had been thoroughly repaired, new lavatories added, and the existing one remodelled. The playground had been drained and gravelled. Incandescent gas lamps had been installed.

The number of schools increased rapidly: some merged and new ones were built. For example, St. Andrew's Girls

Talbot Heath School 1936.

Alma Road School after a parachute mine fell on it on November 16th 1940. The mine fell during the night when no-one was in school. The raid killed more than 50 people in the surrounding area.

The Kinson Village School staff and pupils in 1914.

Five illustrations from the 1924 prospectus for Bournemouth Collegiate School for Girls.
Top left: The Laboratory, *lower left*: The Boarders' Sitting Room, *centre*: School House, *top right*: the Tennis Courts, *lower right*: a single bedroom.

New BOURNEMOUTH SCHOOL FOR GIRLS—

LEFT Originally in two adapted houses, Woodcote and Ascham, on Gervis Road, Bournemouth School for Girls was extended into these purpose-built buildings in 1933.

ABOVE Bournemouth School for Girls moved into its present site on Castle Lane West and was formally opened in April 1961.

and Malmesbury Park Schools merged to become Alma Rd School. When it opened in March 1908 with 698 children, rising to 1033 in 1910, it was a very large school for the time outside London. In 1931, Bournemouth gained Kinson (adding Kinson, East Howe and Ensbury Park Council Schools and Talbot Village CE School) and the remaining area of Holdenhurst Parish. Holdenhurst Council School, although becoming smaller, remained open during the war years (partly to accommodate children evacuated from Southampton and Portsmouth) and then closed in 1948.

The children's health was regularly monitored. Medical inspections and records of children's' absences provide a vivid picture of the impact of infectious diseases such as measles, German measles, chicken pox, scarlet fever, influenza and mumps. Schools closed, for example the new Winton and Moordown School shut in June 1912 because of scarlet fever and closed again for a week in March 1914 for chicken pox. The regular visit of the school nurse and doctor was a very important way of identifying children with chronic conditions. Even in the 1950s, pupils could disappear from the classroom if they were diagnosed as having tuberculosis for example.

From All-age Elementary to Secondary Schools

Many of the early schools eventually became all-age elementary schools, each trying as best they could to respond to the increases in school-leaving age: in 1893 (11), 1899 (12), 1918 (14), and 1947 (15). Although Bournemouth School for Boys was founded in 1901, and the 1907 Act provided for selection of 25% of children from elementary schools on the basis of completion of a test of efficiency, most children in Bournemouth were educated in the all-age elementary schools. Bournemouth Girls' Grammar School was founded in 1918. Not until the late 1930s was there any recognition in Bournemouth of the implications of the 1902 Act for an 'educational ladder' that could facilitate the transfer of children from elementary schools to a different sort of school, even though the Haddow Report of 1926 had coined the generic name Primary School for schools educating children up to the age of 11.

The 1944 Education established grammar, secondary technical and secondary modern schools. Comprehensive schools could also be opened to combine both academic and technical education. Direct Grant schools were also set up: independent schools which offered 'free places' received direct funding from the Ministry of Education. Primary School pupils took an examination - the '11 Plus' - which allocated places in the secondary schools on the basis of aptitude and ability. Those who met the required level went to the grammar school: those who did not went to the Secondary Modern or Technical Schools. Bournemouth took a different approach. It established a dual system of Grammar Schools and Secondary Bilateral Schools. Its existing grammar schools selected 16% of eleven year olds each year.

The Bilateral Schools provided both for technical

ABOVE Bournemouth School on East Way 1950s.   BELOW Oakmead School 1970s.

Hillview School opening by Mayor Bright 8th April 1931.

education and for pupils who could follow a more academic route towards the General Certificate of Education (GCE) Ordinary 'O' Level examination. The principle was that some pupils would develop later and so should be given the opportunity to transfer to the Sixth Form of the Grammar Schools for GCE Advanced 'A' Levels. Several of the Bilateral schools had been established well before the 1944 Act. Winton Boys School, now Winton Arts and Media College, was founded in 1877. East Howe Mixed Senior School (now Kings High) traces its origins to 1937, whilst Porchester Boys was established in 1940. After the war, as the population grew a number of schools were opened, Oakmead Avonbourne Girls School in 1948, Summerbee Mixed (Now Bishop of Winchester) in 1953 and Glenmoor Girls in 1957. The Catholic Schools remained all-age elementary until 1962 when St. Thomas More opened in Iford.

Unusually, the Catholic private secondary schools developed and amalgamated to become part of the state system. In 1969, the nuns at the Marydale Convent School in Highcliffe were asked by the Bishop of Portsmouth to merge with and take over the Boscombe Convent. At the same time, the first girls transferred from Boscombe Convent to St. Peter's School, to study science courses at A Level. Change was under way, but Boscombe Convent School, as it was now called, continued to thrive and expand.

National discussions about comprehensive reorganisation encouraged the Catholic diocesan authorities to suggest in 1977 that the provision of Catholic schools in Bournemouth would be considerably strengthened, particularly in regard to Catholic Sixth Form education, if the Convent and St. Peter's School were to merge as soon as possible, with a view to the joint schools becoming a Voluntary Aided Comprehensive School. The merger began in September 1977, when the Lower Sixth Form teaching was based entirely at St. Peter's, and was completed by September 1980, when the new St. Peter's Comprehensive School was formed from the existing St. Peter's School, St. Thomas More's Secondary Bilateral School and Boscombe Convent School. The main Convent buildings, which are Listed Grade II, were sold and became the Anglo-European College of Chiropractic. The Convent Junior Department was rescued as a Charitable Trust to become St. Thomas Garnet's Independent School.

By 2009, there were 27 Junior/primary/infant schools, twelve of which were Church schools. There were nine Secondary Schools (three girls only, three boys only and three mixed), two Special Schools and six Independent Schools. The present-day pattern of schools owes a great deal to the many benefactors (often unnamed) who provided funds to rent or build the mainly church schools in the Victorian era. Private landowners, such as the Meyrick and Malmesbury Estates and the Clapcott and Cooper-Dean families, provided much of the land on which schools were built.

PART TWO

Teaching English to the World

One very distinctive feature of Bournemouth's education provision has been the establishment and growth of language schools taking students from anywhere worldwide. The importance of English as the primary language for world trade was a feature of the field of commerce after the Second World War. Many non-native speakers of English saw the need to improve their language skills and as a result their ability to trade in this new environment. An English language course could provide this. Early interest in courses came from Switzerland and Scandinavia. Erhard Waespi is usually credited with setting up the first in 1948 in Bournemouth, quickly followed by several more offering courses at the beginning of the 1950s. It subsequently became part of an educational foundation called Eurocentres under the ownership of Migros, a Swiss co-operative. Anglo-Swiss began in 1954 later becoming the Anglo-Continental School of English in Wimborne Road that we know today. The King's School of English opened its doors to international students in 1957 and Scandinavia Britannica (now Scanbrit School of English) starting in Southbourne in the late 1950s. At the same time, the late Councillor Knops arranged courses for groups of French and Belgian students in local primary schools during the summer months. In the early 1960s, Crosby House initially offered summer courses to French children before becoming the year-round school today called Richard Language College. These were the Bournemouth schools which started the fledgling English language teaching sector for the town.

Throughout the 1960s and early 1970s more international markets were added, as Iran, Kuwait and others from the Arab world involved in oil production realised that their newly established trading partnerships with the USA and Europe would benefit from improved English language skills amongst their work forces. From 1972 onwards, Southern and Central American markets developed an interest in English language courses in the UK through their family connections in Spain and Portugal and the merited reputation for quality and value that these courses had achieved through their external inspection process initially with the then Department of Education and Skills and more latterly the British Council and Accreditation UK. By the mid-1970s Bournemouth International School in Boscombe, Wessex Academy in Westover Road and Poole and the English Language Centre in Old Christchurch Road had joined the early starters of the 1950s.

Following the establishment of the national Association of Recognised English Language Schools in 1976, four Principals, the late Alf Crosby from the King's School of English, Dan Ferris from Eurocentres, the late Geoff Kitchen from the Bournemouth International School and Mike Francis from Wessex Bournemouth and Poole established a local association of schools called Mini-ARELS (the Association of Recognised English Language Schools). By the end of the 1970s, Anglo-World (now Kaplan Aspect) and Anglo-European School of English had also opened and Bournemouth was welcoming students from Japan, the Arab world, Mexico, Colombia, Ecuador, Venezuela, Argentina, Guatemala, El Salvador and Brazil, as well as the continuing European markets. In the 1980s as newer markets opened up in Indonesia, Korea, Thailand and elsewhere in South East Asia, seven more schools opened.

As schools matured in experience, the need for English Language Teaching materials with books on grammar, vocabulary, examinations and language skills was met by

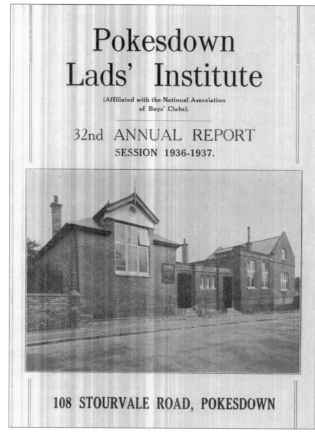

Pokesdown Lads Institute

staff in the schools, one result being the establishment of the Bournemouth English Book Centre which supplies English language schools and universities worldwide.

The global interest in learning English in the early 1980s has enabled the schools to respond robustly to downturns in individual markets. This has stood the industry in good stead as various international events have unfolded. The first Gulf War in 1991 saw bookings fall overnight by as much as 60% in some schools. Such a fall would be catastrophic in most businesses, but the sustained interest

in courses from other markets allowed the schools to end the year with a more survivable downturn of only 10%. Economic downturns in South America and the Far East challenged the schools again in the mid-1990s. Their robustness allowed them to benefit from the emerging interest in English language courses that came from Russia, the new republics and the former Eastern European countries following the fall of the Berlin Wall in the early part of the decade and a similar growth in interest from China by the end of the decade.

About £130 million of the annual tourism income of Bournemouth results from the approximately 25,000 foreign students who come to the largest centre for learning English as a foreign language in the UK outside London.

PART THREE

Institutes to University

To meet the late-Victorian need for technical training, a School of Science and Art was established at 2 St. Peter's Road in 1885. Bournemouth West School of Science and Art on Poole Hill was set up in 1889. By 1892, it had 254 pupils and was recognised in 1893 as a School of Art and Science by the Government Department for Further Education. The Bournemouth East School of Science and Art, known as the Drummond Road Art School, was originally founded as The People's Institute and run along the lines of a Mechanics' Institute until it became a School of Art in 1891. Pokesdown Art and Technical School started in 1897. Bournemouth and District Pupil Teachers' Centre was approved in 1904 but closed in 1909 as it was thought more appropriate that boys should be trained at Bournemouth School.

Programme of Classes for the Session commencing 18th September, 1901.

SUBJECT.	TEACHERS.	Days of Meeting.		CLASSES OPEN.	FEES (per term)	REMARKS.
		Day.	Hour.			
ART AND SCIENCE.						
The course of study comprises Free-hand, Model, Plane and Solid Geometry; Perspective, Drawing in Light and Shade from Models and Casts; Design; Painting in Oil, Monochrome and Water Colours; Clay Modelling; Leather & Repoussé Metal Work, &c., &c.	Mr. A. Lister Lodley	Monday	2.30 to 4.30	Sept. 23	10/-	15/-, two lessons per week
		Wednesday	6 to 9	Sept. 18	2/-	
		Friday	2.30 to 4.30	Sept. 20	2/-	15/-, two lessons per week
		Saturday	6 to 9	Sept. 21	2/-	
Building Construction ...	Mr. R. Cooper	Friday	7 to 9	Oct. 4	2/-	
Physiography ...	Mr. W. J. Woodhouse	Thursday	7 to 8	Sept. 19	2/-	Commencing Sept 14th 1901
COMMERCIAL AND TECHNOLOGICAL.						
Ambulance, Men ...	Dr. McCall	Tuesday	7.15 to 8.15	Oct. 22	5/-	
„ Women ...	„	Friday	7.15 to 8.15	Oct. 25	5/-	
Arithmetic (Commercial) ...	Mr. C. R. Pearce	Wednesday	6.30 to 7.30	Oct. 2	2/-	Book-keeping may also be taken for an inclusive Fee of 4/-
Book-keeping ...	„	Wednesday	7.30 to 8.30	Oct. 1	2/-	Shorthand may also be taken for an inclusive Fee of 3/-
Carpentry and Joinery ...	Mr. R. Cooper	Tuesday	7 to 9	Oct. 1	2/-	The Carving Class may be attended for a further Fee of 2/-
Cookery, plain ...	Miss E. Margrave	Thursday	6 to 8	Oct. 3	1/-	
„ advanced ...	„	Saturday	2.30 to 4.30	Oct. 5	7/6	
Dress-cutting and Needlework	„	Saturday	6 to 8	Oct. 5	2/-	
French ...	M. F. Pepin, B.A.	Tuesday	8 to 9	Oct. 1	2/-	
Home Nursing ...	Dr. McCall			After Christmas		Due notice will be given
Shorthand ...	Mr. C. R. Pearce	Wednesday	8.30 to 9.30	Oct. 2	4/-	See note to Book-keeping
Wood-Carving (including Clay-Modelling)	Mr. E. Arnold	Thursday	7 to 9	Oct. 3	4/-	Students may attend the Carpentry Class without further Fee.

The Pokesdown Art School on the corner of Christchurch Road and Hannington Road, and the programme of courses for 1901-02

Late 19th century Council minutes and reports show that Bournemouth was supporting university education mainly via University Extension Lectures for which there was a specific committee and a separate funding allocation - £223 (just under 10% of the whole Higher Education budget). HE then meant education beyond the school leaving age of 12 years. A small number of school leavers went on to the HE Schools. Courses were mainly in engineering, art, and a wide range of trades, supported by science and technical classes. Oxford University Extension Lectures which began in 1888 were attended by more than 11, 000 people up to 1914 when Oxford University 'passed a decree to confer the privilege of affiliation on the University Extension Centre in Bournemouth'. In 1908, correspondence with the Royal Colleges of Physicians and Surgeons requested recognition for the Poole Hill School (then the Science College) 'as an Institution for the instruction of medical and dental students in Chemistry and Physics.'[10]

In 1903, the Education Committee inherited the three Science, Art and Technical Schools previously grant-aided by the Technical Instruction Committee, and opened a School of Commerce at Avenue Chambers, in Avenue Road, in rooms rented from the Council's Tramways Committee. There was a very strong view that all this work should be amalgamated. Two properties in Gervis Road (Ascham House and Woodcote) were offered by Mr. J.J. Norton JP for a Central School of Science, Art and Technology. Opposition by residents prevented the properties and sites being used as proposed. Five years later, the Authority purchased two adjoining Lansdowne properties, Peachley (£4000) and Strathearn (£4100), at the corner of Meyrick Road and Christchurch Road. On 31st January 1910, the School Buildings Committee reported that Sir George Meyrick had approved the plans and the Local Government Board had approved a loan of £22,955 repayable in 30 years. Building started on 4th April 1910 and the Bournemouth Municipal College was opened formally by the President of the Board of Education on 29th May 1913. The four separate institutes were then closed and work centralised in two

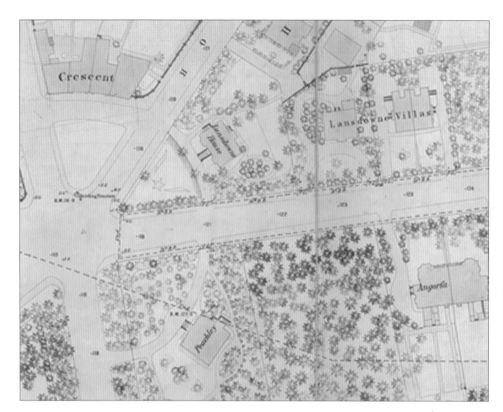

ABOVE Peachley in 1870 - one of the properties given to provide land for a Technical College at the Lansdowne. Reproduced with the kind permission of the Ordnance Survey.

ABOVE RIGHT The Municipal College and Central Library 1913.

new buildings, the larger providing accommodation for Art, Science, Commerce and Domestic Science and the smaller for Technology. A new central library was added and a clock tower (at an extra cost of about £1,200) since the Education Committee felt that such an important building should be an architectural credit to the town.

The payment and priority given to specific subjects is particularly interesting. The Education Committee

Minutes in October 1909[11] record the general hourly pay as 2 shillings and sixpence per hour. However, the hourly rate for Power and Heat Engines (Advanced), Geometry and Machine Construction (Adv.) and Science was 6 shillings (the highest rate). The next highest hourly rate (5 shillings) was paid for two subjects, Builders' Quantities and Commercial Geography. Teaching German paid 4 shillings, but French only paid 3 shillings.

In 1929, the Education Committee approved the establishment of a day commercial course at the college. By 1939, the Municipal College of Technology and Commerce was providing full-time courses for a range of 'Inter' subjects with BSc General, Special and Engineering

degree courses. In 1940, it began courses to train men and women for the war effort, the first providing workshop instruction for making munitions, quickly followed during 1941-2 by full-time courses for radio mechanics, with special reference to radar. In 1942, the College began training engineering cadets who were required to have good educational background and given an intensive course to allow them to continue to engineering degrees.

In 1958, a catering unit was built in the former playground of Bournemouth School for Girls and in 1962 the Department of Commerce and Languages moved to the former Prince's Hotel in Knyveton Road. The Department offered London University external degrees:

foundation stone for the Bournemouth College of Technology's new buildings was laid at Talbot Campus in Poole! Construction of new buildings on what was the largest farm in Talbot Village was completed by September 1976. Following County reorganisation in 1974, the College merged with Weymouth College of Education to become the Dorset Institute of Higher Education. Higher National Diploma and Certificate (HND/C) and Science degree courses remained at the Lansdowne. When Weymouth College closed, degree courses then

Aerial photograph of the College Site 1930s and a prospectus from the same period.

BSc (Econ) with specialisms in Geography, Economics, Politics and from 1963 BA General (3 subjects from English, History, Geography, Law, French and Economics). In 1973, the London degrees were replaced by two courses: BA (Hons) Combined Studies and BSc Catering validated by the Council for National Academic Awards (CNAA).

Bournemouth had earlier set up a committee to foster its case for a university when a group of new ones was proposed nationally in the 1960s. The bid was unsuccessful and when the Polytechnics were also established, Bournemouth narrowly missed being in the first thirty.

Nevertheless, the Borough recognised the need for new premises and on 31st October 1973 the

ABOVE Bournemouth University – Poole House. The first of the buildings occupied on the Talbot Campus in 1976, with the Geological Terrace in the foreground.

LEFT Bournemouth University, the Sir Michael Cobham Library.

validated by the University of Southampton and the nationally renowned HND in Practical Archaeology, moved to Bournemouth and were integrated with the CNAA courses. The Further Education courses were transferred to a new Bournemouth and Poole College of FE in 1974 with premises at the Lansdowne and in Poole, and the Art College became The Arts Institute (now the Arts University College at Bournemouth).

The late 1980s saw a very intensive period of course development with many unique and innovative courses

developed in conjunction with related industries. The emphasis was on degrees which provided both rigorous intellectual development and vocational education, and included one of only two undergraduate degrees in Tourism Studies in the late 1980s. For courses to be approved by the CNAA, staff had to provide strong evidence of scholarship and/or professional expertise in their field. As a result, in 1990, the Dorset Institute was re-designated Bournemouth Polytechnic and then became Bournemouth University with inauguration on 27th November 1992.

Innovative and unique Masters programmes in such areas as European Tourism Management, European Enterprise Management and Coastal Zone Management and strong research and consultancy in Archaeology and Computer Animation provided a firm foundation for the development of the University. The buildings were extended on the Talbot Campus site during the 1990s and a number of office premises as well as the former Bournemouth Fire Station were taken over by the University in Holdenhurst and Christchurch Roads. By 2009, the University had over 17,000 students and claimed a strong reputation for its wide range of high quality undergraduate and postgraduate courses geared to the professions and for its high levels of graduate employment.[12]

ELEVEN

AN ADAPTIVE ECONOMY

Michael Stead and Vincent May

A national land use survey was carried out in the 1930s and this shows in red the areas described as agriculturally unproductive. The areas of close-built housing contrast with the much larger area in purple (houses with gardens, orchards, nurseries and allotments). Areas in brown are arable land (mostly north of Castle Lane) and yellow depicts areas of heathland and similar rough ground. Reproduced from the 1932 Ordnance Survey map.

Chapter Eleven

TOWNS DO NOT GROW without people developing businesses, providing for the everyday needs of the general population and stimulating their growth. Bournemouth is no exception, but it did not start from

The west side of The Square in 1864 and (*below*) approximately the same view four years later, showing some of the town's earliest shops.

an existing fishing harbour or a port, like most of the towns along the South Coast of England. It grew, as other chapters have shown, because people saw the commercial opportunities within the resort and adapted and built upon changes in the wider economy. Although manufacturing industry and unsightly buildings, such as gasworks, power stations and brickworks, provided employment and essential services, they were generally sited outside the early town. This practice has continued to the present-day, with for example university buildings just inside Poole, out-of-town shopping centres along the northern axis of the town, industrial estates in West Howe and sewage treatment plant along the River Stour. The aircraft industry which employed many Bournemouth residents from the 1940s onwards was concentrated within Christchurch at Somerford and Hurn. As will become apparent later, when office developments were seen as acceptable, their establishment was prevented by regional planning policies.[1] Businesses relocating from London and the South-East were built in Poole instead. Two centuries after its very small beginnings, Bournemouth is part of a large internationally important conurbation stretching along the coast from Highcliffe in the east to Upton in the west and inland to Ringwood, Verwood and Wimborne, but its core remains non-industrial.

The Early Economy

In 1800, William Dean, of Littledown House, William Castleman, an attorney and George Adams set up a bank, the Christchurch, Wimborne and Ringwood Bank. William Castleman's son Edward was married to Ann Fryer. Her parents were William Rolls Fryer, a Dorset banker, and Elizabeth Gulliver, daughter of the area's most famous smuggler, Isaac Gulliver. Like all such banks at the time, it provided loans to farmers for drainage and land improvement[2] as agriculture expanded and became more mechanised. However, George Bruce also speculates that the bank also made loans to 'notable smugglers'[3] which contributed to its prosperity. One of Dean's three daughters, Mary, married William Clapcott of Holdenhurst in about 1803 and joined the bank at the same time.

William Dean died in 1812 and his son-in-law succeeded him as a partner in the bank. Over the next six years, the bank began to lose money, especially as Clapcott, like many others of the time, speculated in overseas land and mining, and the bank failed in 1827. However the contribution of this family to the present-day economy should not be underestimated. Sadly it is often overlooked in the history of the town because much of the estate did not become part of the resort until 1931, when Holdenhurst was absorbed into Bournemouth. Sale

ABOVE Enoch White's Nurseries on Holdenhurst Road in 1865 is typical of the businesses which sprang up along the main roads established at the time of the 1805 enclosure.

LEFT Outside the town, the main settlements were still small. This photograph is of a farm and pond on the road to Wick in 1885.

of land for housing developments in the 1920s and 1930s, alongside very generous support of charitable causes, including land for schools in the late 19th century, and the sale of the Littledown House land to Bournemouth Council in 1973, have left an indelible mark on the infrastructure of the town.

At the same time as the Christchurch, Ringwood and Wimborne Bank began to struggle financially, the Tregonwells had begun to develop their small sea-bathing place at Bourne and the heathland had been enclosed. Nevertheless, most economic activity between 1810 and 1850 was still concentrated in the villages of the Stour

Cecil Biles, the last miller at Throop, 1980.

Tregonwell Estate Accounts June 1846

Debit		£ s d	Credit		£ s d
June 6th	Piper's Bill for sweeping all the Chimneys at the Mansion	1 6 -	June 7th	Received for 1 Months Rent for Cottage at Moordown	- 5 -
	Joy's Bill for Sawing ~~~	2 12 -	13th	Recd of Mr Boyle for 1 month Do	- 5 -
20th	Obscured 6 Weeks	3 - -		Recd of Mr Osborn for 1 Month Do	- 5 -
	Baverstock 6 Weeks	2 18 6	15th	Recd of Mr Timson for Pasturing of Donkey 32 weeks at 6 fr Week	- 16 -
	Man & Boys Assisting mowing etc	- 15 -		Recd for ?? of Mr Pirkin	- 11 7
	Butler 6 Weeks	2 8 -			£2 2 7
	Mrs Holdsworth 6 Weeks	1 10 -			
	Jane Coney 4 Do.	1 10 -			
	Beer for Men while Mowing & Haymaking	- 11 5			
	Thos. Conways Bill for Brick	5 1 9			
* 9 April	W. Osborn for Sawing	10 17 9			
*	Best for Gravel and Thatch	3 10 9			
	Bakley for Corn	4 - -			
		£40 .1 .2			
	Dedcnt from Cᵗ Acct	2 2 7			
	Paid As fr Acct Book	£37 18 7			
	Wm Rebbeck's signature				

valley. In 1841 in the nearby villages along the Stour, there were six laundresses, four chain-makers, working at the Fusee factory in Christchurch, five bricklayers, three brick makers and 219 agricultural labourers.

Bourne in the early 19th century was not dissimilar in some ways to the Bournemouth it would become. The 1841 census shows a place where people were trying to decide what the way forward would be. With a complement of seven coastguards, customs and excise was one of the biggest fields of employment, although these were the dying days of the great smuggling industry. The beer seller and inn keeper in the marine village would have needed to be far more clandestine than their predecessors if they had dealings with contraband. There were wealthy residents of independent means. Some like Nathaniel Polhill would go on to play a significant role in building Bournemouth.

Significantly four of the wealthiest residents were women, including Henrietta Tregonwell and Mary Clapcott, both of whom did more than their husbands or fathers to establish the reputation of Bournemouth. It was also a woman, Maria Tomer, who ran the Bath Hotel and was the town's first 'house agent'. One of Mrs Tomer's most significant guests was Harriet Thynne, sister-in-law to the 3rd Marchioness of Bath.

In 1841, contact with the network of aristocratic families was about the closest thing anyone could have to a modern broadband internet connection, with family names and pedigrees being much like email addresses, so Harriet was just the sort of society lady whose good report would be imperative for the success of a fashionable resort. Her husband Charles' cousin Georgina's husband Frederick West (perhaps the connections were more like those over-long webpage addresses) was also in Bournemouth, living next to Mrs Tregonwell, and his children Georgiana and Cornwallis West were staying at the Bath Hotel, with their 'aunt' Harriet. These connections linked via marriage to to the Earls of Shaftesbury, the Duke of Westminster, and Winston Churchill's stepfather, and bring members of all these families to Bournemouth.

Scattered through the exclusive streets of Bourne in 1841, there was also a clergyman and an attorney, and in the lower orders a butcher and a blacksmith, three gardeners, a lodging-house keeper, an ostler and

two bakers. Bourne was a work in progress, and had the nucleus of the construction industry which was soon going to advance across the vast heath. There was a builder, a carpenter, two bricklayers and a labourer. But it seemed that people had not decided quite what form

Bell's Grocery on Poole Hill in 1855.

Bournemouth was going to take, because William Hillier had West Hill Farm, where the Highcliff Hotel now stands. By 1851, William had moved to Lytchett Minster to make bricks and tiles. The burgeoning building industry was a god-send to the impoverished people of Dorset.

In Bourne itself, William Rebbeck was already a house and estate agent (established in 1845), as well as agent for the Tregonwell Estate. The estate accounts for June 1846 show that almost all the costs came from the traditional activities of rural England (see opposite page).

Sydenham's Library and Reading Room, the Belle Vue Boarding House and the Bath Hotel all existed by 1850. Eliza Hardman was listed as a bathing machine proprietor with one bathing attendant. George Fox was not only a stationer (established in 1846), but also a dealer in minerals and fossils. Nine individuals were involved with building trades, including brickmaking, bricklaying and carpentry. The Reverend Edward Bayly and Susan Welch were involved with what is described as a boarding school and one individual is listed for each of the National Schools in Bournemouth and Holdenhurst.

Hunt and Co's 1851 *Directory* shows that in the present-day area of Bournemouth, including Kinson, there were 30 farmers, almost all in the villages and 13 in such related trades as dairyman, miller, blacksmith and maltster.

The Winton Blacksmiths in the 1890s.

Townsend Cottage in Holdenhurst.

There were 14 butchers, grocers and bakers, and six inns. There were two shoemakers in Holdenhurst, one in Kinson and James Sydenham is described as a bootmaker. The only solicitor was in Kinson and the only surgeon in Bournemouth.

By 1861, Holdenhurst parish had twelve laundresses, as by now Bournemouth was producing enough dirty sheets for a complete laundry industry to grow up around Moordown. There were six glove knitters, seven dressmakers, a coal dealer and a potter with four pottery labourers (one of the few manufacturing activities at the time). The most important jobs were in building: a brick & lime carrier, a brick maker & burner, a brickyard labourer, nine bricklayers (there were ten more in Kinson), a bricklayer's apprentice, thirteen bricklayer's labourers, seven sawyers, seven carpenters (with another nine in Kinson), two builder's labourers, sixteen carters and forty general labourers. As the building trades grew, the number of agricultural labourers had fallen, to just seventy.

Commercial and Industrial Beginnings

The first bank to open a branch in the town was the Midland in 1850, followed by the Wilts and Dorset Banking Company Ltd and Barclays in 1859. The Boscombe Conservative Cooperative Land and Building Society was set up in 1851, followed a decade later by the Portman Building Society. The town was beginning to attract the businesses which supported its first phase of expansion and the 1860s saw other beginnings, including the Scientific Motors Ltd Garage in 1863, Ottershaw's Garage in 1864 and the Bournemouth Brewery in 1866. Henry Joy's Southbourne Terrace (where W.H.Smith's store now stands alongside The Square) provided the first row of shops in 1863, followed in 1866 by his Joy's Arcade, now simply The Arcade. Bright's Store opened in 1866. Then in the late 1870s, all the major banks begin to set up branches, a reaction to the rapid expansion of the town as a tourist resort and a rapidly increasing resident population.

Towns need services, but as Keith Rawlings has said[4] the late Victorian council was not prepared to have in the town industrial buildings such as the Bournemouth Gas and Water Company. This company provided the first gaslight in the town's streets in 1864, 50 years after London. Electric street lighting took even longer to reach all parts of the town. The gas works was in Poole, but was then sited in 1898 at Bourne Valley in Poole with 60 subscribers and producing enough electricity for 3000 lamps, but parts of Kinson had no electric street lighting until 1950s. The Bournemouth and Poole Electricity Company also built a power station in Christchurch in 1903. Water supply towers were built in the Upper Pleasure Gardens, providing

Old Christchurch Road. Adelaide Villas and Church Glen in 1860 before Joy's Arcade was built.

This 1888 view across the Square from Terrace Mount shows very well the town as it become, with a mixture of developments around Old Christchurch Road and, in the background, housing and commercial developments between Richmond Hill and the Lansdowne. The shops in Southbourne Terrace can still be seen today, but the tree-lined Richmond Hill has been replaced by shops and offices.

The water tower in Stourfield Gardens which was one of the areas reserved for turbary in the Enclosure of 1805 and later became one of the five municipal parks.

the first piped water to Bourne in 1863 and at Palmerston Road in Boscombe. The first ferro-concrete water tower in the country was built later in Meyrick Park and for many years also served as the location for the sunshine recorder for the resort. The Bournemouth & District Waterworks Company (founded in 1863) built waterworks in Iford Lane to pump water from the river up to a water tower

The old waterworks on Iford Lane, where in 1898, Vladimir Tchertkov set up a printing works. Books which were banned in Russia were printed here and then smuggled back into the country from which he and a group of others had been exiled. He not only printed many of Tolstoy's works, but also kept the original manuscripts safely at Tuckton House.

at Seafield Gardens in Southbourne. The waterworks were abandoned because the water was too silty, but became the printing press for Tolstoy's works when the Russian refugee Count Vladimir Tchertkov took it over in 1900 and set up the Free Age Press. Apart from the church towers and spires and the chimneys of the brickworks, these were the tallest landmarks in the town.

Potentially the most important feature of the town's services was the one hidden from view, the sewers. The 1856 Improvement Act said that it was 'expedient that provision should be made for the more efficient paving, sewerage, drainage' and it was not at all in keeping with a healthy image that the streets were dirty and polluted. Thomas Hawkseley, the most distinguished water engineer in British history, provided advice on the Commissioners' first drainage scheme and another famous engineer, Sir

Joseph Bazalgette, advised them on the drainage works in the growing eastern part of the town. By the 1880s Bournemouth had 46 miles of sewers taking the sewage from almost all the buildings into three long drains (outfalls) 'well into the region of tidal currents.'[5]

Once the dirty water disappeared it was forgotten, and the citizens were reluctant to pay for improvements. For the year 1896-7, the town spent £1613 on sewerage, but many properties still had drains which carried water to the cliff-top. By the 1930s, most foul sewage was discharged after mechanical disintegration into the sea through a number of outfalls. Sewage from Northbourne & Kinson went to a sewage treatment works at Ensbury built in 1926. Most surface water ran into the River Stour or the Bourne Stream. Bournemouth saw the benefits of a

Castlehurst in Castlemain Avenue in 1899 with a carter's truck in front.

By the end of the 19th century, the Square and the streets around it (seen here from Old Christchurch Road) had developed into a busy shopping area. An invalid carriage is just to the right of the lady with an umbrella, and there are numerous horse-drawn carriage and wagons and a lone tram.

ABOVE The Square in about 1900, where Leverett and Frye, Grocers and Fruiterers, advertise a wide range of alcoholic beverages, not the least being Gilbey's Invalid Port.

ABOVE LEFT & LEFT Two views of Christchurch Road, Boscombe, in 1910.

joint sewerage board with Poole & Christchurch because this would ensure the quality of water along the whole frontage of the resort and its neighbours. Talks began in 1934, progress was slow and nothing more happened until 1955 when Bournemouth decided to construct its own sewage treatment works at Holdenhurst. Work started in the 1960s when a sewer eight miles long was built behind the cliffs to intercept all foul water and take it inland to the wastewater treatment plant at Holdenhurst. Once treated, the clean water would be discharged into the River Stour. Most of the sewers were diverted by 1974, except for those from Alum Chine and Southbourne which were connected in 1976. Some so-called combined sewers still

ABOVE LEFT Robert's Grocers at 262 Windham Road in 1910.

LEFT Beale's 'Fancy Fair'.

ABOVE Rebbeck's Corner in about 1905, with Old Christchurch Road and the spire of St Peter's Church in the centre.

discharge during storms.[6]

By 1903, Mate's *Directory* is dominated by service trades such as accountants, shops and estate agents. 71 builders and contractors are listed alongside 10 bookbinders, 61 boot and shoemakers, 37 cabinet makers, and 9 trunk manufacturers. There are 19 farriers and smiths, 13 saddle and harness makers and one horse clothing manufacturer. There were by then over 170 hotels and boarding houses, an increase of 234% since 1871.

Bournemouth of the early 20th century is the Bournemouth of John Elmes Beale. He came to Bournemouth when it was frequented by dukes and earls, and he established a department store with a reputation for providing the essentials for fine living. He built his business by solid industry, selling tin buckets and wooden spades from his 'Fancy Fair' to the masses who were brought to Bournemouth by the railways. Another

BOURNEMOUTH — Hotel Metropole. — LL.

The BOURNEMOUTH HYDRO

View from Marine Balcony

Close to Bournemouth Hotel

The Burlington Hotel Boscombe

J.W.S. 1856.

A BED FOR THE NIGHT

A sample selection of some of Bournemouth's hotels

Opposite page (top left): The Metropole (1906), (top right) The Bournemouth Hydro (1916), (centre) The Durley Dean Hydro (1900), (bottom left) The Burlington Hotel (1856), (bottom right) Hotel Mont Dore,
This page: (top left) Woodleigh Tower Private Hotel (1913), (top right) Highland Private Hotel (1930), (bottom left) The Towercliffe Hotel (1930), (bottom right) The Grosvenor (1930)

prestigious business, the multi-billion pound 'Forte Group', was an example of where you can get, by starting with some hard graft on the streets of Bournemouth. Rocco Forte moved from Scotland to live in a Winton side-street and took over a branch of Malmesbury and Parson's Dairy at 108 Old Christchurch Road, where from 1927-1932 he ran the J. & R. Forte Ice Cream Parlour. This provided the capital for his son Charles to open the first milk bar in London in 1933, which expanded into the famous catering and hotel businesses.

One important but poorly researched aspect of the early

RIGHT A Vickers Viscount under construction in Vickers-Armstrong's production hangar at Hurn airport in 1953. Courtesy of Bournemouth Aviation Museum

BELOW A BAC One-Eleven on roll-out at Bournemouth Hurn airport in 1963. Courtesy of Bournemouth Aviation Museum

ABOVE The Argyle Family Laundry soon after the Second World War broke out.

BELOW Landcheet Stores in Latimer Road at the beginning of the Second World War.

20th century life of Bournemouth is the role of refugees from Europe. The Russians with their printing works in the old waterworks off Iford Lane, the Jewish community who provided a significant number of the hotels as well as being involved in commerce throughout the town and many others brought a strong sense of how to succeed. Refugees from Europe not only broadened the industrial base of the town but played a vital role in engineering design. For example, Ludwig Loewy came to Bournemouth in 1933 and set up The Hydropress Company in 1935. He and his brother were born in Bohemia in what is now the Czech Republic. There, they designed machine tools, forging and extrusion presses and rolling mills, but came to Britain in the mid 1930s to escape the oppression which was spreading through their home country. Ludwig persuaded the British Government to build extrusion presses for aircraft production, an action which together with similar action by his brother in the USA has been described as decisive in the outcome of the war. There have been few industries in Bournemouth's history, but even fewer have been praised as highly as Ludwig and his brother were in a speech by United States Senator Joseph Liebermann in 2005. They 'were problem-solving engineers whose work revolutionized the way we build airplanes and rockets and helped us win World War II, the Cold War and the Space Race. It is people like the Loewys that move us forward. People with the knowledge and vision to see a barrier to break or a problem to solve and say: "Here is how we can fix this. Here is how we can make this better." '[7] Ludwig was living in Bath Road when he was naturalized in 1942 and died shortly afterwards.[8] The company, Loewy Engineering Ltd, subsequently moved to Wallisdown Road in Poole.

The Second World War brought a marked change to the economy. Government offices were moved from London to avoid the Blitz. Large numbers of service men and women were based in and around the town. The airfields at Christchurch and Hurn, the aircraft industry itself and the Military Engineering Experimental Establishment (MEXE) at Christchurch brought workers from other parts of the country as well as providing local employment.

Post-war Development –
What the town might have become

The shape of the town before the Second World War was largely a result of the early separation of places such as Winton, Springbourne and Boscombe from the hotel dominated cliff-top and the original Commissioners' core. After the war, Bournemouth, by now within a boundary which remains to the present-day, could look forward to rebuilding and developing within a new framework of legislation enacted by the Labour Government headed by Prime Minister Attlee.

As John William Moore, managing director of Wilkins Bakery and Mayor of Bournemouth, sat in his parlour in 1946 reading a document just delivered to the Council, he was presented with proof that the town fathers had turned for help in re-invigorating the economic fortunes of Bournemouth to a man who viewed industry as a distasteful activity. It should be confined to places where it could do no harm. The document was focused on correcting what he saw as the faults of Bournemouth: namely where it was built, the shape of its roads and the design of its houses.

That man was the newly knighted, renowned town planner Sir Patrick Abercrombie, best known for his role in the post-war re-planning of London.[9]

Abercrombie, in his *Plan for Bournemouth Poole*

Sir Patrick Abercrombie's design for the approach to Boscombe Pier.

Amongst Sir Patrick's Abercrombie's proposals for redeveloping the town were his plans for the Lansdowne .

and Christchurch in 1946, defined the industry of the conurbation as 'the ministration of National Health', not a new description for in 1934 Smith had described health and pleasure as the resort's 'staple manufactures'.[10] Abercrombie elaborated: 'the pursuit of health and recreation, absolutely essential to national well-being on holiday and in retirement from work, . . . will increase in intensity and in extensiveness and this favoured coast will respond.'

Abercrombie defined three types of industry: 'basic' industry which underpins economic prosperity and results in exportable products; 'local' concerned with the needs of the area, and 'balancing' industry, introduced to diversify and to give maximum employment.

He judged that a 'basic' economy, with heavy industry, best suited Poole and Hamworthy. Light industry would be strictly confined to several areas in the conurbation where it was most needed. The centre of light industry would be a zone north of the railway in Bournemouth, where it would become 'an industrial cell within the recreational pattern of public open space'. A new area in west Bournemouth was 'advised' for light industry, but no other part of the town. Local industry, such as petrol stations and car repairs, would be allowed to survive as a very small part of residential districts and on trading estates, providing alternative employment for families in the leisure industry.

Abercrombie assumed Bournemouth to have spread amorphously. He felt obliged to impose upon it a structure of 28 Neighbourhood Units of about 8,000 people each, 'within which the local inhabitant could go about his or her daily work or the child walk in safety to school.' Although this was not taken up at the time, some of the later estates, such as Townsend, follow a similar model.

Abercrombie revealed his antipathy towards 'industry' in his detailed plans for the Winton Neighbourhood Unit, which is offered as an exemplar of what should happen across the conurbation. 'Business' would be separated from streets carrying traffic, and there would be business centres in the neighbourhood units. In decreeing that 'small compact groups of shops could also be located in residential areas and this policy would be effective in eliminating the promiscuous spotting of individual shops', he makes corner shops sound like a disease.

We now recognise that land-uses have networks. There is a causal nexus that links the smart office of the accountant to her client the newsagent and to his customer the garage mechanic. People had put their lives into developing this messy but functioning network, yet Abercrombie decreed that 'straggling business along major streets, inconvenient for shoppers and harmful to neighbouring uses should be eliminated'.

Also in his sights was 'shabby and unsightly development with advertising signs, dilapidated or flimsy temporary structures, vacant and neglected properties and poorly cared for vacant lots, which damage the whole city and reduce property values' and the 'uncontrolled shifting of business centres' and uneconomic overbuilding of small stores and shops'. Now that nearly 70 years of Town Planning has failed to cure towns of vacant lots, we accept that the rubble-strewn fenced-off site awaiting redevelopment is always with us.

In Abercrombie's Utopian version of Winton 'all the light industry has been removed from the area, as

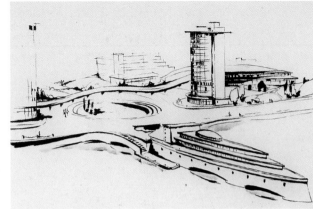

The plan and the reality. On the right is Sir Patrick Abercrombie's design for Bournemouth Pier. The futuristic boat in the foreground is a far cry from the paddle steamer *Waverley*, the world's last sea-going paddle steamer and still a regular visitor to Bournemouth.

this is scheduled definitely as a residential unit. The only industries for which space is allowed are those indispensable to the daily life of the inhabitants such as service garages, laundries, small jobbing builders, bakeries etc.'

Abercrombie's vision of Bournemouth failed to recognise that the centrally located Victorian heartland constituted a vital leisure industry, which had been devastated when all the major hotels had been requisitioned for troop accommodation during the war, and which needed to be sympathetically revived.

One of the worst decisions made by the first developers, Abercrombie explained, was to build Bournemouth in the wrong place: 'A less suitable place than the present 'Square' for a busy town centre could, in many ways, hardly be conceived'. He then suggested that Bournemouth town centre should be moved to the Lansdowne. The Square was to become the 'West Precinct' and there would be two new traffic bridges over the Bourne Stream: one (which

was never built) close to the present bandstand, and the other (which was) at Pier Approach.

It might be unfair to divorce Abercrombie from the issue he saw as a paramount problem – vehicular traffic. Britain's population between 1928 and 1938 went from 44.3 million to 46.2, and car numbers rose from 2.05 million to 3.09. By 1938, Britain had 1 car for every 15 people. Bournemouth had 1 car for every 3.8, prompting him to write: 'the enormous increase and influx of modern traffic into its tangled streets and ill-designed centres has largely contributed to and greatly aggravated a post-war planning problem of the utmost difficulty and urgency'.

Despite all the inadequacy, as Abercrombie saw it, of how Bournemouth had been allowed to grow, Bournemouth had managed an exceptionally successful growth since its Victorian genesis. So Abercrombie's beautifully painted plans and wonderfully constructed models for his new version of Bournemouth were put away in filing cabinets and store rooms, waiting for the time when they could be

consigned to the depths of a distant depot. The council in Hull had done much the same, and in 1956 it fell to the Borough Engineer and Surveyor, W. L. Clowes, to write a Development Plan for Bournemouth.

Clowes' Development Plan

Clowes did not expect the Development Plan to be revolutionary in character, but sought 'to enhance the character of Bournemouth as already established in the past.' His vision was to increase the existing 100 acres of industrial land to 142 acres, and to include Class III and IV industries, as defined in the Use Classes Order 1950.

Class III, light industry, was any activity that could go on 'without detriment to the amenity of that area by reason of noise, vibration, smell, fumes, smoke, soot, ash, dust or grit'. Light industry was needed, but not where it

Insurance offices and Crown Courts at Castle Lane East.

would depreciate the town's primary function as a health and pleasure resort'. The zones proposed for light industry would be at Wallisdown, between Ringwood Road and Francis Avenue (where Max Factor established premises), at Muscliff between Castle Lane and Broadway (Unigate), at Springbourne, around Holdenhurst Road (Wilkins Bakery), in the town centre near the railway stations (Kennedys, B&Q), and south of Boscombe Station.

Class IV, general industry, would be at Wallisdown. Both Wallisdown and West Howe had areas set aside for surface mineral working.

Clowes noted that less than 1% of the population of Bournemouth insured for work was employed in agriculture and fishing, whereas the national figure was over 5%. National employment in engineering and textiles was nearly 16 times than in Bournemouth, but employment in jewellery, woodworking, printing and local government was similar both in the town and nationally.

Building, theatres, and laundries were numerically above the national average. Bournemouth's main employment was in four areas: transport and communication took nearly 12% of the insured workforce, the national figure was barely 8%. The distributive trade employed 19% compared to a national 10%. Professional services were well represented, over 13%, in contrast to 17% nationally. As would be expected, Bournemouth's greatest employment was in hotels and catering at nearly 20%, dwarfing the national figure of 3%.

Despite the war, building, distribution and hotels were all recovering. The only reversal of trends was in government service, which had risen ninefold in Bournemouth during the war, as civil servants scurried to the south coast to escape the Blitz, and then swiftly moved on when Bournemouth was bombed too.

The Town Hall, offices and apartments on Richmond Hill: November 2009.

Clowes' plan, with modifications, was finally approved in 1956 and served Bournemouth for nearly half a century. The industrial zones he intended for Springbourne and Boscombe were never built. Instead an industrial estate was built at Yeoman's Road. His heliport in King's Park remained an aspiration only.

His successor, E. C. Whittaker, revised the Clowes plan in 1966. In our days of global greengrocery, Whittaker's statement on agriculture has become astonishing: 'The majority of the land north of Castle Lane is at present used for agriculture and grows a quantity of the fresh vegetables used daily in Bournemouth.'

Whittaker admitted that one of the biggest challenges had been whether to allow the growth of backyard light industry. A small workshop with a couple of employees could present few problems, but when the owners wanted to enlarge the business and bring in more workers, this

Old Christchurch Road remains the town's principal shopping street, a role it has enjoyed since the first shops opened in the early 19th century.

could be detrimental to the neighbourhood. Generally, such expansion would be constrained. As one solution, Clowes' industrial estates had been a great success: 'the privately owned factory estate at Wallisdown has been, to a large extent, occupied by new industries, some of them formed by existing Bournemouth companies.'

Functioning industrial land had risen to 123 acres on the 142 acres set aside for industry. Whittaker proposed an increase to 197 acres. This compared to 1417 acres of public open space, 1679 acres of agriculture and 7107 acres of housing. One far-reaching development was the arrival of 'Your store for Super Value – Woolco'. Woolco opened at the Hampshire Centre in 1967. To many people, Woolco <u>was</u> the Hampshire Centre. Designed with parked cars in mind, the Centre was based on the model of the American shopping mall. At the time, it was a rare example of out-of–town shopping.[11] Reaction in 1967 to Woolco was polarised. Some argued that Bournemouth had enough shops in the town centre, others were attracted to it because of the easy parking and different style of shopping.

The Hampshire Centre was demolished in 2003 and redeveloped on a larger scale as Castlepoint with ASDA, Marks and Spenser, Sainsbury's and B&Q as its largest units. In 1982 when the Hampshire Centre was still the only out-of-town shopping mall in the area, there were 1826 shops in Bournemouth Borough, four areas accounted for 52.2% of the shops and 74.89% of the floorspace, almost 50% being in Bournemouth centre.[12] By 2005 the same four areas accounted for 51.4% of the shops and 66.8% of the floor space. Castlepoint had 3.1% of the total 1443 shops but 25% of the floorspace. Although the number of

The Square, the heart of the town.

shops had fallen by 21%, the area of floorspace had risen by 21.3% with Castlepoint accounting for 25%. Boscombe and Winton had both increased in floorspace, but Bournemouth had fallen from 84527 to 70893 sq m.[13]

The next significant set of proposals for the town were set out in the North Bournemouth Plan, which provided for the Yeoman's Road industrial estate, and then the Bournemouth Local Plan. The *Bournemouth Development Plan* of 1966 (known in daily office life as the 'Town Map') was barely in place when the Local Government Reorganisation of 1974 moved Bournemouth and Christchurch from Hampshire into Dorset. New County Councils were established with an extraordinary reach of powers. The books on the shelves of Bournemouth's libraries went from the control of the Borough Librarian at the Lansdowne Central Library to the County Librarian at Dorchester. The large-scale decisions about town planning in Bournemouth were to be taken at a county level, as set out in the *South East Dorset Structure Plan* of 1980, and its First Amendment of 1990.

Fine detailing, so long as it conformed to the Structure Plan, was carried out at Bournemouth, and so the Town Map was joined by a variety of ancillary planning policies, most significantly two Local Plans for Boscombe and the Town Centre. Conservation Areas were designated from 1974 onwards. In a rather belated response to the rampant Abercrombieism, which had seen many of Bournemouth's Victorian and Edwardian villas replaced by blocks of flats, areas were designated where the Council would seek to preserve the existing character. The new Local Plan 'Conservation and Townscape' set out 25 policies to protect the historic environment.

The Borough Local Plan 1995

In 1995 the Bournemouth Borough Local Plan was published. Its most significant objective was, arguably, to 'enhance the economic and environmental well-being of the borough' that is to develop the local economy and increase the number of available jobs. The Council could do very little proactively, beyond promoting the town and ensuring that local bureaucracy did not hinder job creation. There had been more employment during the 1980s, until it was reversed by the national recession of the 1990s, with unemployment rising to 16% compared to a historic rate of 6%. By 1993 there were 7,892 unemployed people in Bournemouth, a slight fall to 13.3% as service industries began to become more important.

The Plan said that manufacturing industry had always been a small part of the local economy, because there was no available land. Manufacturing and construction accounted for less than 14% of Bournemouth jobs in 1987. Although the Structure Plan had identified Yeoman's Road and Castle Lane East as major locations for light industry, there had been a change in the nature of industrial employment since the 1980s. So Castle Lane East was proposed instead for 'companies which require locations set in high quality landscape surroundings with good access to the strategic highway network'. What it got was Tesco, insurance companies and the Crown Courts, alongside the Royal Bournemouth Hospital.

Most existing jobs were in the fields of service industries, such as tourism (which brought a strong seasonal factor to the economy), banking, and insurance, and of distribution, education, public administration and medical services. Planning permission would normally be granted where this would increase the opportunity for job creation. It was noted that 'there is an increasing role for women in the field of employment'. There was to be a policy normally to grant permission for day nurseries, which have since gone on to become something of an industry in themselves.

Between 1981 and 1987 employment in agriculture, forestry and fishing fell from 600 to 300. Energy and water supply jobs fell from 310 to 260, and in the other industries (mineral extraction, manufacture, metal goods, vehicles) jobs fell from 7100 to 5800. Hotel/catering and distribution jobs also fell, from 19,600 to 17,700, but banking and finance increased from 21,700 jobs to 28,500.

Office development was seen as vitally important for future job opportunities and a need was identified for 'major office development'. Bournemouth Council had been promoting the town as a 'major provincial location for banking and similar commercial operations' since before the Structure Plan, which led to Bournemouth becoming home to the European HQ of Chase Manhattan/J.P. Morgan. Shopping was also seen as a 'major growth sector in the local economy', although it came with its own problems, as there was pressure for out-of-town retail schemes, and for shopping units on sites allocated for offices and industry. Lastly tourism was saluted, for maintaining a major role in the economy of the town, with a special mention for the BIC, which had given Bournemouth a regular high-profile role in the politics-by-the-sea of the annual party conference season.

The historic residential and commercial buildings around Holdenhurst Road were replaced by a variety of tall office blocks, including the distinctive McCarthy and Stone 'radio-set' building. However, because less than half the office development envisaged by the Structure Plan had taken place, the office designation of the Lansdowne area was strengthened.

Bournemouth still had higher unemployment than neighbouring areas, and so a commitment was made 'to encourage the retention of employment-generating potential' meaning that areas zoned for industry would remain as industrial zones.

The Plan identified 11 significant shopping areas, such as Winton and Southbourne, that would be protected by limiting the non-retail uses that would be allowed, such as cafes and banks. A further 17 small shopping centres, such as Wimborne Road, Northbourne and Bennett Road, were to be protected by a presumption in favour of keeping the existing shopping uses. Retail warehousing was to be encouraged in Ringwood Road.

The plan identified that tourism, in 1984, had generated £180 million income for Bournemouth, and provided 16,000 jobs. A tourist survey had identified the following types of visitor: language students staying up to several months, holiday-makers staying up to two weeks, conference and business visitors staying for a week or less, visitors staying with relatives, and day trippers. The 1.7 million tourists and 1.4 million day-trippers were 95% British residents.

The strength of the tourist industry was its high quality, with clean and tidy gardens, streets and beaches, but it lacked wet-weather or child-oriented facilities. Remedying these weaknesses was outside the scope of the Local Plan, but it would 'promote conditions which achieve an attractive environment for holiday makers'. Hotels proposing to include sports and conference facilities and access 'for the disabled' were to be encouraged. Bournemouth did get the ever-controversial IMAX and a nice new sea-life themed mosaic in the newly designed Square. Because there was a concern that guesthouse accommodation was being changed to rest homes and nursing homes, 'Tourism Core Areas' were proposed to prevent the loss of tourist facilities. Proposals for new language schools were also to be viewed favourably.

Agriculture, which was once the principal activity of

the area, had been reduced to a strip of dairy farming and market gardening along the Stour, but would be protected against loss to other uses.

Local Development Framework

After extensive public consultation and several re-draftings, the Plan was finalised as the *Bournemouth District Wide Local Plan*. By this time, its replacement was already being hatched, in the form of a portfolio of documents, capable of being independently updated. This was the *Local Development Framework – the vehicle for shaping the future of Bournemouth*. Due for publication in 2010, and intended to guide Bournemouth's fortunes over the period to 2026, this is currently the subject of its own consultation, published as *The Bournemouth Plan - Core Strategy Issues and Options Consultation Document*' which has to 'respect and implement a number of external influences'.

Let's allow it to speak for itself: 'The Bournemouth Plan sets out the vision ... for the spatial development of the area [to] steer other planning documents to ensure that ... the vision becomes a reality.' Anyone with an interest in the future of Bournemouth was invited to give views and provide options 'to meet the Regional Spatial Strategy targets for the borough.' Now let's speak for it: Regional Government ordered Bournemouth to shoehorn 14,600 new homes into the town, to provide pitches for gypsies and travellers, and to create 23,000 new jobs, whilst protecting wildlife habitats. The publication of a proposed gypsy pitch prompted an immediate march on the Town Hall by irritated neighbours. Proposals to define a protective zone around heathland habitats effectively prohibited any development in Bournemouth. For several days the whole machinery of town planning stalled entirely, until it was decided to interpret the heathland policy creatively.

The Plan's *Bournemouth Profile* showed that the major employment sectors in 2007 were distribution/hotels, public administration/health/ education and banking/finance. Bournemouth had a 'progressively ageing population', needed 'more affordable private and social housing', and suffered from 'car dependency'. The existing industrial estates in the town were 'largely built out and show low vacancy levels' – meaning that more sites for industry were needed. The main issues identified for industry were whether zoning protection should be given to small industrial sites not already identified in any policy document, and whether new industry should be sited in the Green Belt. Whether to concentrate support for tourism in the Town Centre, extend it to Boscombe or to the whole borough required further discussion.

Under the new Plan, climate change, health and learning have become town planning issues, with discussion focussing on the provision of homes with on-site renewable energy sources, cycle lanes, and Bournemouth University, particularly the Lansdowne Campus.

To continue to be economically successful, Bournemouth needs a supply of raw materials and labour and an inspiring set of objectives. In many ways the town's venerable motto 'Health and Beauty' seems to still offer some of the answers. However, one of the greatest challenges is that having built up to the edges of the Green Belt the town has no further expansion to make, and it is not clear if brownfield re-development (replacing low density houses with higher density flats) will stimulate the economy before it overwhelms the infrastructure: can the roads and the sewers carry the increasing traffic that is being imposed upon them?

As Bournemouth is increasingly subject to outside pressure, needing to conform to agendas that are set in the South West Region, or even at European Union level, there is a need for those who shape policy to understand better Bournemouth itself and the historic circumstances which underlay its development. It is worth looking back to the pre-Abercrombie era, when the fate of the town was firmly tied to the waistcoats of the leading citizens. A brief look at the mayors of Bournemouth in the first half of the 20th century shows that most of them worked in retail. There were twelve shop-keepers (five of them grocers) and three major storeowners; three were hoteliers, as well as two builders, two doctors, two carpenters and two who were retired. The remaining four were a lawyer, a solicitor, an estate agent and a baker. Each owned or ran a business in Bournemouth and came into the political world through the doors of commerce. They act as a fingerprint of the town, for despite its occasional famous resident or visitor, these were the men who had come to stay and play an active role in shaping the fortunes of the place.

However, the town set its sights firmly on maintaining its green image when two separate decisions were made. First in May 2008, it was announced that Bournemouth would be the United Kingdom's first Fibre City and the largest Fibre City project in Europe. Little did the Improvement Commissioners realise that when they laid the first sewers in the middle of the 19th century that they were providing the infrastructure for this 21st century innovation. Using the existing sewers means that broadband links can be made to all businesses and more than 88,000 homes at speeds of between 50 and 100Mbps.[14] Surfing via the sewers sounds unlikely but is both pragmatic and innovative.

Then in July 2009, Bournemouth decided to develop a 'Green Knowledge Economy' - focussing on economic growth through the development of green industries. This would be developed in cooperation with Dorset and

Poole councils as well as the private sector to develop a 'Green Knowledge Economy' action plan for the area. The emphasis would be on clean technologies, energy management, renewable energy, noise control, sustainable transport and environmental consultancy.

Bournemouth could already point to a number of positive moves towards this vision. Marks & Spencer's had opened its first eco store in Bournemouth and the BIC had invested significantly in energy efficiency. In 2008

Bournemouth was the first UK district council to sign up to the UN Earth Charter. The Council had also been one of the first to convert itself to a low carbon economy in 2003. Several local companies had significant environmental credentials, including JP Morgan.

The Council saw the key to successful development of green industries was that it would not need expensive sites or have to draw upon large pools of unemployed labour. It could grow on smaller sites, led by creative people in areas

Windsurfing at Boscombe against a backdrop of the Victorian Undercliff Parade, the pier, and the redevelopment of Honeycombe Chine. The sand pile was awaiting use in the construction of the surf reef, which opened in November 2009.

of high environmental quality. Bournemouth's historical insistence on avoiding traditional industries was now seen to provide the foundations for successful future economic production.[15]

NOTES

CHAPTER 1

1. K.A. Hanna (ed.) *18. The Christchurch Priory Cartulary* Hampshire Record Series (2007).
2. The Right Hon. Earl of Malmesbury *Memoirs of an Ex-Minister* (London 1885), p.7.
3. The Volunteer Act 1794.
4. R. Dale *Stourfield Memories* Bournemouth Local Studies Booklet No.613 .
5. A.B. Granville *Spas of England and Principal Sea-Bathing Places 2. The Midlands and the South* (1841) p. 516.

CHAPTER 2

1. G. Bruce *A Fortune and a Family: Bournemouth and the Cooper-Deans* (1987).
2. C.H. Mate and C. Riddle *Bournemouth 1810-1910 The history of a modern health and pleasure resort* (Bournemouth 1910).
3. Roger Gutteridge kindly provided this information.

CHAPTER 3

1. H. Dobell *The Medical Aspects of Bournemouth and its Surroundings* (1885) p. 34.
2. H. Harries Climate In D. Morris (ed.) *A Natural History of Bournemouth and District* (1914) p. 125.
3. W. Watson Smith *The Book of Bournemouth* (1934).
4. E. Hawkins *Medical Climatology of England and Wales* (1923).
5. Y. Burney *Climate and Health Resorts* (1885) p. 82.
6. A.B. Granville *The Spas of England and Principal Sea-Bathing Places 2. The Midlands and the South* (1841) p. 512.
7. Dr. Aitken 1840 paper quoted by Granville p. 534.

8. A.B. Granville *Op.cit.*, p. 524.
9. Report on Comparison of Sunshine recorded on Meyrick Park and roof of café, Bournemouth Pier.
10. *First Annual Report of the Bournemouth Meteorological Society* (1868) p.15.
11. *Second Annual Report of the Bournemouth Meteorological Society* (1869) p. 7.
12. H. Harries *Op.cit.* p. 125.
13. H. Dobell *Op.cit.* p. 34.

CHAPTER 4

1. H. Dobell *The Medical Aspects of Bournemouth and its Surroundings* (1885), p. 327.
2. A.B. Granville *The Spas of England and Principal Sea-Bathing Places* (1841).
3. C.H. Mate and C. Riddle *Bournemouth:1810-1910* (1910), p. 86.
4. For more information about Bournemouth's climate, see Chapter 3.
5. M. Graham *The Royal National Hospital*, Bournemouth Local Studies Publications.
6. Dr Kinsey-Morgan published an article in the journal *Nature* on 4th February 1897 in which he refers to the important part climate plays in the aetiology and cure of lung diseases. He shows the advantages Bournemouth offers to consumptive patients, or to persons suffering from any form of chest disease.
7. Report of the Medical Officer of Health year ending 1890. Bournemouth Library.
8. C.H. Mate and C. Riddle *Bournemouth:1810-1910* (1910) p. 189.
9. Annual Report for the year 1917, Heritage Zone, Bournemouth Library.

10. On the same page as this article there also appears the following: 'The report of the ladies' visiting committee of the Highworth and Swindon Guardians has drawn attention to the state of the isolation ward where some 20 children were confined owing to the prevalence of ringworm. Nurse Wilkins stated that she found nine of the children all in one bed. There were some placed at the top, some at the bottom, and the others were arranged round the sides. An inquiry will probably be held.' It must be hoped such things did not happen in Bournemouth.
11. *The Hahnemann Convalescent Home and Dispensaries, Thirty Ninth Annual Report*, issued April 1918, Heritage Zone, Bournemouth Library.
12. *The Times* newspaper around 1890.
13. Mr Kneese was the manager of Mont Dore at this time. Records of the passengers on the Titanic show a Miss Kneese whose father was hotel manager in Bournemouth. Miss Kneese survived the maiden voyage as she only travelled on the journey from Southampton to Cherbourg.
14. www.cwgc.org .
15. F.P. Dolomore Seaside Health Resorts in *The Souvenir Book of the Royal Sanitary Institute 33rd Congress*, July 1922.
16. W.C.H. Vernon Shaw *Report on an Outbreak of Enteric Fever in the County Borough of Bournemouth and in the Boroughs of Poole and Christchurch* (1937).
17. *The Bournemouth Public Health Report 2005/6* (Bournemouth NHS Teaching Primary Care Trust, the Bournemouth Partnership and Bournemouth Partnership: March 2006).

CHAPTER 5

1. J. Soane The General Significance of the Development of the Urban and Social Structure of Bournemouth 1840-1940, Unpublished Ph.D. thesis, University of Surrey (1978).

2. R. Borsay *The English Urban Renaissance, 1660-1770* (1989) pp. 284-295.

3. J.C. Loudon (ed.) *Humphrey Repton: Landscape Gardening* (1840).

4. Gervis Estate 1840-1850 Plan and Elevations of Westover Villas – Hinton Admiral Estate Office; Gervis Estate 1838 Plan of Bournemouth. Dorset History Centre.

5. Quoted from one of Burton's Reports by C.H. Mate and C. Riddle *Bournemouth 1810-1910 – The History of a Modern Health and Pleasure Resort* (1910).

6. D. Bouillard *Le Site Balnéaire* (1985) pp. 9-10, 172-184, 277-282.

7. P. Brannon *The Illustrated Historical and Picturesque Guide to Bournemouth* (1856) p. 6.

8. Registrar General: Census Enumerators Returns for Christchurch (1851).9. G. Rosen Disease, Debility and Death. In H.J. Dyos and M. Wolff (eds.) *The Victorian City* (1985).

10. *Blackwood's Magazine* (1884) p. 74.

11. J. Soane *Fashionable Resort Regions: Their Evolution and Transformation* (1993) p. 25.

12. Registrar General: Census Reports for Hampshire (1871 and 1911).

13. *Bournemouth Echo* 28th November 1923.

14. *Bournemouth Echo* 31st July 1926.

15. W. Watson Smith *Book of Bournemouth* (1934) pp. 48 and 55.

16. L.A. Birch Tale of Two Valleys *Picture Post* (1950) pp. 34-41.

17. *South West Spatial Strategy Report* (2006 and subsequent editions).

18. *Bournemouth Characterization Study* Bournemouth Borough Council Report (2007).

CHAPTER 6

1. G.F. Berkeley *George Berkeley: My Life and Recollections, Part 2* (1865).

2. Butlin's Plans More Holiday Camps at Ryde and Bournemouth, *The Caterer and Hotel Keeper*, 8 June 1938, p. 11.

CHAPTER 8

1. R. Roberts Leasehold estates and municipal enterprise In Carradine, D (ed.) *Patricians, Power and Politics*, (1982) p. 179.

2. R. Roberts *Ibid*. p. 180.

3. J.K. Walton, *The British Seaside: Holidays and Resorts in the Twentieth Century* (2000) p. 58.

4. A. D. Edwards Public health of Bournemouth In D.Morris (ed.) *The Natural History of Bournemouth* (1914) p. 96.

5. V. J. May Replenishment of resort beaches at Bournemouth and Christchurch, England, *Journal of Coastal Research*, Special Issue 6, (1990) pp.11-16.

6. V. J. May Urban beaches: a European perspective on the uses, values and futures of urban beaches. In L. Ewing, T. Herrington and O. Magoon (eds.) *Urban beaches: balancing public rights and private development* (2003) pp. 39-51.

7. J.K. Walton, *Op.cit*.

8. R. Harrington Beyond the bathing belle: Images of women in inter-war railway publicity *The Journal of Transport History*, Vol. 25, (2004) pp. 22-45.

9. American Red Cross no date *Furlough in Bournemouth*.

10. *Combat Journal: The Story of the Timberwolf Regiment of the 78th Lightning Division in World War II 1944-1945*, p.14.

11. J.B.Priestly I look at Bournemouth *Picture Post* (21st June 1941).

12. www.hotel.info

13. Dorset New Forest Tourism Data Project, The Market Research Group (2009).

14. www.bournemouth.co.uk

15. www.bournemouth.co.uk

16. www.bournemouthsurfreef.co.uk

CHAPTER 9

1. Much of this chapter has been derived from the comprehensive publications written by Michael A. Edgington, with his agreement. For more information, see his *The Citizen-Soldier: a history of the Bournemouth Volunteers, 1860-1908*, published in 1988, *Bournemouth and the First World War: the Evergreen Valley, 1914 to 1919* (1985) and *Bournemouth and the Second World War, 1939-1945*, (1994).

CHAPTER 10

1. This part of the chapter is based on the Local History Group's publication *Bournemouth's Victorian schools: forerunners of education for all*, (Bournemouth Local Studies No. 720: 1992) written by Jack Parsons and John Young, and *Education in Bournemouth 1903 to 1945* (No. 735: 1996) and *Post War Education in Bournemouth 1945 to 1974* (No. 738: 1997).

2. D. Gillard *Education in England: a brief history* (2007) provides a very useful summary of the Act as well as subsequent changes.

3. J. Parsons and J. Young, *Bournemouth's Victorian schools: forerunners of education for all*, (1992) p. 37.

4. J. Parsons and J. Young, *Ibid*. p. 40.

5. www.rc-churches.net/boscombe/history.

6. J. Parsons and J. Young, *Op.cit*. p.42.

7. J. Parsons and J. Young, *Ibid*. p.43.

8. Talbot Heath website www.talbotheath.org

9. For more details see Terry Smith's *St. Peter's School-Independent Days* (1998).

10. www.eurocentres.com

11. Bournemouth County Borough Higher Education Committee Minute 23 p. A 389 .

12. www.bournemouth.ac.uk

CHAPTER 11

1. For example, *The South East Study* (1964).

2. *First report on a land use and transportation study of Southeast Dorset and Southwest Hampshire - April 1967*. The Bournemouth County Borough Council, Dorset County Council and Hampshire County Council.

3. K. Rawlings *Just Bournemouth* (2005).

4. A. Kinsey-Morgan *Bournemouth as a Health Resort* (1889) p. 34 quoted in J. Hassan *The Seaside, Health and the Environment in England and* Wales (2002).

5. Smith, S.W. *The Book of Bournemouth* (1934) p. 41.

6. www.fibrecity.eu

7. www.bournemouth.gov.uk/News/press_office.

ACKNOWLEDGEMENTS

This book would not have come into being without the authors, but many others have also played important roles in bringing it to fruition. In particular, John Walker has been a constant source of advice on dates, local detail and content, as well as reading everything critically.

There is also a significant number of individuals of all ages who provided advice on content, style and interest. They know who they are and we hope that they enjoy reading this book to which they contributed so much. The support of the staff of the Bournemouth Libraries Service who have provided advice and information on many occasions is gratefully acknowledged. Working closely with the Streets of Bournemouth Project has made it possible to access illustrations which without the Project's support would not have been available.

The overall appearance of the book owes a great deal to the creativity of David Burnett at Dovecote Press and we thank him for his help and that of Elizabeth Dean in bringing the book to fruition.

Sources of the illustrations in this book (except where explicitly acknowledged with the illustration) are Bournemouth Libraries: all illustrations with the exception of the following: American Red Cross: 131 right, 146 below right; Bournemouth Airport Archive: 119, 146 below, 146 above, 182 below right; Bournemouth Borough Council: 7 coat of arms, 144, 147 top right; Bournemouth Daily Echo: 99 right; David Bailey: 4, 36, 41 above, 47, 51, 95, 123, 132, 133, 168, 185 left, 187, 188; John Barker: 39 top left; Vincent May: 8 map, 12, 13, 19, 20 left, 24 bottom right, 54, 56, 68 top right, 78 top left, bottom left, 79 above, 84 bottom left, 84 top left, 104, 108 top right, 109 above, 128 below, 120 above, 134 above, 134 left, 168 left, 176 centre, 186 top left, 186 bottom right; Louise Perrin: 58, 60, 63, 64, 65, 68; Mike Phipp: 120 bottom left; John Soane: 71 right, 75, 77 top left, 82 below; William Law Photography: 191. If we have inadvertently not acknowledged an illustration, please accept our apologies.

INDEX